# A Guide to
# Pregnancy and Parenthood
# for Women on Their Own

# A GUIDE TO

# *Pregnancy and Parenthood for Women on Their Own*

## Patricia Ashdown-Sharp

**VINTAGE BOOKS**
*A Division of Random House*
*New York*

A Vintage Original, September 1977
FIRST EDITION
Copyright © 1975, 1977 by Patricia Ashdown-Sharp

All rights reserved under International and Pan-American Copyright
Conventions. Published in the United States by Random House, Inc.,
New York, and simultaneously in Canada by Random House of Canada
Limited, Toronto.

Library of Congress Cataloging in Publication Data

Ashdown-Sharp, Patricia, 1941–
A guide to pregnancy and parenthood for women on their own.

Includes bibliographical references and index.
1. Pregnancy. 2. Abortion. 3. Contraception.
4. Adoption. 5. Unmarried mothers. I. Title.
RG525.A798       362.8'3       76–62491
ISBN 0–394–72272–8

Manufactured in the United States of America

# Acknowledgments

My thanks, most of all, to the many women in the United States and Britain who talked to me frankly about their pregnancies, their abortions, their experiences of marrying while pregnant, having their babies adopted or bringing up children on their own. Their feelings and experiences provided the basis for much of the discussion in the book and gave invaluable insights into how the system works both for and against women in this position. All were only too happy to pass on to others what they themselves had found out the hard way.

My thanks also to all the organizations mentioned, the government departments and volunteer groups that provided so much information. Among the many individuals who helped, special thanks to: Dr. Christopher Tietze and Edward Weinstock of the Population Council; Harriet Pilpel and Eve Paul of the law firm of Greenbaum, Wolff and Ernst; Robin Elliott and Arlene Gilbert of Planned Parenthood Federation of America; Judy Meers of the American Civil Liberties Union; Gwen Davis and Joseph Reid of the Child Welfare League of America; Judy Riggs of the Children's Defense Fund of America; Richard Lincoln and Patricia Donovan of the Alan Guttmacher Institute; Catherine Day-Jermany of the Legal Services Corporation and the NOW task force on poverty; Valerie Greer, former director of the One Parent Family Project, New York City; Carol Jauch, director of the Single Parent Resource Center, San Francisco; Kristin Luker of the University of California, San Diego; Helen Marieskind, editor of *Women and Health*; George Williams, former director of Parents Without Partners. An extra special thank-you to my editor Anne Freedgood and my friend Eva Zucker for their encouragement, criticism and extreme patience.

# Contents

Introduction   ix

1. Diagnosing Pregnancy   3

2. Deciding What to Do   19

3. Marriage   32

4. Abortion   41

5. Pregnancy   66

6. Adoption and Fostering   87

7. Bringing Up a Child on Your Own   99

8. Contraception   141

Source References   183

Index   189

# *Introduction*

In little more than a decade, women have experienced a revolution that, in the sheer enormity of its consequences, rivals all the great social and political upheavals of history. The revolution has centered on sexual freedom, not only freedom to enjoy sex both within and outside marriage but, more specifically, the right of women to decide for themselves whether or not to have children. As Margaret Sanger wrote as long ago as 1920: "No woman can call herself free until she can choose consciously whether she will or will not be a mother."

This book is about that choice. It is written as a self-help guide for women who wish to make independent decisions about pregnancy, parenthood and birth control, and its bias is toward those who, accidentally or by intent, are pregnant or who are bringing up children without the support of a man. This does not mean that it is exclusively for unmarried women. A widowed, separated or divorced woman may be just as disconcerted as a teen-ager to find herself unintentionally pregnant or, on the other hand, may deliberately plan to have a child without marrying again. A married woman also may confront dilemmas posed by unplanned pregnancy. And women in every situation have the problem of what to do about birth control. Independent does not necessarily mean man-less. It means being well-informed about our options so that we can more easily make the decisions that most affect our lives.

The essence of the sexual revolution in recent years has been the new technology of modern contraceptive techniques and the impact of Supreme Court decisions which, between 1965 and 1973, endorsed the constitutional right of women throughout the nation to practice contraception regardless of marital status and obtain abortions on request. No one can deny the historic importance of these developments. But they have taken us only halfway down the road toward real choice. The right to *avoid* motherhood is only half the equation; what of the right to bear and raise children? This question is central to the predicament of women who are pregnant or who are bringing up families without the support of men. To answer it, we must explore why women are now in the contradictory position of losing some of their old options before the newer options, which would guarantee a genuine freedom of choice, are fully available to them.

That contradiction is evident at all levels. According to conventional wisdom, the invention of the contraceptive pill twenty years ago should by now have made unwanted pregnancy a thing of the past. Yet every year in the United States, nearly one million women still have abortions, and one in four of all women who become pregnant are not married at the time. Premarital sex is now supposedly taken for granted; yet in 1975 Betty Ford could still create a furor by casually mentioning in a television interview that she "wouldn't be surprised" if her nineteen-year-old daughter Susan had had an affair. The very fact that some ordinary women, not just the Vanessa Redgraves, have begun deliberately to have children outside marriage, not only by giving birth but by adopting children, is itself a measure of the growing independence of women. Yet the vast majority of women bringing up children on their own suffer immense economic hardships. We are, in fact, in the middle of a "transition gap"—a period of enormous progress for women and a period of unparalleled uncertainty brought about by rapid change.

In 1971 British feminist Juliet Mitchell wrote a gloomy prophecy: "The current wave of sexual liberalization *could* become conducive to the greater general freedom of women. Equally, it could presage new forms of oppression." An immediate example of this is the way that the emergence of female contraception and legalized abortion has created a different kind of imbalance between the sexes, particularly for unmarried couples. Avoiding pregnancy is now *her* responsibility, not his. No matter that the pill gives her side effects, or that other contraceptives often fail, or that he didn't stop to find out whether she was using anything in the first place: if she gets pregnant it must be her fault. A new stereotype has replaced the old—he feels no obligation to marry her. In this context, it hardly comes as a surprise to discover that among more than one million American women who become pregnant outside marriage every year, over one half (53 percent) have abortions and over one third (37 percent) give birth "illegitimately," but only one tenth get married before the child is born. A woman today is far more likely than in the past to be left holding the baby or, its modern equivalent, arranging for an abortion.

It is not the aim of this book to suggest that any woman should, or should not, become pregnant or have a child on her own. Nor does it attempt to forecast what might happen to society if women in any significant numbers began to do so as a matter of choice. Rather, it is offered as an antidote to the extreme positions taken by both sides: to the conventional view of women as wives and mothers which seeks to perpetuate the penalties and injustices used for generations against women outside marriage, and to the excessive feminist view that sometimes persuades women they can, and even should, take on more than they are yet ready for.

As with everything else, there is a *system* to pregnancy and parenthood outside marriage. With sufficient information you can learn how to make that system work for you, or help change the system where you find it operating against you and others in a similar position. But the key is to understand yourself as far as you are able, think through the consequences of the alternatives open to you, and make your own decision, not according to other people's ideas but to fit the reality of your own circumstances and needs at a particular time in your life. You should also recognize that as women's options increase, decision-making becomes more complex: old values may conflict with new; new freedoms may bring new anxieties. This is not necessarily bad. Many women have found more confidence and maturity in the challenge. The fundamental assumption of this book, in fact, is that pregnant women or mothers on their own are neither social deviants nor the victims of unfortunate circumstances. In a very real sense they are pioneers Their experience is the most accurate measure we have of the relative independence of *all* women in society.

# A Guide to
# Pregnancy and Parenthood
# for Women on Their Own

# 1

## Diagnosing Pregnancy

Something has made you suspect that you may be pregnant. Probably your period has not arrived, or perhaps you just *feel* pregnant: some women say they know intuitively the exact moment they conceived. Or you've had sexual intercourse without using a reliable contraceptive and now you're wondering . . . could you possibly be pregnant?

Whichever it is, if you're a single woman, you are probably worried —unless you deliberately plan to have a child outside marriage. However, you cannot know for certain until a pregnancy test has confirmed your suspicions. In fact, it is vital to know one way or the other *as soon as you possibly can.* This may sound obvious. But some women (particularly teen-agers) tell themselves they can't be pregnant because they don't want it to be true, or they shut the possibility out of their minds as though not thinking about it will make the whole thing vanish. But ignoring the first signs can have unfortunate results. You may risk your health if you don't seek medical care early. You may find you are too late for the abortion procedure that, otherwise, you might have chosen. If you drift along until your baby is almost due, you may find yourself facing all kinds of problems that you don't know how to handle. Above all, an early diagnosis means maximizing your options: you will have time to think things over and make a real choice, so that the outcome of your pregnancy is more likely to be what you feel is best for you.

Recent research has produced a new pregnancy test that can accurately detect pregnancy even before a woman misses her period. However, hospitals and clinics are often slow to adopt new techniques, so you may find that only the standard urine tests are available in your area. The earliest these tests can produce an accurate result is when your period is about fourteen days overdue—which is unfortunate because it often means fourteen days of uncertainty. In the meantime you will be looking for the symptoms of pregnancy, perhaps hoping that it is all a false alarm, or wondering if there is any way of "bringing on" your period. So let's begin with these matters before going into how to get a pregnancy test.

## THE SYMPTOMS OF PREGNANCY

Women differ a great deal in the symptoms they experience in early pregnancy. The following are the ones doctors look for:

*Missed period* This is the commonest sign, but it doesn't happen for everyone. A woman may have a few drops of blood, or even what looks like a not-so-heavy period, at the usual time or a little late, and still be pregnant. Bleeding of some sort in early pregnancy is more common than is generally believed. It usually happens because the level of the hormone progesterone (which normally causes the suppression of periods throughout pregnancy) is not sufficiently high.

*Sickness and nausea* You may be sick in the mornings, afternoons or evenings. What is usually called "morning sickness" can strike at any time. Or you may feel nauseated without actually vomiting. Tastes and smells that never bothered you before—alcohol or cigarette smoke, for example, or even everyday foods like coffee—may now make you feel queasy. You may lose your appetite, or you may develop a craving for one type of food.

*Breast changes* Your breasts may feel uncomfortable or especially tender, as they possibly do before a period. They may feel fuller than usual, with soreness or a tingling sensation. The nipples may darken by about the eighth week of pregnancy. By about twelve weeks, a little watery fluid can sometimes be squeezed from the nipple.

*Passing urine frequently* You may find you want to go to the bathroom more often than usual. In pregnancy this is caused by hormone changes and by the enlarging womb pressing on the bladder; in the later months the urgent need to urinate every half-hour or so can become a nuisance.

*Mood changes* Some women can recognize pregnancy by a change of mood. You may feel depressed, lethargic, irritable and run-down.

It can happen that a woman never suspects she is pregnant until much later on—perhaps because she bleeds a little at the time her period is expected or because her periods are normally irregular and she experiences no other symptoms. Some women don't gain weight much in the first few months. However, around the twelfth to fourteenth week underclothes and waistbands are likely to start feeling tight. After that, the swelling of the body gradually becomes more noticeable. By about twenty weeks the movements of the fetus may be felt; these start as slight flutterings and become stronger toward the end of pregnancy.

A late or missed period does not always mean that you are pregnant. Nevertheless it is foolish to decide on your own that it must be a false alarm. It is possible to become pregnant when the chances seem strongly against it, even if you used a contraceptive or it was the first time you had sexual intercourse. (According to the best estimates, the chances of becoming pregnant after only one act of intercourse during a month are between 2 and 4 percent, unless the act took place in the middle of the cycle between periods, when they rise to 20 percent.[1]) Even in fact, if you didn't go all the way: semen can occasionally get into the vagina without full intercourse taking place.

The pill is supposed to be virtually foolproof as long as it is taken faithfully, but some women who get pregnant swear they never missed taking one. (Occasionally, a mistake occurs in the manufacture of pills.) If you have *any* reason to suspect you may be pregnant, it is best to make sure.

## CAN YOU "BRING ON" A PERIOD?

Over the past few years attempts have been made to find a modern, medically sound way of "bringing on" periods—in other words, to insure as early as possible that a woman's egg, if it *has* been fertilized by the man's sperm, does not continue to develop into an unwanted pregnancy. Three techniques have been developed so far: two are used shortly after unprotected intercourse and the third when a period is overdue. All these methods are controversial and have drawbacks, which have led many doctors to be sceptical of their value. It is therefore worth discussing each in some detail.

### *"Morning-after" pills*

The popular name is not quite accurate. This treatment is actually a five-day course of ten pills which must start *within seventy-two hours* of sexual intercourse. They are prescribed only as an "emergency" procedure and not as a routine means of birth control. In other words, you cannot get hold of a supply to keep as a standby in case you have sex without contraception, but a doctor may prescribe them if you seek help immediately after the event. Some doctors and hospitals prescribe them routinely to women who have been raped.

The "morning-after" pills most commonly available contain a high dosage of diethylstilbestrol (DES)—and it is this artificial estrogen that has caused controversy. In the early 1970s a link was established between DES and cancer of the cervix or vagina: the cancer was found in about one hundred women whose mothers had taken DES in pregnancy during the 1940s and 1950s, when it was believed that the drug could help prevent miscarriage. In 1975 the Food and Drug Administration (FDA), having reviewed the evidence, approved the use of DES as a postcoital treatment. The FDA noted[2] that women whose daughters had developed cervical or vaginal cancer had taken DES generally for longer periods and in higher doses than is necessary for "morning-after" treatments; the only evidence of cancer developing in women who had themselves taken DES occurred in those who had been given the drug for five years or more to treat a rare gynecological abnormality, gonadal dysgenesis (incomplete development of the ovaries).

Nevertheless, the FDA approved DES only as an "emergency treatment" and warned that it should not be used repeatedly. The FDA also insisted that patients should be given information leaflets warning that if the pregnancy continues in spite of the treatment, and the fetus is female, there will be an increased risk of the child developing cervical or vaginal cancer later in life. In reaction to this known link between DES and cancer, some other estrogens have also been used in "morning-after" pills with reportedly effective results.[3] But the pills most generally available are still those containing DES.

It is not only the kind of estrogen contained in "morning-after" pills that has caused controversy, but also the fact that the dose is so powerful, since estrogen is the ingredient in the contraceptive pill that has been linked with thromboembolism (blood clotting). According to Lucile K. Kuchera of the University of Michigan, who has conducted one of the largest tests of DES treatments, "there is as much estrogenic activity in the ten tablets of stilbestrol totaling 250 mg as in a ten-month supply of some of the oral contraceptives currently used."[4] A further drawback of the treatment is that it can (but does not always) cause unpleasant side effects, such as vomiting, headaches, dizziness and diarrhea.

"Morning-after" pills seem to be effective in preventing pregnancy—providing that the course of pills is begun within seventy-two hours of sexual intercourse, and also that intercourse has occurred *only once* since the woman had her last menstrual period. In Kuchera's study, 1,217 women fulfilled these conditions, and none became pregnant. But the pills appear much less effective if the course is begun later or if the woman has had unprotected sex several times since her previous period. In the same study, eighty-one women were in one or other of these situations, and six of them became pregnant. These six women all had abortions. In fact, doctors will always recommend abortions for women who have undergone the "morning-after" treatment and still find themselves pregnant: any powerful drug such as this increases the risk of damage to the fetus.

So how worthwhile is the "morning-after" treatment? These are the arguments for and against:

For: It is of benefit to a woman who is especially upset at the possibility that she might be pregnant—particularly if she has been raped. It is the only immediate postcoital treatment currently available.

Against: The chances are high that the woman is not pregnant at all —particularly if she has had unprotected intercourse only once since her last period (in which case the chances are 96 percent to 98 percent *against*). In most cases, the treatment is more drastic than is warranted for simply providing immediate relief from anxiety. It may be safer to offer a woman menstrual extraction (see p. 8) or early abortion *after* she has missed a period or had a positive pregnancy test. The long-term effects of so high an estrogen dosage are not fully known.

If you want the "morning-after" treatment, you must, of course, get to a doctor or clinic as soon as possible. Try your own gynecologist or call any Planned Parenthood clinic (address in the telephone directory) to see if they prescribe the pills—not all will. Some student health centers provide this treatment. If you have been raped, a rape crisis center (see p. 29) can advise you.

### Copper IUDs inserted postcoitally

This procedure, prompted by the disadvantages of "morning-after" pills, is still experimental and not generally available. So it should be said at once that you cannot "bring on a period" simply by getting a doctor to insert a contraceptive intra-uterine device (IUD) into your uterus. However, recent research suggests that pregnancy may be averted if an IUD is inserted into the womb soon after unprotected sexual intercourse. The difference is apparently a question of timing. IUDs are thought to work *after* a woman has conceived—by preventing the implantation of the fertilized egg into the wall of the uterus. Theoretically, therefore, if an

IUD is inserted during the time the fertilized egg is traveling down the Fallopian tubes into the uterus—which takes up to seven days—it should be just as effective and safe in preventing implantation as an IUD that has been there all along. But by the time a woman realizes her period is overdue, it is already too late: implantation has occurred several days before.

The experimental program conducted by Dr. Jack Lippes in Buffalo, New York, from 1972 on, is the only one so far to put this idea to the test. Lippes inserted copper IUDs into the uteri of ninety-seven young women, none of whom had borne children. Half of the women had had sexual intercourse within the previous forty-eight hours; the rest up to five days before. None became pregnant.[5] Lippes (inventor of a popular IUD, the Lippes Loop) claims two main advantages for this method. First, he says, minor side effects commonly linked with IUD insertion are fewer and more short-lived than side effects linked with "morning-after" pills. Second, the device is left in place and so continues to protect the woman against unwanted pregnancy. This last argument may prove especially attractive to family planners, in which case postcoital IUD insertion may in the future become available at birth-control clinics.

Considerably more research is required before the effectiveness and safety of the method are proved. But there are some obvious drawbacks. *It excludes most sexually active women.* Lippes himself recommends[6] that the procedure should be performed only within five days of un-protected intercourse and should not be done if the woman has had sex more than once since her last period. This is to make sure that implantation has not yet occurred, for the reasons explained above. *It may not work. It is not suitable for all women.* (IUD insertion can cause complications in women who already have venereal or pelvic inflammatory diseases—see pp. 159–60) *It may not be necessary. It commits a woman to the IUD for contraception.*

### Menstrual extraction

An overdue period can certainly be brought on by means of menstrual extraction. This procedure is also known as menstrual regulation, en-dometrial aspiration, interception, etc. Actually it is an extremely early abortion, performed during the two weeks before a standard urine test can confirm whether a woman is really pregnant.

When extraction was first introduced in 1971, many women and some doctors welcomed it as a great breakthrough, seeing it as a useful halfway measure between contraception and abortion. By 1974–5 the procedure was falling out of favor, mainly because too many women turned out not to be pregnant after all and had therefore taken an unnecessary, if small risk. However, in 1976 the tide turned again. The new blood tests that can diagnose pregnancy accurately as soon as a woman's period is one day late, or even earlier (see p. 12), have now made extractions feasible for the first time—although, once pregnancy has been confirmed, the procedure should be (and is likely to be) called precisely what it is, a very early abortion.

*How it works* A woman's egg is normally released from her ovaries once a month. If it is not fertilized by sperm, the egg is flushed away in her menstrual period. But if it has been fertilized, it implants itself into the wall of the uterus (womb), and the endometrium (the uterine lining which comes away each month in the form of menstrual blood) remains in place to feed and support it. The purpose of menstrual extraction, as the name implies, is to remove the endometrium and thus ensure that the woman is not pregnant. To do this, a thin plastic tube (known as a cannula) is passed up through the vagina, through the cervix (neck of the uterus), and into the uterus itself. The endometrium is extracted by suction. In essence, extraction gives you your period in a few minutes instead of over several days, while removing the tiny egg that, if fertilized, is the very beginning of a pregnancy.

*When should it be performed?* Timing is important. Most conscientious doctors will not perform extraction when a period is only a day or two late unless a woman is in a state of extreme anxiety. Research has revealed[7] that only about 50 percent of women are pregnant when they have extractions within seven days of an overdue period (counting the day the period was expected as day one), although this goes up to about 85 percent if it is done between seven and fourteen days. As the procedure is not without risk, most doctors now prefer to wait until a pregnancy test proves positive—which means delaying until at least the fourteenth day if only the standard urine test is available. However, if the earlier blood test can be used, the optimum time for extraction is between the seventh and fourteenth day.

*Effectiveness* The procedure is highly effective, and you can be reasonably sure that you are no longer pregnant once it is done. Very occasionally, extraction fails to remove the fertilized egg. Studies show that this happens to about three to five women in every hundred (about 4 percent), most often when extraction is performed within the first seven days of an overdue period.[8]

*Clinical practice* The procedure must be performed by a doctor, preferably one who is properly trained and experienced in the technique. It can be done without an anesthetic, but most women find this painful; when a local anesthetic is used, it usually feels no worse than a passing period cramp. Normally you can go home within an hour or two.

*Safety* In the early days it was often argued that the technique was so safe and simple that it could be done not only by doctors but by women themselves. Many feminists believed that here at last was a way of "putting abortion back into the hands of women." Some women in self-help groups, with or without instruction, performed extractions on each other, sometimes on a regular monthly basis to avoid troublesome periods; a few performed one (or attempted to perform one) on themselves. These practices are generally frowned on today. Research has found that the operation, though simple, is not free of risk. About two women in every hundred develop some complication such as infection or bleeding.[9] Perforation of the uterus, a major complication that happens when the cannula accidentally pierces the uterine wall, is not unknown. But if pregnancy has been definitely established, there is no question that suction at this very early stage is the safest type of abortion procedure when done by a qualified person.

*Acceptability* Many women make a distinction between "bringing on a period" and abortion. It is far easier to accept the removal of a microscopically tiny egg than an embryo with more human characteristics. A few people have therefore suggested that extraction could be relied on as an alternative method of birth control. Yet in a British study of women who had had extractions at a London teaching hospital, nearly all who were specifically asked whether they would consider using it routinely reacted strongly against the idea, and some thought the question was a joke.[10]

*Cost* The simplicity of the technique led most people to assume that extractions could be performed at a fraction of the cost of suction abortions. Clinics now say that this is a myth. They maintain that extractions require the same equipment, staff and time as suction abortions and therefore cost the same. Accordingly, most now charge the same—usually over $120.

## HOW PREGNANCY IS DIAGNOSED

The most common method at present is a urine test. The newest is a blood test. A much older method, long discredited and now officially banned in the United States, involves a course of hormone pills. The fourth way is an internal examination by a doctor: this cannot usually give an accurate result until you are at least eight weeks pregnant, but it may be necessary to confirm the result of a urine or blood test and check how far the pregnancy has progressed.

## Urine tests

These tests work by detecting a hormone called HCG (human chorionic gonadotropin) manufactured by the developing placenta (the tissue that nourishes the growing egg). By about the sixth week of pregnancy, a sufficiently high level of HCG has been produced for it to be detected in the woman's urine. A urine test, therefore, is simply a matter of mixing a few drops of urine with chemicals to discover if there is any HCG present. If the mixture remains clear, the result is "positive," which indicates that you are pregnant. If it coagulates, the result is "negative," which indicates that you are not.

Urine tests are 95 to 98 percent accurate. They are more accurate if done with the first urine specimen of the morning, which is more highly concentrated than later specimens. However, they occasionally give wrong results. A false negative usually means that you have been tested too early, so if your period does not arrive, it is best to have another test. Some abnormalities of early pregnancy (such as threatened miscarriages or ectopic conceptions—see p. 12) cause HCG levels too low to be detected by urine tests. So if you feel pain or miss two periods, you should be examined by a doctor. A positive result is hardly ever wrong. But it very occasionally happens if a woman has blood or some other protein in her urine (from cystitis, for example) or has been taking certain drugs (such as some antidepressants or antihistamines). A woman going through the menopause in her late forties or fifties might get a false positive because of hormonal changes, although some women of this age have conceived.

It should be noted that two other factors are on occasion responsible for wrong results: human error and human greed. A technician may read a result wrongly (though it is difficult to mistake a positive and negative result in modern tests); the chemicals may have been stored too long; or the bottle containing the urine may have been contaminated or imperfectly washed (any trace of detergent can affect the result). There is also some evidence that a few abortion clinics have deliberately falsified test results for financial gain: this possibility is discussed on p. 17.

## Blood tests

This new technique is known clinically as "radioassay." One version of it—"radioreceptorassay" (RRA)—was developed at Cornell University Medical Center in New York City by Dr. Brij B. Saxena and Dr. Robert Landesman. It offers women several unprecedented practical and medical advantages:

- It can detect pregnancy in some cases as early as four to six days after fertilization and is "virtually 100 percent accurate" by the time a woman's period is one day late.
- It can predict a threatened early miscarriage before the woman herself suspects anything is wrong.
- It can detect ectopic pregnancies (which develop abnormally in the Fallopian tubes instead of in the uterus) early enough to prevent serious complications and also makes exploratory surgery unnecessary.

Blood tests work on the same principle as urine tests: they detect the pregnancy hormone known as HCG. Stored HCG, used as a control, is made radioactive and put with a "receptor" produced from the ovaries of pregnant cows. This preparation is then mixed with a drop of blood, taken from a finger or vein. After a period of incubation, the level of radioactivity in the mixture is measured on a gamma counter which picks up the "bleeps" of gamma rays emitted by the radioactive HCG sample. Any HCG that is present in the woman's blood will compete with the radioactive HCG and neutralize some of it, causing the level of radioactivity to drop—so a reduction means that the woman is pregnant. If the level remains the same, she is not pregnant.[11]

Unlike urine tests, blood tests cannot be carried out in physicians' offices. The procedure involves expensive equipment (gamma counters) which only hospitals and larger clinics or laboratories are likely to possess. The cost will certainly be higher than for urine tests.

## Internal examination

If you have already missed two periods a doctor can usually tell whether you are pregnant by looking for the normal body changes that occur in early pregnancy: the uterus and the cervix become softer, and the cervix enlarges somewhat and changes from pale pink to a bluish color. Even if you have missed only one period, a doctor may want to see if any of these changes can yet be detected.

To examine you internally, the doctor presses your lower pelvic area with one hand and feels inside your vagina with two fingers, while you lie on the examination table. He usually wears a thin surgical glove lubricated with cream in order not to hurt you. It may feel a little uncomfortable, but it doesn't take longer than a minute or two. Tension increases the discomfort (and makes it more difficult for the doctor to give an accurate diagnosis) so it will help if you can be as relaxed as possible. If there *is* any pain, you should say so.

The doctor should ask you several questions: the date of your last period and whether your menstrual cycle is usually regular; any symptoms you have experienced; details of your medical history including the number (if any) of all previous full-term pregnancies, miscarriages and induced abortions. It is important to give as much accurate information as you can, bringing your medical records with you if possible. The doctor needs as full a picture as he can get. For example, he is not simply being curious in wanting to know whether you have been pregnant before. During the examination, he is looking for a slight enlargement of the cervix and uterus. If you have been pregnant before, your cervix will already be slightly enlarged. So if you pretend you have never been pregnant (when you have), you will be misleading the doctor: he may think that this enlargement is a sign of a present pregnancy, rather than a previous one, and diagnose accordingly.

Occasionally an internal examination may reveal a tumor or some other condition that produces symptoms similar to pregnancy. But if, after an internal and verbal examination, the doctor says that you are pregnant, you can be almost 100 percent certain that he is right. Very rarely, a woman has an abortion and is found not to be pregnant after all, even though a doctor has diagnosed pregnancy in good faith. At one time doctors tended to be cautious about confirming pregnancy until a woman had missed two periods and definite signs of a growing embryo could be felt. Today, many women who want abortions come along for pregnancy tests much earlier, and doctors may take a few more chances in their diagnosis. They reason that if a woman has had a positive urine test and missed one period when she is normally regular, she is almost certainly pregnant; and if she wants an abortion, it is better to do it as soon as possible, because delay increases the risks.

## Where to go for a pregnancy test

If for any reason, financial or emotional, you hesitate to consult a doctor, there are several other places you can go to to determine whether or not you are pregnant.

- Planned Parenthood birth-control clinics perform pregnancy tests as a matter of routine. They are used to helping unmarried women (including teen-agers) and can be relied on more than most to be sympathetic and discreet. They operate in most states (except Arkansas, Louisiana, Maine, Mississipi, North Dakota, South Dakota, Wyoming) and their numbers and addresses are in the telephone directory. If the nearest clinic is too far away to travel to, it is still worth investing in a call: they may be able to refer you to a sympathetic doctor in your own area. Or look in the Yellow Pages (under "Birth Control Information") for other services, preferably the nonprofit ones.
- Women's health centers can also be relied on, providing they are truly women-oriented, nonprofit organizations. Check the list on pp. 25–26 or call your nearest chapter of the National Organization of Women for information on women's clinics in your area.
- Student health centers often provide pregnancy testing services for enrolled students. Call your campus clinic.
- Zero Population Growth is a political and educational organization concerned with population problems and birth control, but its chapters can sometimes refer you to reputable clinics which offer pregnancy testing. If there is a local chapter near you, it will be listed in the telephone directory.
- Abortion clinics always offer confidential pregnancy testing (often advertised in newspapers and in the Yellow Pages under "Birth Control Information") but see p. 58 first.
- Birthright, the organization that offers counseling to pregnant unmarried women who do *not* want an abortion, sometimes provides pregnancy tests. If there is a local chapter, it will be listed in the telephone directory.
- Most hospitals perform pregnancy tests, usually in their family planning or maternal health clinics. Call the main number of the hospital, say you want a pregnancy test and you will be referred to the appropriate department.
- The Department of Health usually runs clinics where you can get a test, or they can refer you to a hospital. The local health department is listed in the telephone directory under the name of your city or county.

## If you are a minor

If you are a teen-ager, your immediate concern may be your parents. Do you tell them you think you are pregnant, or not? Let's assume you'd rather find out for sure before saying anything at all. Can you get a pregnancy test without your parents' (or guardian's) consent? And, if it turns out positive, can a doctor inform them of your pregnancy without *your* consent?

Both questions depend mainly on the law. When you want a pregnancy test, what matters is the age at which your state will allow you to consent to "pregnancy-related medical care" in your *own* right. (This statutory age is not always the same as the statutory age of majority, when you legally attain adulthood—eighteen years in most states. Nor is it necessarily the same as the statutory age at which you can consent to sexual intercourse, or marriage, or contraception, or abortion or even other types of medical care. The law varies not only between states but even between these categories, which makes for much confusion.) As of January 1976 different state laws—as affirmed by legislation, court decisions or the opinions of attorney generals[12]—allow you to get a pregnancy diagnosis without parental consent at the following ages:

*At any age:* Alabama, Alaska, Arkansas, California, District of Columbia, Georgia, Hawaii, Illinois, Kansas, Kentucky, Louisiana, Maryland, Massachusetts, Michigan, Minnesota, Mississippi, Missouri, Montana, New Hampshire, New Jersey, New Mexico, New York, Ohio, Oklahoma, Pennsylvania, Texas, Utah, Virginia.
*From age 12:* Delaware
*From age 15:* Oregon*
*From age 16:* South Carolina*
*From age 18:* Arizona, Colorado, Connecticut, Florida, Idaho, Indiana, Iowa, Maine, Nevada, North Carolina, North Dakota, Rhode Island, South Dakota, Tennessee, Vermont, Washington, West Virginia, Wisconsin*
*From age 19:* Nebraska*, Wyoming

In practice, some doctors insist on parental consent before they will treat a minor, even when their state law does not require it, while others will diagnose a minor without parental consent even if she has not yet reached the required age.

No legal action has ever been brought against a doctor for giving

*The following states also permit diagnosis without parental consent at any age if you are married or "emancipated"—usually defined as living apart from your parents and supporting yourself financially, or already the mother of a child: Arizona, Colorado, Connecticut, Florida, Indiana, Iowa, Nevada, N. Carolina, N. Dakota, S. Carolina, S. Dakota, Vermont, Washington, Wisconsin. Married only: Nebraska, Oregon. Emancipated only: Maine, Rhode Island.)

sex-related treatment to a minor of any age. It is now extremely doubtful whether any such action, if brought, could be successful.

A different question is what can happen if the pregnancy test turns out to be positive. Can a doctor then inform your parents of it without your consent? This again depends on state law. At present Massachusetts is the only state which specifically *prohibits* doctors from giving information on a minor's care to anyone without the minor's written consent, except when her (or his) condition "is believed to be so serious that life or limb is endangered." Most states leave it to the doctors to decide. But several states have given doctors the legal right to tell parents of a minor's pregnancy—whatever the minor's wishes—and have declared that doctors cannot be held liable in any consequent lawsuit for damages.

These laws have so far not been challenged in any court to test whether they are constitutional. Yet they are inconsistent with court decisions on the constitutionality of parental consent requirements for treatment for abortion and contraception (see p. 180). And sometimes they seem directly in conflict with related laws in the same state: Hawaii, for instance, allows a minor to get a pregnancy test legally without parental consent no matter how young, yet insists that the doctor inform the parents if the test is positive when the minor is under eighteen.

The American Medical Association has not laid down any specific ethical guidelines on minors, but it takes the view that doctor-patient confidentiality "should prevail unless the law requires otherwise." At present only Hawaii "requires otherwise" and its law is opposed by many doctors who have campaigned for years to get it changed. So if you go to Planned Parenthood or an otherwise sympathetic clinic or doctor, you can be reasonably sure that your parents will not be told behind your back. The younger you are, the more likely a doctor is to try to persuade you to tell them yourself—in your own interest. The important thing, however, is that you are not discouraged from having an early pregnancy test just because you think a doctor *might* tell your parents without your consent.

### The cost of pregnancy tests
This varies enormously—anything from zero to over $20. The higher prices charged do not seem justified by a technician's time (it takes only a couple of minutes to complete the test) or a doctor's time if the consultation consists only of telling you the result. So it is worth shopping around to compare prices.

Consulting a private physician is the most expensive way of getting a urine test. (Blue Cross allows as "usual, customary and reasonable" between $15 and $20 on the average.) Private hospitals charge similarly. Planned Parenthood fees vary from city to city but are usually in the same range, which is about standard for other nonprofit birth-control or abortion clinics and womens' health centers.

### If you cannot afford to pay

If you are eligible for Medicaid, this will cover the cost. If you are not eligible but nevertheless poor or too young to have money of your own, you can usually get a free or low-cost test through a public hospital. Alternatively, Planned Parenthood provides tests on a sliding scale according to your income and circumstances or, if necessary, free tests: its policy is never to refuse treatment for financial reasons. Zero Population Growth affiliates sometimes refer to clinics which offer free tests. Birthright (the nonabortion organization) and some abortion clinics offer free tests—but see the warning below.

### Possible rip-offs

In 1974 the Department of Consumer Affairs in New York City conducted an investigation into several abortion clinics: women investigators who were not pregnant had pregnancy tests at these clinics and were told the tests were positive.[13] Reports published in other parts of the country[14] also show evidence that profit-conscious abortion clinics have falsified pregnancy-test results. Consequently, some of these clinics have been closed down.

Don't think that *every* abortion clinic offering free tests gives fraudulent diagnoses or that *every* physician is on the take. Such practices are the exception rather than the rule. Planned Parenthood can be relied on to give a genuine service; so, too, can those other birth-control or abortion clinics and womens' centers that are *truly* nonprofit. The difficulty is deciding in advance whether they are or not. If you have to go to a clinic or doctor you are uncertain of, here are some precautions you can take:

- Check which clinics are reputable. Planned Parenthood and the National Organization of Women (if either has affiliates or chapters in your state) can usually give you this information, or call the department of consumer affairs or the health department of your state, city or county.
- Call before going to a clinic and ask about the cost of pregnancy tests

and, if these are offered free, whether you will have to pay if you decide *not* to have an abortion. Also ask about the cost of an abortion and whether this covers all the necessary tests and anesthesia: this may indicate how profit-conscious they are.

- Avoid any clinic that tells you that a pregnancy test is unnecessary.
- Get suspicious if a doctor seems to be pushing or edging you into an abortion before you have had time to think about it, particularly if he does this before you know the result of your test.
- If anything else makes you suspicious (like having a positive test without in any way feeling pregnant), have a test done by someone else quickly as an independent check.

# 2

# *Deciding What to Do*

It may take a little time to get used to the idea that you are definitely pregnant, even if the possibility has dominated your thoughts for the past week or so. Perhaps the first thing to do is to try to get into a sufficiently calm state of mind to find out what you honestly feel about it. Each of the options open to you—marriage, abortion, adoption or bringing up a child on your own—is discussed in the following chapters. This chapter is designed to help you collect your thoughts and work toward the solution that is right for you.

## IMMEDIATE REACTIONS

By no means do all women today become panic-stricken when faced with a pregnancy outside marriage. Yet at the same time, few remain absolutely calm and sure of themselves. The situation is often just as disconcerting for a widow, divorcée or separated wife as for an unmarried woman. At one level, this is hardly surprising: if you didn't plan to get pregnant, naturally you feel caught off-guard. But pregnancy is a momentous event in any woman's life, married or single, and it helps to try to understand your initial feelings, which may include any of the following, or even several mixed up at the same time.

### *Pleasure*
A single woman often feels pleased and proud about her pregnancy, even when the circumstances seem disastrous and she is seriously considering abortion. This can be very unsettling, but without delving too deeply into psychology it is possible to make several guesses as to why it happens. Maybe it's because it makes her feel more *womanly:* fertility may be just as important to a woman as virility is to a man. Maybe it's because it makes her feel more *adult:* getting pregnant is a sign of physical (though not necessarily emotional) maturity. It may have a lot to do with

her feelings of *love:* many women find that becoming pregnant by the man they love is an especially intense experience. Or perhaps it is because, deep down and for reasons she cannot entirely explain, she simply wants a child.

### Doubts and fears

Some kind of initial panic is very common whether a woman is married or single, especially with a first pregnancy. Suddenly she is very aware of what it means to be a woman. Pregnancy can make you feel vulnerable and conscious of the responsibility of bearing a child. You may feel scared of what pregnancy, abortion or childbirth entail physically. But above all, pregnancy is usually a turning point because it prompts so many questions about yourself and what you want out of life.

### Embarrassment

Convention still expects women to become pregnant only within a marriage, and prejudice can be strong against those who do so outside it. The double standards that prevail on the subject of extramarital sex often seem hypocritical and unfair: to many people it's apparently all right for men, but not for women; it's all right if you're discreet but not if you're found out. Until these attitudes change more than they have so far, many women will feel embarrassed (sometimes deeply) at becoming pregnant outside marriage. Many will also take this strongly into account when deciding what to do about the pregnancy.

### Apathy

It can be paralyzing to be confronted with a situation that demands you to make an important and difficult decision. You may find you become very apathetic—wanting to sleep a lot, feeling listless and unable to concentrate, not caring about anything or anyone, wanting to be alone. Some of these reactions may be the physical symptoms of pregnancy, but you may also be trying to escape facing up to the problem by pushing it out of your mind. And you cannot afford to do that. If you want to end the pregnancy, you should be thinking out what abortion means to you and contacting someone who can help as soon as possible. If you want to have the child, that should be a conscious decision, too.

### Activity

Far from feeling lethargic, you may throw yourself into all kinds of activities—working very hard, going out a lot, surrounding yourself with people and things to do. Yet this too may be escapism: *anything* to take your mind off making a decision.

## Instant decisions

One kind of panic reaction is to rush into marriage or have an abortion without really thinking out what either means. Both offer a way of avoiding pregnancy outside marriage. Either may be the right choice in your own case, but you should be as sure as you can be so that you do not regret it later. Check your impulse against the issues discussed in Chapter 3 and Chapter 4.

## Running away

Panic may make you want to run away from home because you feel you can't face anyone knowing about your pregnancy, particularly if you are very young. This may be unnecessary if you have an abortion. If you continue the pregnancy, you have to decide whether going away is a good idea. But there is no advantage in rushing off as soon as you know you're pregnant. Think it over first.

## Suicide

Some women become so frightened that they think about killing themselves. In fact, very few actually attempt it, perhaps because they soon realize that pregnancy is not the end of the world. But if you feel you just can't go on, it is useful to call a suicide prevention organization such as the National Save-A-Life League which offers free counseling and a twenty-four-hour emergency telephone service. Similar organizations are listed in the telephone directory under "Suicide."

## WHO DO YOU TELL?

You may prefer to sort things out for yourself before telling anyone about your pregnancy, or you may feel this is something you can't handle on your own. Certainly you will have to tell someone eventually, but remember this is *your* pregnancy and what you choose to do about it should be *your* decision. Other people may have plenty to say, but they are not you. Many women have found that once other people are involved, their own choice somehow starts slipping away. Instead of honestly considering their own feelings, they let themselves be influenced by the opinions of others.

If you want to keep control over your decision, think out carefully who you want to tell and how they are likely to react. Right now you need practical help and understanding. You do not need people getting upset or panicky. There may be several people to turn to: the man who made you pregnant, your family, friends, or professionals whose job is to help with personal problems.

## The man who made you pregnant

Perhaps he is the most natural person to tell. You may want to discuss whether you should marry. Even if marriage is out, you may still want him to take part in the decision. On the other hand, he may be the last person you want to contact now. If you've already split up, or if you are in the process of getting a divorce from him, you may feel there'd be no point. You may be involved with someone else by now, and so may he. If you're still together, you may worry that the pregnancy will cause him to leave you. Or perhaps you simply don't want him to influence your decision.

Men react in many different ways to the news that they have made a woman pregnant. Some walk out, some behave callously, some are frightened by the demands that may be made on them, and some, not knowing what they should do, do nothing at all. Some strongly resist the idea of abortion or adoption for their child.

Most important, however, is your own attitude. Ask yourself why you want to tell him about the pregnancy and what you expect him to do. You may simply feel that his share of the responsibility is equal to yours, and so in all fairness he should share the decision-making. That's fine. But some women tend to think the decision should come *entirely* from their lovers. Others feel the only thing to be decided is whether their lovers will marry them. For example, a teen-ager may spring the news on her boyfriend in the most alarming way: "My father will kill me— and he'll kill you, too, when he finds out!" What she usually means is that she wants to present her parents with a package deal: "I'm pregnant, but we *are* going to be married." The danger in this approach, if he does agree, is that she has now virtually committed herself both to marriage and to motherhood without really thinking out whether either would be a good idea in her case. Both of these questions—the ones that really matter—are discussed in the next chapter.

Sometimes a woman regards the man's reaction as a test of how he feels about her. If he loves her, surely he will marry her. If he loves her, surely he wouldn't walk out or suggest an abortion or just dither around? This may be true up to a point, but it isn't usually as simple as that. Pregnancy is always a big test of any couple's relationship. It is also a test of how well they know themselves. It usually takes a little time and a lot of heart-searching for a woman to decide what an unintended pregnancy means to her. It can be much the same for a man. Think hard about your own feelings before you break the news. If you can stay reasonably cool, he may turn out to be sympathetic and helpful. It is always difficult for a woman in this situation to feel on equal terms with a man: she is pregnant, and he is not. But you have a mind of your own, and you should use it. After all, you more than anyone else is affected by the circumstances.

### Your parents

Parents often have more influence on their daughter's decision than anyone else, whether they know about the pregnancy or not. She may choose abortion, or to give birth secretly and have the child adopted, rather than risk her parents' anger or disappointment, or because she can't bear to hurt their feelings or upset them. She may marry in haste in order to lessen the shock to them. She may find it particularly difficult to be honest with them if she is pregnant by a married man or expecting a child of mixed race. If she tells them about it, she may come under strong pressure to do what they think best. They may feel they have every right to a say in the decision if, for example, their daughter is very young, or wants to have the child and bring it up in the family home.

So is it best to tell them or not? If so, how far should they be involved ion the decision? Only you can decide this, taking into account your relationship with them, your age and degree of independence from them, your circumstances and what you intend to do.

If you tell your parents, try to understand how they feel, and why. They may blame themselves, perhaps feeling guilty for not communicating with you or not discussing sex in the past. It may take them a long time to realize you are no longer a child. If you are very young it may be even harder for them. They may worry about how the pregnancy will affect your education, their finances and the rest of the family, particularly if you have younger brothers and sisters. If you want to keep the child and they are opposed to the idea, they may not only be thinking of what the neighbors will say; they may also be more fully aware of what it means to bring up a child.

At the same time, your parents should try to understand your feelings, too. You are pregnant and asking for their support. You do not need endless recriminations about how it happened and why. Nor will it help if you are made to feel overly guilty about hurting their feelings and upsetting their lives, or for having had a sexual relationship at all. You may be genuinely sorry to disappoint them, but you cannot go on acting out their fantasies of the sort of person they think you *should* be. You are an individual with values of your own. Your pregnancy, and how you cope with it, is an important event in *your* life.

You may find your parents much more helpful and resilient than you imagined they would be, once they get over the first shock. If you are afraid to tell them but feel you must, you might talk first to a counselor who specializes in this sort of problem (see below). Sometimes parents themselves have very little idea of what can be done and who can help. They may find it easier to cope if some contact has already been made and the alternatives have been discussed. Professional help is also useful if you and your parents cannot agree on what should be done about the pregnancy.

### Friends

You may prefer to turn to a friend first of all. Sometimes it can be enormously helpful to have a sympathetic friend who will just listen while you get it off your chest. Talking it out often clarifies your ideas about what you really feel and what you should do.

Good friends often rally round in other ways. They may give you the moral support to approach a doctor, an abortion clinic or a counselor for the first time. They may lend you money or provide temporary accommodation if that is what is needed. Remember, however, that a friend cannot *always* be relied on to give good advice, and perhaps should not be expected to do so.

If you have a friend who has gone through this herself, she may seem like the ideal person to help you. Certainly, she is likely to have more understanding of the problems than most people. But try not to be influenced too much by her experience. Every woman in this situation must work out the best solution for herself. Your friend's circumstances may be quite different from yours, and her personality may make her cope better, or worse, than you would in carrying through a similar decision.

### Professional advice

Any of several different groups of people can help with personal problems. It isn't easy to explain the differences between them because they vary so much and turn up in a number of professional guises—some of them working so informally that to call them "professional" makes them sound more official (and in some cases more trained) than they actually are. "Pregnancy counseling" may be exactly what it promises—an appraisal of all the alternatives—or it may lean toward one solution rather than another. The following, although perhaps differing in their points of view, all offer help with pregnancy problems:

*Women's centers,* which may also be called women's counseling services, crisis centers and hotlines, are run by women for women. There are now a great many throughout the country, offering paraprofessional counseling on a wide range of problems facing women today. These services may be free or priced according to ability to pay. Most names begin with the word "Women's" or the name of the community (for example, Cleveland Women's Counseling Service) so they are easy to find in the telephone directory; alternatively, they may be listed in the Yellow Pages under "Pregnancy," "Abortion," "Birth Control" or "Counseling." A list of centers throughout the country is also kept by the Women's Action Alliance (see p. 136).

*Planned Parenthood* voluntary birth-control clinics operate in nearly all states and have extended their service into pregnancy-counseling and referrals. Some offer special services for teen-agers. Counseling is either free or according to ability to pay. Local affiliates are listed in the telephone directory. National headquarters is Planned Parenthood Federation of America, Inc., 810 Seventh Avenue, New York, N.Y. 10019 (tel: 212–541–7800).

*Clergy Consultation Service on Abortion* began in 1967 to help women obtain medically safe abortions at a time when they were illegal almost everywhere. Today, this national network of ministers, rabbis and lay people continues to offer free counseling on problem pregnancies, including information on alternatives to abortion and referrals to responsible organizations that can help. Local groups are listed in the telephone directory. If not, contact headquarters at 55 Washington Square South, New York, N.Y. 10012 (tel: 212–477–0034).

*Abortion counselors* at clinics and hospitals should, if they are any good at all, offer all-around pregnancy counseling, although their bias may inevitably be toward abortion. Nonprofit clinics may charge a small fee (adjustable according to ability to pay) for counseling if you do not go on to have an abortion.

*Birthright or Lifeline* groups grew out of the anti-abortion movement and offer free counseling and practical help to women who do not want abortions. They are listed in the telephone directory or may be contacted through Catholic Charities (see below).

*Church welfare organizations* offer counseling on a wide range of problems, including pregnancy, and referrals to sources of help. (Catholic organizations will not help with abortion.) Contact through listings in the telephone directory under "Catholic Charities," "Federation of Protestant Welfare Agencies," "Federation of Jewish Philanthropies."

*Catholic Alternatives,* 30 East 23rd Street, New York, N.Y. 10010 (tel: 212–777–3511) is at present the only Catholic organization offering counseling and support to Catholic women regarding abortion. It plans to open similar services in other parts of the country.

*Social workers* are attached to state, city or county departments of social services or social welfare, hospitals and voluntary organizations throughout the country. They are specially trained in giving practical and personal help on all kinds of problems, including pregnancy. Some are in private practice and are listed in the Yellow Pages under "Social Workers."

*Departments of social services, social welfare, family welfare* all employ people who can help discuss the situation. Some offer free special counseling on pregnancy problems. These will be listed in the telephone directory under the appropriate government department or under the listing for frequently called numbers and emergency services.

*Adoption agencies* now often give all-round pregnancy counseling as the number of women who give up children for adoption has declined. This does not mean that all agencies will give unbiased counseling, but many recognize the need for objective help at the early decision-making stage.

*Community counseling organizations, crisis centers, hot lines* have proliferated throughout the country to meet the demand, especially from young people, for free nonjudgmental counseling on a wide range of problems such as drugs, sexuality, relationships, pregnancy. Some are oriented to ethnic groups. Many are listed in the Yellow Pages under "Counseling," or may be contacted through community information projects.

*Professional counselors and therapists,* like private physicians, charge for their services. They are listed under "Counseling" or "Psychologists" in the Yellow Pages or may be contacted through the department of social services.

Counseling does not mean telling you what to do. Ideally, its purpose is to clarify how *you* feel and what *you* want, so that you come to know what seems best for you. During an informal chat (or perhaps more than one if you need longer to talk and think about it) a good counselor will encourage you to talk about yourself and your problems. She or he will probably ask some questions; you are not obliged to answer them, but it will help if you can be as frank as possible.

Sometimes the problem can be easily settled by specific information. Sometimes it is more complicated and may center on your relationship with the man or your family as well as the pregnancy itself. Or you may be torn about what is the "right" thing to do. Good counselors can help you unravel these tangled emotions so that you understand more clearly why you are confused. They may also strengthen your awareness of yourself as an individual with the right to your own decisions. If you would like them to discuss the situation with the man or your parents (with you or separately), they will do that too. They may make suggestions, but counselors should not influence your decision with their opinions or prejudices—though some may try.

Like doctors and priests, counselors and social workers work on the basis that what a client tells them in private is confidential and not to be divulged to anyone else without the client's consent. If you are a young teen-ager, a counselor may feel that it is in your best interests for your parents to know about your pregnancy, but they should try to persuade you to tell them yourself or offer to break the news with your consent.

### How to approach them
Telephone for an appointment. All you need say is that you are pregnant and want to talk to someone about it as soon as possible. If you feel nervous, remember their job is to help you, not to judge you. You will probably know soon after you meet the counselor whether this is a person you can talk to and trust. If the person you see makes you feel uncomfortable, or you find you cannot communicate easily with each other, try someone else.

## SEX AND THE LAW
If you are under the age of consent for sexual intercourse, or if your pregnancy is the result of forcible rape or incest, the man who made you pregnant has broken the law and runs the risk of prosecution. It is important to know the implications of all three situations.

### If you are below the age of consent
All states have set a minimum age below which a woman cannot consent to sexual intercourse without her partner being open to the charge of statutory rape. This is different from forcible rape in that it does not

matter whether she agreed to sex or not: it depends entirely on her age. Most states have fixed the age of consent at sixteen to eighteen, a few at fourteen.

These laws were intended to protect young girls, particularly from much older men. But they are obviously frequently broken, often by young couples of the same age. Many teen-agers have sex willingly, which is why some people suggest that the age of consent should be lowered or abolished. It is also the reason the police do not investigate the case of every underage girl who becomes pregnant. Usually they start inquiries only if a complaint is made against the man concerned.

The age of the man is important. Some states do not prosecute men who are the same age as their girlfriends, and some require it to be established that the girl was a virgin before statutory rape can be charged at all. In general, the younger the girl and the older the man, the more likely the risk of prosecution. In most cases a man cannot defend himself by claiming that he thought the girl was older.

The complaint is usually made by the girl's parents or guardians. It would be very unusual for a doctor or social worker/counselor to make a complaint or give information to the police: it is against the ethical code of both professions. However, the only way a girl can guarantee that her boyfriend is protected from the law is to refuse to admit that he was responsible for her pregnancy or ever had intercourse with her. This too has its dangers: if she has the child, the declaration could be used at a later date to deny her child support from the man.

## Forcible rape

In law, rape means proving that a man used violence or the threat of violence to overcome a woman's resistance, or deliberately gave her drink or drugs to make her incapable of defending herself. The penalties for convicted rapists range from a minimum of one year's imprisonment to a maximum (in fourteen states) of life imprisonment or death.

If you want to prove a man raped you, it helps if you went to the police immediately after it happened, if a doctor examined you and found signs of forced intercourse, or if you have witnesses who found you in a distressed state at the time. Otherwise it is only your word against his. In this case, the police might be reluctant to prosecute, your lawyer might advise you not to proceed and, if the case came to court, the judge might direct the jury not to convict. In about half the states, the law does not technically require corroboration of the victim's testimony, but the judge always instructs the jury to weigh this testimony very carefully, with the result that it tends to be regarded with suspicion if there is no other evidence to consider.

Is it worth trying to prove a man raped you? In principle, yes—if it prevents the man subjecting other women to the same distressing, and perhaps harmful, experience. In practice, there are disadvantages. In court you can expect to be cross-examined not only on the alleged rape but on your sex life in general. Only very few state laws protect a woman against this ordeal in which she may justifiably feel that it is she, rather than the man, who is on trial.

The psychological traumas of being raped and the humiliation of trying to obtain justice have led in recent years to the setting up of many rape crisis centers. These are usually run by women and are a valuable source of help after a terrifying experience. They offer counseling, legal advice and emergency medical attention to prevent venereal disease or to insure against pregnancy. The Rape Crisis Center, P.O. Box 21005, Washington D.C. 20009 (tel: 202-347-4278) keeps a list of rape crisis centers throughout the country.

## WORKING TOWARD A SOLUTION

The real problem of becoming unintentionally pregnant, whether or not you are married, is that it confronts you with the necessity of making an important decision. It means dealing with all kinds of questions about yourself that may never have arisen before and, above all, being as honest as you can with yourself. This is no bad thing—in fact, it can be an enlightening experience. You may find, as many women have, that it gives you the best incentive you've ever had to examine your deepest feelings and to take a good look at the way your life is going.

Of course, you may know from the start exactly what you want to do. Even so it is best to put the decision to the test by considering the alternatives carefully, if only to make it less likely that you will regret your choice later on. Your decision may be influenced to a certain extent by circumstances outside your control—the man's reaction or your dependence on your parents. Sometimes your choice will change as your situation alters: for example, the sudden chance of getting a home of your own may enable you to marry or keep the child when both seemed impossible before. But the essential thing is to work out what this pregnancy means to you *at this particular time in your life*.

You should be prepared for the fact that you may have to compromise. Sometimes, what you would ideally like to do is not possible in the circumstances, and you will have to settle for something else. This can be hard to accept, but it must be recognized. While women today have more choice in the matter than ever before, each choice involves practical problems and imposes emotional demands that may be difficult to resolve. This can be seen more clearly from the simplified chart below. The issues it raises are discussed in greater detail in following chapters.

### Marriage

| FOR | AGAINST |
|---|---|
| Avoids unmarried pregnancy. Child born into two-parent family. More security. Personal fulfillment as wife as well as mother if it works out well. | May be risky grounds for marriage, divorce figures discouraging. Pregnancy may still cause financial, housing and emotional problems. Effect on child (and any children born later) if marriage is unhappy. |

### Abortion

| FOR | AGAINST |
|---|---|
| Avoids unwanted pregnancy. Normal life can be resumed immediately. Safe and simple if done early, according to best available evidence. | Moral objections to abortion. Possible emotional conflict. Long-term effects not fully known. |

### Adoption

| FOR | AGAINST |
|---|---|
| May give child better chance in life. Avoids difficulties of bringing up child alone. Normal life can be resumed again with fewer restrictions than child inevitably imposes. | Usually grief and maybe guilt at giving child away. Uncertainty that child would necessarily have better life with another family. Child loses contact with natural origins, unless adopted by other members of own family. |

### Bringing up a child alone

| FOR | AGAINST |
|---|---|
| Possible benefit to child of own mother's care. Possible self-fulfillment and personal development through being a mother. Child maintains own identity through natural family. | Usually serious practical and emotional difficulties for mother, possibly affecting child. Possible resentment against child if mother feels trapped. |

Note: The pros and cons of two half-way solutions are discussed later. The child may be placed with a foster family until the mother can look after it herself (pp. 96–98). The question of living with the child's father, or another man, without marrying him is discussed on p. 37.

# 3

*Marriage*

Little more than a decade ago, abortion was illegal and an illegitimate child was considered (at least in white, middle-class families) the ultimate disgrace. Therefore, if you inadvertently became pregnant, a speedy marriage was socially desirable. Today, in a more flexible world, that is no longer generally true.

By 1972, the number of "conceptions legitimized by marriage" (statistical language for children conceived before marriage but born afterwards) had fallen to just under 130,000. This represented only 12.5 percent of all first births within marriage in that year, compared to 22 percent in 1966.[1] As these figures preceded the 1973 Supreme Court ruling on abortion, we can assume that the total is even fewer today. Yet it would be quite wrong to conclude that women who do not marry while pregnant are all strong-mindedly rejecting marriage in a new-found spirit of independence. Thousands very much want to be married. (Some become pregnant, deliberately or unconsciously, in an effort to precipitate marriage.) Most single women when pregnant at least consider getting married, if given the choice. A great many do not have the choice.

This last point is of utmost importance because it is not generally recognized that while a pregnant single woman's options in all other directions have greatly increased, her option to marry has actually lessened. Paradoxically, the same factors that freed pregnant women from the tyranny of forced marriage have turned the trend in the opposite direction: the pressure now is to have an abortion or go it alone. And as Kristin Luker points out in her survey of abortion patients[2]: "In direct contrast to the past, when social custom pressured men to 'make honest women' out of women they had impregnated, our present contraceptive technology has increasingly created an ideology that says an unwanted pregnancy is the woman's fault."

32

Whether this is a good or bad thing depends on your point of view. No one wants to feel that she has blackmailed a man into marriage, and indeed, statistics show that young marriages (where the bride is under twenty) and marriages that begin with pregnancy are both far more likely to end in divorce than others.[3]

On the other hand, society has not yet arranged matters so that a woman is equally well protected whether she marries or not. In most cases, her opportunities and earning power are far less than a man's; with a child they drop even farther. And so it is little wonder if she sees pregnancy as a way to get back her old conventional advantages—to acquire a higher status and standard of living, as well as protection for her children. Once again, we are back in the "transition gap" or, as Kristin Luker calls it, the "option squeeze"—a "period in which women are likely to feel the loss of traditional options before the real availability of new options becomes an accomplished fact."

This may explain something of your present predicament if (perhaps in spite of a normally independent outlook) your instant reaction to the news of pregnancy is: Will he marry me? Yet the fundamental question, surely, is whether you want a child. Marriage will not stop your being pregnant; it simply stops you being unmarried.

This may seem an overly simplistic way of looking at it. You may point out that it is impossible to separate your feelings about your pregnancy from your feelings about the man. Or that you are perfectly willing to have a child, but not on your own. Or that, as you see it, the choice comes down to giving a child two parents or not having a child at all. All these points are valid. But it is also worth asking yourself whether you want a child for its own sake or whether you see the pregnancy as a way of resolving an uncertain relationship between its father and yourself. Everything depends on whether you and the man feel ready for marriage and whether both of you welcome the idea of having a child at this time. This is something only you can decide for yourselves, but there are several points you might take into consideration.

## IF YOU BOTH WANT TO GET MARRIED

There is no reason why you should not get married if that is what you were planning to do anyway. Sometimes pregnancy brings a couple closer together and makes them realize, perhaps for the first time, that they would like to formalize the relationship. However, this does not necessarily mean that the pregnancy won't cause problems.

What if you have little money and can't afford the additional expense of a child? What if your husband-to-be is still in school and won't be able to work for some time? What if you needed to depend on *your* earnings for a year or two after marriage in order to set up a home? What if you want time to adjust to each other before starting a family? For reasons such as these, some couples decide that it is better for the woman to have an abortion or, more rarely, to have the child adopted, even though they have every intention of getting married eventually.

Of course, you may see it quite differently. You may be delighted at the idea of a baby right now. Or you may not be able to accept the alternatives of abortion or adoption. You may worry that you would never forgive yourself for having ended this pregnancy or given your first child away. And so you may be determined to manage somehow, whatever problems get in the way.

Sometimes a young couple who want a child solve the immediate housing problem by moving in with parents. This can work quite well —if their family recognizes them as a married couple with the right to privacy, and if the couple is strong enough not to let tensions affect their relationship with one another or with the child. But it can also be extremely difficult for several generations to live together under one roof, particularly if conditions are cramped as a result.

It is also a good idea to think about how a child might complicate your early married life. The first year or so of marriage is often a trying time. Learning to live together is not always easy, and it takes time to realize that quarrels and upsets are not necessarily the end of it all but are just part of the normal process. Having a baby can sometimes add to the difficulties and demand much more understanding, simply because it means getting used to *two* major changes in your lives at once.

This is why it is so important to talk it over thoroughly together and to be as honest as you can be about how you both feel. If you agree that what you want to do is right for both of you, there is no reason why the marriage shouldn't get off to a good start, whether you continue the pregnancy or not.

But what if you can't agree? What if one of you wants an abortion and the other wants a child? This can cause a lot of distress and is likely to test your relationship to the utmost. If you want to stay together but cannot reconcile your separate views on what should be done, it may be worth seeking professional advice, as suggested on pp. 24–26. If all else fails, the final decision must be yours. You are the one who is pregnant.

You, more than the man, will feel the effects of having an abortion or having a child.

## IF YOU ARE NOT SURE ABOUT MARRIAGE

If you are less than sure that you want to get married, you need to think about it very carefully indeed. Two of the reasons for your hesitation could be: you don't feel ready for marriage, or you are uncertain whether you want to marry the particular man who made you pregnant. In these circumstances, most advisers would say: *Don't!* They are probably right, and yet you obviously have some reason for contemplating it at all.

If you are very young, it could be that someone is putting pressure on you to marry—your parents or the man himself. Even today many parents are so concerned to get a pregnant daughter respectably married that, if the man is willing, she is hardly given a chance to think of an alternative. On the other hand, they may be so utterly opposed to her marrying the man who made her pregnant that they may unwittingly push her into it by creating a kind of pressure in reverse.

Quite a few teen-agers use pregnancy as a way of punishing their parents, or getting back at them for some real or imagined hurt. If their parents can't bear the boyfriend, he seems all the more attractive. Because the atmosphere at home has become intolerable, the idea of moving out and setting up a home with someone else becomes highly appealing. So some girls rush blindly into marriage as an escape, or as a gesture of rebellion, without giving sufficient thought to the really important issues.

Marriage may seem sensible also because you feel this may be your last chance and, though this man is not your ideal, he wants to marry you and could prove to be a good husband. If you are in your thirties and have never married, this can be a matter of real concern. (You may feel, too, that this could be your last chance to have a baby.) Sometimes much younger girls believe this may be their last opportunity to marry. Most people would write this off as nonsense, but it may be a more serious worry for a pregnant girl who wants to keep her child: if she doesn't marry her current boyfriend, will her status as a single mother reduce her chances of getting married in the future? Some single mothers don't marry, although not always because they don't have the opportunity. The majority do get married sooner or later, but a growing trend is for single mothers to choose not to.

Another possible reason for thinking about marriage is that you honestly feel you would like to complete this pregnancy and have the child but are terrified of doing it alone. Sometimes being pregnant without the emotional and practical support of a man can be difficult and lonely (see Chapter 5). Usually it isn't easy to bring up a child on your own (see Chapter 7). So marriage may seem the safest, or perhaps the least complicated, thing to do. On the other hand, your problem may simply be not being able to decide what your true feelings are for the man. Your hesitation may be no more than the normal apprehension many women feel at the brink of committing themselves to marriage, or it may be that you have genuine doubts about the person. It isn't always easy to tell the difference, but there is one test you can apply: If you've ever caught yourself wondering about divorcing him in the hazy future, then the chances are that deep down you have real doubts about the marriage.

Any of these reasons, and perhaps several more of your own, may explain something of your present dilemma. You therefore have to decide if marriage to a man you are not sure about is a good idea in *any* circumstances—including pregnancy. For a start, you could get married and promptly miscarry (as many women have). Then how would you feel about your husband?

Sometimes a compromise may be possible. If you want to continue the pregnancy, you can consider postponing the decision about marriage until later on. Often the first news of pregnancy throws a couple into such confusion that they cannot work out how they really feel about each other until they've calmed down. Some couples don't decide to marry until after their children are born; some choose to live together instead. Neither one of these may entirely solve what may well be your biggest worry—security—but it might give you a chance to see more clearly if marriage is the right thing to do.

## IF YOU ARE SURE BUT YOUR BOYFRIEND IS NOT

This is probably the most unhappy situation to be in. Many women are shocked to find that pregnancy changes everything between themselves and the father. Sometimes the man opts out completely; sometimes he appears indifferent, or incapable of offering any opinions on the subject. In a way, this is not surprising. Most young men are terrified of being pushed into marriage before they feel ready to cope with it. For them, marriage implies having to support a wife and children for years to come.

Although in many modern marriages it is taken for granted that the wife will work and help support the family too, a pregnancy suggests that she may not be able to do so, just at this early stage in his career when his earning power is probably at its lowest. It could be that his reaction is simply the fear of being trapped by too much responsibility too soon. If he is no longer young, he doesn't want the responsibility, period.

On the other hand, perhaps he was not so deeply in love with you as you thought he was. Or even as *he* thought he was. Pregnancy forces any couple to work out what really matters to them, when otherwise they might have let time decide. It is better for him to stop and think now than do the "honorable" thing and rush into a marriage he may later regret. You may feel furious and rejected if he appears to think that it's your fault and therefore your problem, but that response should demonstrate to you that a happy marriage with him would be unlikely.

## IF YOU ARE LIVING TOGETHER

Living together "without benefit of marriage"—or cohabitation as it is formally called—is still illegal in twenty-seven states, although these archaic laws are only occasionally enforced. Nevertheless, the latest census figures (1970) show that about a quarter of a million people are now living together, and this is almost certainly an underestimate. For an increasing number of couples, cohabitation is an acceptable and desirable way of life.

If you are already cohabiting, you have one big advantage. You know what it's like living together and should have a reasonable idea whether you want to stay together permanently. Of course, it isn't always as simple as that. Some couples live together *because* at least one of them is unsure about getting married. Sometimes pregnancy makes them realize they would like to get married; or they may feel that a child is the only justification for marriage anyway. Other times it causes as much soul-searching as in a couple who don't know each other nearly so well.

It may be that marriage is impossible at the moment: if one of you is still married to someone else, you would have to get the divorce settled first. Or perhaps you are against formal marriage on principle and can see no reason why pregnancy, or a child, should make much difference. There are many couples who, for reasons like this, stay together and raise whole families without getting married legally.

However, you must accept the fact that a single mother who is living with a man has less security than a woman who brings up a baby on her own. If you are financially independent, of course, there's no problem. But what if you can't work, or don't want to work, while your child is very small? You cannot claim AFDC as a mother on her own might, because the authorities assume that a mother living with a man is also being supported by him. You would therefore be entirely dependent on him and have no money of your own. That may not worry you if he is willing to support both you and the child, and you are happy with the arrangement. But what if you later split up? You will probably find it difficult to obtain maintenance and a legal share in the home. And what if he dies? You cannot inherit from him unless he has made a will in your favor, and you might not even be able to continue living in your home.

This may strike you as a materialistic way of looking at it, but you have to consider the future of your child, too. Financial security may not in itself be a good enough reason for marrying, but you both should think seriously about the consequences to you and the child if you don't marry, and perhaps make alternative legal arrangements for more protection. *The Cohabitation Handbook* by Morgan D. King (Berkeley: Ten Speed Press, 1975) provides some useful ideas in this direction. A lawyer can also advise you.

## IF HE IS ALREADY MARRIED

In this situation everything really depends on how honest he is about his real feelings and intentions. Perhaps he was always honest with you about the fact that he would never leave his wife and family. If so, you know quite clearly that marriage is out.

But what do you do if he is still promising to divorce his wife and marry you, and you don't know whether to believe him? The only thing you can do is to try to forget for a moment all the things he's *said* and take a searching look at everything he's *done* since you began the affair. Is he still living with his wife, or has he already left home? Is he secretive about your meetings, or doesn't he appear to mind if anyone he knows sees you with him? Does he welcome you phoning him at work or meeting him there? Does he ever see you on weekends and holidays?

The main thing to bear in mind is that divorce is usually a very difficult step for a man to take, even if his marriage is unhappy and he genuinely cares for you. Apart from the financial considerations (how will he support two families?), he may be struggling to come to terms with his own sense of failure for the breakdown of his marriage, guilt over his wife, love for his children. For some men, if their girlfriends become pregnant, the pressures and conflicts are too much to bear. So they may do nothing—perhaps preferring to endure things as they are rather than face up to so many overwhelmingly demanding decisions.

It is a different matter if he has already left home or is already living with you. You may not be able to get married yet, but you will probably be able to work out whether you want to eventually, and make a decision about the pregnancy according to your circumstances and feelings. But if he is still living with his wife, it would be best to make up your mind about the pregnancy as though you were on your own—which, unfortunately, is actually the case.

### IF YOU ARE THINKING OF MARRYING SOMEONE ELSE

Perhaps you are going steady but became pregnant by someone else for reasons that no longer matter. You may decide to have an abortion without telling your current man. Or you may decide to tell him the truth. Obviously you risk losing him. But it may not happen like that. He may care for you so much that he would be prepared to marry you and keep the child rather than split up. In this case, you should try to have a very frank talk before deciding to marry. Will he really be able to forget and forgive the circumstances in which the child was conceived and treat him or her in exactly the same way as any children of his own? On the other hand, he may lay down conditions: he will marry you only if you have an abortion or have the child adopted. This might be exceptionally difficult for you. If you genuinely want to marry him (and not just because you are pregnant) you will have to decide what those conditions mean to you and to your relationship with him.

### IF YOU ARE UNDERAGE

Most states require that a person who is under eighteen must obtain parental consent to be married, although in some states the legal age is still nineteen, twenty or twenty-one. Some states have laws that permit parental consent to be waived if the woman is pregnant, even if she is as young as twelve or thirteen. There are also states that prohibit marriage below certain ages (usually sixteen or eighteen for boys, fourteen or sixteen for girls), even if a child is expected or already born.

If your parents refuse their consent, listen to their reasons and ask yourself whether what they say makes sense. They may be right! Certainly they must feel strongly about it if you are pregnant. If you find it impossible to discuss it with them without having an argument, ask someone whose opinions you trust. Alternatively, you could seek professional advice (see p. 26), particularly if you are very young. This might help convince your parents (or anyone else involved, such as a social worker or teacher) that you are mature enough to make a decision like this. Sometimes everything seems very uncomplicated when you're young. If you want to get married, what's wrong with that? If you want a baby, why shouldn't you have one? Unfortunately, it *is* more complicated than it may seem. Do ask yourself whether your desire to get married isn't mixed in with some other motive: wanting to drop out of school, wanting to be the first among your friends to marry, or wanting to get away from home and live a life of your own. Sometimes marriage seems easier than staying at school or remaining with your parents. It isn't!

Some girls marry very young and enjoy growing up with their husbands, perhaps looking forward to still being young when their own children are teen-agers. But often a young couple find themselves growing up differently, perhaps coming to resent their lost freedom, perhaps finding they have little in common after a few years. This may be the main reason for the high divorce rate among such couples. It also may be that so many divorced or separated mothers find themselves at a disadvantage on the job market because they did not make the most of their training opportunities earlier on.

However, if, after careful consideration, you still wish to marry and your parents still refuse, you may be able to apply to a court to have any parental consent requirements waived on the ground of your pregnancy. A social worker or a lawyer can advise you on your state law and how to approach the court.

# 4

❧

# *Abortion*

Abortion has been legal in every part of the United States since January 1973 when the U.S. Supreme Court struck down restrictive state abortion laws as unconstitutional. In effect, this landmark decision gave all women the right to abortion on request, regardless of reasons, up to about the sixth month of pregnancy—a right restricted only by the willingness of a qualified physician to perform the abortion. In practice, however, some women are still prevented from exercising that right because abortion services are lacking in their home areas and they cannot afford to travel elsewhere.

Abortion may seem the easiest way out of an unwanted pregnancy, but you have to be clear in your own mind that it is really what you want. Ending a pregnancy provokes a variety of emotions and strong opinions. It has caused bitter controversy for years and is likely to do so for some time to come. However, the *only* person who can possibly know what it means to you is yourself. So it is important to understand what abortion is about and what it means in relation to the different stages of pregnancy.

## ABORTION AND THE STAGES OF PREGNANCY

How far your pregnancy is advanced is calculated from the first day of your last menstrual period (LMP) because it is assumed that you were not pregnant when you last had a period. If you actually conceived two weeks after your last period, your pregnancy will be two weeks less advanced than the doctor says it is—but he will calculate from your LMP anyway to be on the safe side. Therefore all references in this chapter to length of pregnancy—known medically as gestation—mean the number of weeks that have gone by since your LMP.

Traditionally doctors accepted twenty-eight weeks gestation as the upper limit to when an abortion might be performed because if born then few babies would be "viable"—that is, able to survive outside the womb with suitable care. Now, with improvements in medical care, a few have been known to survive at twenty-two to twenty-four weeks, so most doctors today regard twenty weeks as the upper limit.

However, doctors usually make an important distinction between abortion during the first twelve weeks of pregnancy and abortion later. For convenience, doctors divide the nine months of pregnancy into three-month periods, each known as a "trimester." The first trimester is defined as the first twelve to thirteen weeks, the second trimester as from thirteen to about twenty-four weeks, and the third trimester as the remaining weeks of pregnancy. It is now well established that legal abortion during the first trimester is a relatively safe and simple operation, but beyond that the risks increase. The earlier it is done, the easier it is for both women and medical staff to accept abortion emotionally. Speed is therefore essential in deciding to have an abortion.

At what stage is abortion justified? This is purely a matter of individual belief. Some people take the view that abortion means taking the life of an unborn child and so regard it as akin to murder whenever it is done. Others hold that it depends on when you think life actually begins: Is it with conception, with the "quickening," or with birth? Others believe that it is the woman's circumstances and feelings about her pregnancy that justify an abortion rather than the stage at which it is performed.

What of *medical* thinking? As a profession, doctors have been less concerned than lawyers and theologians as to the question of when precisely life begins. Instead, their interest has centered on whether abortion is ever ethically justified and, if so, under what circumstances (see p. 55). In general, theirs is the *scientific* standpoint that fertilization and pregnancy is a continuous process, and there is no single point which can be identified as the start of life. This becomes clearer if we look at birth control methods which are supposed to "prevent" pregnancy. Contraceptive creams (p. 171) used in the vagina destroy live sperm from the man before they can fertilize the woman's egg. The function of both the contraceptive pill (p. 142) and the IUD (p. 155) depends partly on destroying a fertilized egg by preventing it from implanting itself into the wall of the womb. "Morning-after" pills (p. 5) certainly work by aborting a newly fertilized egg *after* conception. The fine line between preventative and abortifacient methods of controlling fertility is already blurred.

So each woman must decide for herself at what stage abortion is justified, according to her own feelings and the medical facts. The following account of the development of a fertilized egg into an embryo and then into a fetus throughout normal pregnancy is based on an authoritative medical textbook[1] and the latest statistics on the survival rate of prematurely born babies[2]:

Around the end of the *second week* after the last menstrual period, an egg (ovum) is released from the ovaries and, if a sperm penetrates it, the egg is fertilized. The fertilized egg then consists of a single cell and is known to medicine as the zygote. It takes about seven days for the egg to move down through the Fallopian tubes into the womb. At the end of the *third week,* the egg implants itself into the wall of the womb. At this stage (if removed from the womb) it is invisible to the naked eye, but may be detected under the microscope.

From the *third to the eighth weeks* it is known as the embryo. At the end of the fourth week it is just visible, and at the end of the fifth week it is the size of a small dot: the spine and nervous system are beginning to form but no human characteristics are detectable. At six weeks small buds, which will become arms and legs, are visible.

At *eight weeks* the bones have begun to form and elementary hands and feet appear. The embryo is now about one inch long and at this stage becomes known as the fetus. By ten weeks it is one and one-half inches long and the ears and limbs are formed.

At *twelve weeks* the fetus has more than doubled in size to about three and one-half inches. The face is now properly formed, fingers and toes are separated, and the fetus makes some spontaneous movements.

It is *sixteen weeks* before the sex of the fetus can be easily distinguished. Although heartbeats and vigorous movements are present, they can only rarely be detected by the woman. The fetus measures about six inches and weighs about six ounces at this point.

By *twenty weeks* the woman can usually feel the movements of the fetus (although it can occur at any time between the sixteenth and twenty-second week). This stage is known as the "quickening," and the woman may feel for the first time that life has truly begun. The fetus weighs about ten ounces and all its organs are functioning properly. But it is still not viable—that is, able to live outside the woman's body.

By *twenty-four weeks* the fetus measures about twelve inches and weighs about one and one-half pounds. If born, the fetus will attempt to breathe but will almost certainly die shortly after birth. Only about three percent of fetuses born at this stage will survive with intensive care.

Most doctors draw a medical line against abortion here unless the woman's life would be endangered by continuing the pregnancy. The Supreme Court has ruled that any state legislature may, if it wishes, prohibit abortion after this stage except where necessary to preserve the life and health of the woman.

By *thirty weeks* the chances of survival after birth would be about 60 percent with suitable medical care, while at *thirty-two weeks* this chance rises to about 90 percent and at *thirty-six weeks* to 97 percent. Full term for a normal human pregnancy is *forty weeks*.

*Note:* If you want an abortion and are uncertain about the date of your last menstrual period, ask the doctor you consult to examine you to see how far on you are. Never lie about the date of your LMP to the doctor. It will not help you get an abortion more easily. The physician who decides to perform the abortion will, in any case, examine you to confirm the length of pregnancy. But if you try to pretend that you are less far on than you actually are, there is a danger that the abortion might be delayed—and delay increases the risk to your health (see pp. 49–50).

## KINDS OF ABORTION

There are four different kinds of abortion: spontaneous, self-induced, criminal, and legal. There are also several different methods that are used for legal abortions.

### Spontaneous abortion

This is the medical term for what we usually call a miscarriage. It happens when the body expels the embryo or fetus of its own accord. Precisely why miscarriages occur is not fully understood: it seems that the body has a delicate mechanism for rejecting an embryo that is imperfect or has not established itself properly in the womb. It has been estimated that between 15 and 25 percent of all pregnancies miscarry, most often before the twelfth week. Early signs are backache, abdominal pains and bleeding. At this stage the pregnancy can sometimes be saved by resting in bed. If you suspect you are having a miscarriage, you should call a doctor immediately.

If you are unwillingly pregnant, a miscarriage may come as a relief. Nevertheless, it is important to consult a doctor, to protect both your health and your peace of mind. Sometimes it is necessary to use vacuum suction or a D and C (dilation and curettage) to remove the remains of an incomplete miscarriage; any tissues left behind can cause infection

It may also be sensible to have a pregnancy test to make certain you are no longer pregnant; sometimes a pregnancy continues normally in spite of unusual bleeding.

## Self-induced abortion

Since the beginning of time, women with unwanted pregnancies have attempted to bring on miscarriages or abort themselves, using a variety of methods. You may have heard of a few yourself. *Don't try them.* They hardly ever work and some are extremely dangerous. Gin and hot baths, drugs and laxatives, herbal drinks and violent exercise are all useless unless a miscarriage is already imminent. Swallowing quantities of birth-control pills will, if anything, support the pregnancy instead of ending it. Even the remedies that sound "medical"—so-called abortifacient pills, potions and suppositories sold by some druggists—are expensive and have no effect whatsoever, except perhaps to make you feel sick.

Sometimes a woman is desperate enough to attempt more dangerous methods. It is important to know just what these can do to you. Inserting a sharp instrument up through the vagina, introducing soap pastes or douche solutions or chemical suppositories, drinking strong household fluids, can all cause terrible internal injuries, infection, excessive bleeding, shock and death. It is possible to damage yourself badly without getting rid of the pregnancy; anything powerful enough to destroy a fetus may also kill you.

## Criminal abortion

It is also risky to go to a criminal abortionist (a person who is not a physician). Before the 1973 Supreme Court ruling, when most states prohibited abortion except to save a woman's life, many physicians performed abortions that were illegal under the laws of their state but were, nevertheless, medically safe. Today we can define an illegal abortionist as someone who has no formal medical training; as confirmed by the Supreme Court in November, 1975, such a person can be prosecuted under the criminal code of every state. It may be that in the future we will see an increase of paramedics in abortion—that is, people without formal medical credentials—who have been specially trained to perform early abortions. However, at present no state has authorized the training of paramedics for abortion purposes.

It is impossible to judge how much illegal abortion there still is in this country. Christopher Tietze, director of abortion research at the Population Council, has calculated that 70 percent of the legal abortions performed on resident women in New York City during the two years after its abortion law was liberalized in 1970, actually replaced illegal abortions which had previously been performed.[3] Further evidence of a substantial reduction can be seen in the decreasing number of women who are admitted to hospitals with septic complications of the uterus or incomplete abortions—very often the result of the illegal abortionist's handiwork. Known deaths from illegal abortion fell from thirty-nine in 1972 to five in 1974. It is also a matter of common sense that most women would choose to have a legal abortion rather than risk going to an illegal abortionist. Not only is it medically safer, but usually cheaper.

On the other hand, it is only a comparatively short time since medical abortion has become universally legal throughout the country. Many women may not yet realize that they *can* obtain an abortion legally; the hostile attitudes of some doctors and hospitals still make it difficult to obtain abortions in some areas; a woman's own fears of making her pregnancy known may cause her to drift into the hands of someone who, she hears, "knows what to do," instead of consulting a qualified doctor. So it is likely that illegal abortion is still going on.

## Legal abortion

A legal induced abortion is one performed by a licensed physician in a clinic or a hospital or the physician's own office, according to certain conditions required by law. There are several different methods, depending on how far advanced the pregnancy is, who is doing it and under what circumstances.

*Within fourteen days* of an overdue period, it is sometimes possible to have a very early abortion (otherwise known as menstrual extraction or menstrual regulation) by the suction method (see p. 8).

*Under thirteen weeks* gestation, it is normal to terminate pregnancy through the vagina, using either suction or dilation and curettage.

*Between thirteen and sixteen weeks* many American doctors will not perform abortions by any method, in the belief that complications are more likely during this time than either before or after. But this view is no longer supported by the evidence: the Joint Program for the Study of Abortion 1970–1 shows that the complication rate for abortions performed after sixteen weeks is three to four times higher than for abortions carried out between thirteen and sixteen weeks (see p. 49). So delay does not seem justified. Some American doctors, of course, do perform suctions and D and Cs up to about sixteen weeks.

*After sixteen weeks* a method known as intra-amniotic injection (saline or prostaglandin) becomes necessary. The only other method of abortion used in later pregnancy is hysterotomy—an abdominal operation not often performed in the United States. Occasionally a hysterectomy (not in itself an abortion method) is performed to remove the entire uterus, in effect sterilizing the woman at the same time as terminating her pregnancy.

*Dilation and curettage (D and C)* This involves dilating (stretching) the cervix (neck of the uterus) with a tong-like instrument and scraping out the fetal tissue in the womb with a metal, spoon-shaped instrument known as a curette. The technique has been used for a long time and is not confined to abortion; it is also used to empty the uterus of any tissues left behind after childbirth or a miscarriage and to remove tissue that can be examined to diagnose certain gynecological problems. It is usually performed under a light general anesthetic. Although some doctors prefer this method because they are familiar with it, D and Cs have generally lost favor in recent years to the suction method, which is regarded as being less traumatic.

*Suction* The suction method, which has been in use for many years, also involves stretching the cervix, but a hollow metal tube called a cannula is used instead of a curette to empty the uterus. The cannula is attached to a suction machine which works something like a vacuum cleaner. Either a general or local anesthetic is used. Suction can also be used for the gynecological purposes described above, instead of a D and C. A recent refinement is to use a thin, soft plastic tube which stretches the cervix as little as possible and is less likely to damage the uterine wall than metal instruments. It is this technique that has made outpatient abortion possible, since it minimizes the need for anesthesia. It can be done without any anesthetic, but usually a light local is used, which prevents pain or discomfort while keeping the woman conscious. The procedure itself takes only five to seven minutes. The whole clinic or hospital process, including blood tests, counseling, the abortion itself and recovery time, takes between three and five hours. Most women feel fine afterwards and are able to return to work almost immediately.

*Intra-amniotic injection* This method, used after sixteen weeks, is considered preferable to hysterotomy, at present the only other alternative in the late stages. There are two variations:

*Saline* The abdomen is anesthetized locally; then a long needle is passed through it and into the amniotic sac which contains the fetus. The needle draws off some of the amniotic fluid in the sac, and this is replaced by a saline (salt) solution. The saline brings on contractions of the womb so that the fetus is expelled—a process similar to labor in childbirth. The contractions start some hours after the injection and may continue for some time (up to about forty-eight hours). The fetus is dead on expulsion.

*Prostaglandin* This is a drug that also brings on contractions. It is regarded as safer than saline, which can be dangerous if a mistake occurs and the salt solution is injected into the woman's bloodstream instead of the amniotic sac. Labor may take a shorter time if prostaglandin is used. However, the fetus may live for a short time after expulsion.

Both methods can be unpleasant and distressing, to the woman and to the nursing staff, since the fetus is usually well formed. This type of second-trimester abortion is nearly always carried out in a hospital. The woman remains there several hours after the fetus is expelled. Occasionally a woman reacts badly to a saline or prostaglandin injection, and the procedure may have to be stopped.

*Hysterotomy* This is a major surgical operation, performed under general anesthesia. The fetus is removed through a cut in the abdomen, usually below the pubic hairline, like a birth by Caesarean section. This method has often been used for early abortions. But ideally it should be used only as a last resort—*never* under sixteen weeks and preferably not under twenty weeks unless for some reason a woman cannot have an intra-amniotic injection or in the rare cases where such an injection has already been tried and failed. Sometimes a woman is given a hysterotomy if she is to be sterilized at the same time; this double operation is now thought to increase risk. As the operation leaves a scar on the wall of the womb which becomes a "weak" spot, the woman may have to have a Caesarean birth if she conceives again and continues the pregnancy full term. After a hysterotomy, the woman is required to stay in the hospital for about a week. Two or three weeks convalescence is recommended afterwards. Hysterotomy is more expensive (at least $1,000) and carries more risk than any other method of abortion.

*Hysterectomy* Hysterotomy, which does not normally put an end to childbearing, should not be confused with hysterectomy which removes the entire uterus and is usually carried out on women with uterine damage or abnormalities. It is not used as a method of abortion in itself. However, hysterectomies are sometimes included in the abortion statistics. The likeliest explanation for this is that a doctor may remove the entire womb of a pregnant woman who wants an abortion and no more children, instead of aborting and sterilizing her. However, the risk of death associated with hysterectomy is far higher (about 20 times) than for sterilization by tubal ligation.

## HOW SAFE IS ABORTION?

Any operation—even having a tooth pulled—involves a certain degree of risk. But "safe" is always a relative term. As far as pregnancy is concerned, the only real comparison that can be made is between having a legal abortion and having a baby. In May 1975, a report called "Legalized Abortion and the Public Health" was published.[4] The work of a distinguished committee appointed to examine the medical risks of legal abortion to American women, it is the most comprehensive and detailed review to date of existing evidence available in the United States. The following information summarizes its findings:

### Risk of death
Legal abortion in early pregnancy carries far less risk of death than does childbirth. In 1973 the death rate among American women continuing pregnancy to full term was 14 per 100,000. This is much higher than the 1972–3 death rate for legal abortions in the first trimester of pregnancy—1.5 deaths per 100,000—and even a little higher than the death rate for second-trimester abortions—12.2 deaths per 100,000.

However, the risk of death from abortion rises sharply the farther the pregnancy is advanced. Here are the death rates, per 100,000 in each category, according to length of pregnancy:

| | |
|---|---|
| Eight weeks or less: | 0.4 |
| Nine and ten weeks: | 1.5 |
| Eleven and twelve weeks: | 4.2 |
| Thirteen to fifteen weeks: | 6.9 |
| Sixteen weeks and over: | 16.1 |

The risk of death also varies according to the method of abortion used. Vacuum suction and D and C—the methods used in early pregnancy —carry the least risk. Not only is the risk of dying from abortion in early pregnancy far lower than from continuing the pregnancy full term, it is also much lower than the risk for any other common surgical operation. Compare the death risk for legal abortion under twelve weeks (1.5 per 100,000) with the following rates for other operations.[5]

| | |
|---|---|
| Removing tonsils: | 3 per 100,000 |
| Removing tonsils and adenoids: | 5 per 100,000 |
| Sterilization by tubal ligation: | 5 per 100,000 |
| Caesarean birth: | 111 per 100,000 |
| Hysterectomy: | 204 per 100,000 |
| Removing appendixes: | 352 per 100,000 |

Still another comparison can be made: the most recent statistics show that the risk of death from abortion under twelve weeks is lower than from regularly using contraceptives like the pill and IUDs—3 per 100,000 users.

### Risk of complications

Complications that do not result in death can occur in both legal abortion and in continued pregnancy and childbirth. But the complications are sometimes different, are not always recorded and thus cannot validly be compared. The possible risks of abortion are infection, damage to the wall of the womb, excessive blood loss, overstretching of the cervix, an adverse reaction to anesthesia, and disturbances of the blood-clotting mechanism.

The vast majority of women having legal abortions, however, do not develop complications of any kind. The most reliable evidence we have on this point comes from a study carried out on 73,000 abortions in the United States between July 1970 and June 1971 by the Joint Program for the Study of Abortion (JPSA).[6] This defined a wide range of possible physical consequences of abortion, including some very minor ones, such as a single day of vomiting or fever; these, in all, were categorized as "total complications." It further categorized a number of these as "major complications," such as unintended major surgery, one or more blood transfusions, prolonged illness, etc. The results showed that for every one hundred women having abortions at twelve weeks or less, 5.2 developed complications of some kind, of which 0.6 were major—whereas for every one hundred women aborted after twelve weeks, 22.2 developed complications, of which 2.2 were major. This suggests that a woman's chances of having an abortion free of any complications are about 95 percent during the first twelve weeks of pregnancy, and about 78 percent after twelve weeks.

The JPSA study was completed in 1971—only a short time after the first states introduced liberal abortion laws and two years before the Supreme Court struck down restrictive state laws. So these complication rates are almost certainly even lower today.

## Long-term complications

What about the long-term effects of abortion? Can it affect a woman's chances of having a normal pregnancy and healthy child in the future, as antiabortion writers have frequently claimed and as a few foreign studies have indicated? Unfortunately, in the absence of any conclusive evidence either way, this question cannot yet be properly answered. All that can be said so far is that many women who have had abortions have later had perfectly normal pregnancies and healthy children; but some women who have had abortions later miscarry or give birth to premature or handicapped children or find themselves unable to conceive at all. What is not known is whether this happens more frequently as a result of abortion or whether it would have happened in any case.

Two possible consequences of abortion, infection of the uterus and overstretching of the cervix—which, though rare, can occur as a result of both abortion *and* childbirth—can lead to a greater risk of ectopic pregnancies or miscarriages or premature births later on. But no properly controlled research has been conducted to determine whether there is a greater risk of these conditions from legal abortions (in the United States) or in childbirth itself. Such evidence as is available comes mainly from Eastern Europe, where different conditions prevail. For example, in countries where contraception is rare, repeated abortions (and indeed births) to individual women are far more common than in the United States—and this in itself could account for the far higher long-term complication rates reported in some foreign studies. Another problem is differences in techniques. One Hungarian study, for example, indicated that premature births among women who had previously had induced abortions were nearly twice as high as among women who had not. But all these abortions had been performed by D and C—a method thought to have a higher risk of overstretching the cervix than suction. A still further problem is methodology. Nearly all the available studies can be (and have been) criticized for serious shortcomings in the research data. What is more, the findings of some studies flatly contradict the findings of others. It is worth recording the assessments made in two authoritative reports which reviewed all of these studies in detail. One is the 1975 American Institute of Medicine report, "Legalized Abortion and the Public Health," which stated, in summary:

> The impact of legal abortion on long-term complications is more difficult to evaluate [than short-term complications], particularly in the United States, where the history of non-restrictive abortion practice is too short to provide longitudinal data. Although there is some evidence from Hungary and Greece associating a history of repeated abortions with subsequent premature births, different studies from Japan and Yugoslavia conclude that prior induced abortions cannot be statistically linked to prematurity. Similar contradictory evidence is found on infertility. The data on ectopic pregnancies, particularly from the Ljubljana [Yugoslavia] study, are somewhat more reliable and lead to the tentative conclusion that induced legal abortion does not lead to a greater risk of ectopic pregnancy post-abortion. There is evidence that spontaneous second-trimester abortions [i.e. miscarriage after the 12th week of pregnancy] may be related to previous induced abortions, particularly for teen-agers. But it also appears that a teen-ager is at risk if she carries a pregnancy to term. The length of gestation, method of termination, and other characteristics relating to pregnant women are not adequately sorted out at this time. Thus, the inconsistent findings of these diverse studies do not permit definitive conclusions to be drawn on the long-term complications of legal induced abortion in the United States, and particularly if that abortion is an early, first-trimester abortion performed by suction.

The other assessment was made in a report published in England in 1974 which presented the findings of the Lane Committee, an official committee appointed by the British Government, which held a three-year inquiry into legal abortion in Great Britain. The six-hundred page report[7] devoted twenty-eight pages to analyzing all the available evidence on long-term complications. It described this evidence as "impressive and disturbing" but nevertheless concluded:

> We would consider it inadvisable at the present time to use a possible risk of future complications as a reason for advising a young woman to continue her pregnancy if there are adequate reasons for terminating it under the provisions of the Abortion Act. The extent and severity of long-term complications are not yet established as far as this country is concerned, and we consider

that evidence from other countries is still too much in conflict for general statements about precise risks to individuals to be made with any degree of reliability. If the results of the Japanese studies prove to be true for this country the long-term risks of continuing pregnancy and childbirth may be much the same as those of therapeutic abortion.

*Teen-agers and long-term complications* Can abortion have an especially adverse effect on teen-agers? This is an important question because there is already evidence that women who become pregnant in their teens, particularly if they are in their early teens, are more likely than older women to suffer medical complications, whether their pregnancies end in abortion or childbirth.

One study[8] looked at subsequent pregnancies among sixty-two women who, when they were under sixteen years of age, had become pregnant and had then had either an abortion (fifty women), a baby (eleven women) or a miscarriage (one woman). The fifty who had been aborted later had fifty-three pregnancies between them during the period of the study (1960 to 1971): of these, nineteen ended in miscarriage and seven in premature birth. The eleven who had originally continued their pregnancies later had nine pregnancies between them, all of which went to term. On the other hand, another study[9] made during 1967 to 1969 examined the subsequent pregnancies of 180 school-age mothers, *none* of whom had been aborted: this also found a very high rate of prematurity (27 percent) in their later pregnancies.

In reviewing this scant evidence in more detail (and once again finding shortcomings in the research methods and data), the Institute of Medicine report concludes:

> The fact that teen-age pregnancies have a greater risk of death and medical complications than pregnancies of older women has been documented extensively.... What is not clear, however, is under what conditions and to what extent induced abortion aggravates that risk in subsequent pregnancies. Since nearly one-third of legal abortions in the United States are obtained by teen-age women, it would seem that further research in this area would merit high priority.

## Psychological consequences

The psychological effects of abortion are even more difficult to evaluate than the physical effects. How an individual woman reacts to having an abortion depends on a complexity of factors: the reasons why she is ending her pregnancy, her relationship with the man who made her pregnant, her economic circumstances, how she is treated when obtaining an abortion, the support she has from family and friends, the attitude of her particular culture and her mental outlook. As no two women are in precisely the same circumstances or have exactly the same personality, the variations in reactions are infinite. How can anyone tell what the psychological impact on a particular woman would have been if, instead, she had continued the pregnancy?

The psychological impact of abortion has been examined in a number of studies of which the latest are the most significant since it is reasonable to assume that women feel very differently about abortion when they are able to obtain it legally, in medically safe conditions and in a more generally sympathetic climate of opinion. The studies undertaken in the late 1960s and early 1970s all indicate that abortion does *not* carry a significant risk of psychiatric trauma and that the vast majority of women have feelings of relief after an abortion rather than feelings of guilt or other emotional disturbances. For example, the Joint Program for the Study of Abortion reported a total psychiatric complication rate of between 0.2 and 0.4 per thousand abortions. In this study, out of 72,988 abortions, sixteen major psychiatric complications were reported, including five depressive reactions in women who had suffered major hemorrhage or protracted fever, and two suicides. One suicide was a woman with a history of psychiatric hospitalization.

Perhaps it is inevitable that some women will experience depression after abortion. But many women also become depressed after childbirth —so frequently, indeed, that "postpartum blues" is recognized as a normal medical condition. One study in 1970 reported that every year in the United States there are approximately four thousand documented cases of postpartum psychoses severe enough to require hospitalization —a rate of between one and two per thousand deliveries.[10] This is more than twice as high as the postabortion psychiatric complication rate reported in the JPSA study.

Both the American Institute of Medicine report and the English Lane Committee report, after reviewing the available research literature, are cautious in drawing any hard and fast conclusions. But both point out that legal abortion does not appear to lead to any general increase in mental illness. According to the Lane Committee: "To those distressed by an unwanted pregnancy, abortion usually brings quick, sub-

stantial and lasting relief [and] feelings of regret, self-reproach and guilt
. . . found to be present in about 20 percent of cases . . . are usually mild
and transient." And the Institute of Medicine: "There is no evidence
that abortion is significantly more hazardous psychologically than term
delivery."

## *How you personally can minimize the risks in abortion*

If you decide to end your pregnancy, there are several steps you
yourself can take to make certain that your abortion is as safe as possible:

1. Make sure it is carried out in the first twelve weeks of pregnancy if
   possible, and ideally before the ninth week. The golden rule is always
   "the earlier the safer."
2. If a second-trimester abortion is necessary, try to avoid having a
   hysterotomy unless there are good medical reasons why an intra-
   amniotic injection by saline or prostaglandin would be inadvisable (see
   p. 48), or unless an abortion by the intra-amniotic method fails.
3. Avoid having a sterilization at the same time as an abortion (see
   p. 178).
4. Avoid having a hysterectomy unless there are sound medical reasons
   (like cancer or other serious health-threatening conditions) for removing the entire uterus.
5. Consult a doctor immediately if you suspect that anything is wrong
   after an abortion. It is normal to lose a little blood (like a period) and
   feel some cramping (like a period pain) after a suction or D and C
   abortion. Anything else should be investigated in case further treatment is necessary.
6. Avoid the necessity for repeat abortions, which may increase the risk
   of later miscarriage and premature births.

## *Religious and moral feelings about abortion*

To explore the morality of abortion would take a whole book—and
indeed, so complex are the issues involved that the most extensive work
on the subject (*Abortion: Law, Choice and Morality* by Daniel Callahan,
see p. 64) runs over five hundred pages. Each side of the abortion
argument—those who regard abortion as the murder of an unborn child
and those who support the right of the individual woman to choose
whether or not to have a child—is convinced of the morality of its own
cause and the wrongness of the other's. As Callahan wrote: "Each side
feels that it is the true defender of the common tradition. In the West,

that common tradition is a respect for life and the right of individual choice."

The problem is not necessarily a matter of persuading yourself that whatever you decide is "right." As Callahan again properly remarks: "A woman can, with little trouble, find both people and books to reassure her that there is no problem about abortion at all; or people and books to convince her that she would be a moral monster if she chose abortion." The true dilemma comes in seeing through the rhetoric and recognizing that there is moral "right" in both arguments: abortion *does* mean the destruction of a developing human life—and there *are* many circumstances in which the decision to abort is sensible, compassionate, responsible and just.

To be sensitive to this conflict is, perhaps, to demonstrate a real sense of morality over an abortion decision—even though it might make that decision more difficult. But to insist on one viewpoint and deny the other is surely the ultimate immorality, since it contrives to persuade women that ending or continuing an unwanted pregnancy is a clear-cut issue, and fails to prepare them for any ambivalence they may naturally feel.

This point has been almost totally overlooked, lost between the polarized arguments of two ideologies. So here—no less than the social conditioning of the past—is another source of uncertainty. A woman who, before her pregnancy, held strong opinions on abortion may now find her personal reactions very different from what she expected. Many a feminist, believing in the right of women to control their own bodies, has suddenly found herself pondering the rights of the fetus—just as many a "right to lifer" has suddenly found justification for abortion after all.

To be forced to question one's beliefs may come as a shock, but it probably explains why so many women find the decision-making process on abortion a maturing experience. Today, women who seek abortion have the law on their side and also, to a great extent, the acceptance of society. They no longer have to waste so much emotional energy actually getting an abortion; they no longer have to justify their decision to anyone but themselves. Such freedoms may well allow women to have abortions without the slightest thought of anything but their own convenience and self-interest—a development that alarms the moralist. And yet the reverse might prove equally true. Those same freedoms may incline women to reflect more deeply on the moral implications of abortion, making the final decision all the stronger precisely because it was forged out of intellectual doubt.

## OBTAINING AN ABORTION

How easy it is to obtain an abortion depends on a physician's willingness to perform the operation, what facilities are available in your area and whether there are any problems over cost. Certainly you should have no difficulty if you are within reach of a large metropolitan area and you can afford the medical expenses or are covered for abortion by a health insurance plan or Medicaid.

### Who provides abortions?

An abortion must be performed by a qualified doctor who has been licensed to practice medicine by the state. Ideally, an abortion should be carried out in a place where there are full back-up facilities to cope with the very occasional emergencies that can arise. Not all hospitals perform abortions and those that do often charge relatively high fees. For these reasons early first-trimester abortions are most often performed in special clinics or in doctors' offices.

In many areas where there are no local clinics or hospitals that offer abortion, your choice may be limited to traveling a long way to the nearest clinic or contacting one of the few local doctors who perform early abortions in their own offices. Names and addresses are available from local chapters of Planned Parenthood or the National Organization of Women (NOW), or from any women's centers in the area, or your state, city or county health department.

*Clinics* Abortion clinics that are not attached to hospitals have proliferated throughout the country since 1973. All offer first-trimester abortions performed by suction as an outpatient procedure, but beyond that they vary a good deal.

Nonprofit clinics charge moderate fees and often make adjustments according to a woman's ability to pay. They usually provide a wide range of services including abortion counseling and after-care, pregnancy and VD screening, Pap tests and birth-control information. In this way a woman receives an abortion in the context of all-round health care—an ideal that is basic to the women's clinics that have emerged from the women's self-help movement and are controlled by women who hire and train professional staff sympathetic to the principles of information-sharing and nonexploitative care. The more numerous commercial clinics tend to regard abortion as a money-making business; the standard of medical care is often good but women sometimes complain of impersonal and insensitive treatment and a "conveyor-belt" atmosphere.

All clinics are supervised by government health departments. On the whole they offer a reasonable service—but it is wise, if you can, to ask about the reputation of a clinic from one of the referral organizations listed below, and know what standards count as good care (see p. 60).

*Availability* Clinics are usually confined to metropolitan areas to which women travel from miles around. They are listed in the regional Yellow Pages under "Abortion;" government health departments also keep local lists. No comprehensive listing of nonprofit or women's clinics is available, but those known to be operating at the time of writing include:

*The Feminist Women's Health Centers* began in Los Angeles in 1973 and now have several women's clinics performing abortions in California, Detroit, Salt Lake City, Atlanta, Tallahassee and Ames, Iowa. For information on these and any new clinics elsewhere contact The Feminist Women's Health Center, 1112 Crenshaw Boulevard, Los Angeles, California 90019 (tel: 213–936–7219)

*Preterm,* 1990 M Street N.W., Washington D.C. 20006 (tel: 202–452–8400), was one of the first nonprofit clinics and now has two more branches: 1842 Beacon Street, Brookline, Massachusetts 02146 (tel: 617–738–6210); 10900 Carnegie Avenue, Cleveland, Ohio 44106 (tel: 216–368–1006).

*The Margaret Sanger Center,* 380 Second Avenue, New York, N.Y. 10010 (tel: 212–677–6474) is run by Planned Parenthood of New York City.

*The Emma Goldman Clinic,* 715 North Dodge, Iowa City, Iowa 52240 (tel: 319–337–2111).

*Vermont Women's Health Center,* Box 29, Burlington, Vermont 05402 (tel: 802–863–1386).

*The Delta Women's Clinic,* 1406 St. Charles Avenue, New Orleans, Louisiana 70130 (tel: 504–581–2250), opened amid fierce opposition in 1974 when very few abortions were being performed in Louisiana.

*Referrals* If there are several clinics to choose from in your area, you may want to find out in advance those that are nonprofit, commercial or simply reputable. Or, if there are none where you live, you may want information on clinics further away. To obtain help, contact your nearest Planned Parenthood, Clergy Consultation Service on Abortion, National Organization of Women, or one of the many women's centers which offer abortion referrals. If you can find none of these listed in your telephone directory, contact the Women's Action Alliance (see p. 136), which tries to keep track of women's centers nationwide. Abortion referral agencies are also listed in the Yellow Pages under "Abortion." However, beware of any agency that charges a fee, a practice that is not only exploitative but illegal in many states; women have often been channeled from such agencies to the profit-minded clinics.

*Hospitals* The advantage of having an abortion in a hospital is that facilities for occasional emergencies are close at hand—which is why second- and third-trimester abortions must usually be performed in hospitals. The drawbacks are that only a few offer outpatient services for early abortion and most insist on an overnight stay, which sends the cost soaring. Another problem, particularly in rural areas, is availability.

*Public hospitals* Women with low incomes are especially dependent on public hospitals to provide abortions, yet only a minority actually do so. By 1975—the third year after abortion was legalized throughout the country—fewer than one in five (18 percent) were performing abortions, and there were still nine states in which not a single public hospital had performed an abortion at all.[11] This situation is due largely to present state laws which allow hospitals, as well as individual doctors, to refuse to provide abortions.

*Private hospitals* By 1975 only one-third of the private hospitals that could be expected to provide abortions (i.e. non-Catholic, general, short-term) were doing so.

*Military hospitals* These are now all required to provide abortion services to eligible women according to constitutional principles, under a directive issued by the U.S. Defense Department in September 1975.

*Referrals* You can find out in advance the policy of any particular hospital by contacting the government health department that supervises it. If you need a second- or third-trimester abortion and no hospital in your area will cooperate, contact one of the organizations listed above under clinic referrals.

### Checking the quality of care you will receive

It is natural to feel apprehensive about having an abortion if you've never had one before. The experience can never be said to be pleasant exactly, but you will feel far more comfortable about it if you receive good medical care in a sympathetic atmosphere. Therefore, when you keep your first appointment with a doctor or at a clinic or hospital, it is important to find out what kind of service is offered. The following is a guide to what to expect and, in some cases, to insist upon.

*Counseling* Abortion counseling was pioneered by the first nonprofit clinics and is now accepted as an important part of good abortion care. All good clinics employ counselors and so do some hospitals; sometimes doctors give a certain amount of counseling or it is done by nurses or social workers. But it is not routinely offered everywhere.

Ideally, counseling should perform three functions: ascertain that a woman is sure she wants the abortion and has considered the alternatives; explain what will happen during the abortion so that she knows exactly what to expect; give encouragement and understanding so that she can feel as relaxed as possible in an unfamiliar and potentially tense situation.

In some clinics the abortion procedure is explained at group sessions before individual women are given the opportunity to discuss personal matters with a counselor at a private interview. At others, one counselor is assigned to one woman for all the time she is at the clinic, sometimes literally holding her hand during the abortion itself. Not all women want counseling, and some resent being asked a lot of questions. A sensitive counselor appreciates this. But the questions—about how she got pregnant, her relationships, her reasons for wanting an abortion—are intended to help a woman clarify her feelings and to reassure herself that she is doing the right thing.

*Medical screening* Although an abortion, particularly a first-trimester abortion, is a relatively simple operation, it is important that certain medical checks are carried out beforehand.

*Confirmation of pregnancy* You should be asked the date of your last menstrual period, asked to take a pregnancy test, and be given a pelvic examination (see below) to confirm that you are really pregnant. No doctor should ever perform an abortion without making these checks, even if pregnancy has been diagnosed elsewhere.

*Medical history* You should be asked how many times, if any, you have been pregnant. It is also important to give honest information of any illnesses or conditions you have suffered from, or which run in your family. Occasionally complications have arisen which might have been avoided if the patient had not concealed from the doctor some part of her medical history, such as high blood pressure, asthma or convulsions.

*Medical tests* You should be given a series of routine tests: blood typing, blood pressure, temperature, urinalysis, VD and Pap tests. These are all to ascertain your state of health and determine whether you need any extra medical precautions. For example, if your blood type is Rh negative and you become pregnant by a man who is Rh positive (the commonest type), your body will create antibodies that try to destroy the fetus in this and future pregnancies; you will therefore need a Rhogam injection to prevent you from miscarrying in the future.

*Examination* The doctor should listen to your heart and lungs and then give you a thorough pelvic examination, even if you had one when your pregnancy was diagnosed. The doctor who is about to perform the abortion must confirm gestation personally and check the size and shape of your uterus so that the operation can be performed with maximum efficiency.

*Emergency measures* Although the chances are greatly against it, a first-trimester abortion can occasionally go wrong, and a woman may need emergency treatment. If your abortion is performed in a clinic or doctor's office, it is sensible to ask in advance what precautions have been taken to cope with these rare emergencies. Ideally, the clinic or office should not be far away from the nearest hospital, should have an agreement with that hospital to transfer patients if necessary, and should keep emergency transportation constantly on hand just in case. Some state laws or health regulations require that all these conditions are met.

*After-care* The clinic, hospital or doctor should arrange for you to return for a follow-up visit to check that the abortion is complete (i.e., that no fetal tissue has been left behind in the uterus) and that everything is normal. Or, if you have traveled from far away, they should arrange for a medical checkup where you live. Another sign of good care is when a 24-hour telephone service is provided which you can call if you think that all is not well.

*Birth-control information* A clinic or doctor with your well-being at heart wants you not to need another abortion in the future. They should discuss with you the different methods of contraception and, if you wish, insert an IUD immediately after the abortion or give you a month or two's supply of contraceptive pills to start you off. They should not pressure you into a particular method, but it is a good idea to think this out for yourself beforehand. More detailed information than you would get from any doctor or counselor is discussed in Chapter 8.

### The cost of abortion

The cost of an abortion varies enormously—depending on when it is performed (in the first trimester or later), where it is carried out, whether you have general or local anesthesia and whether there are extra charges for routine tests and Rhogam shots. At the time of writing, the cheapest quality abortions are those performed during the first trimester in non-profit clinics, which charge at least $125 for an outpatient procedure using local anesthesia. The Feminist Women's Health Center clinics currently charge $165. Commercial clinics charge anything from $125 to $500, which may or may not include "extras." Private doctors would regard $150 as "reasonable," but many charge more. Hospital abortions are always more expensive, particularly if a woman is required to stay overnight: a routine first-trimester procedure averages $200 to $350 but may run as high as $600. Later abortions in a hospital are the most expensive of all—$350 and upwards for an abortion by saline or prostaglandin injection, and sometimes more than $1,000 for a hysterotomy.

*Private health insurance plans* If you are covered by a health insurance plan, you should check your policy carefully to see whether it allows benefits for abortion, and on what conditions. A national survey conducted by the Health Insurance Association of America[12] found that most group schemes offered some kind of abortion coverage, though 12 percent offered none. Many set a maximum level of benefit which may not cover the full cost.

*Medicaid* Most states currently permit Medicaid payments for abortion, but whether they will continue to do so remains in doubt. In late 1976 Congress passed an amendment to the 1977 HEW appropriations bill which would stop Medicaid payments for abortion, thus effectively denying poor women their right to abortion. But so far that amendment has been held up by a court injunction. The issue will now go to the Supreme Court and is expected to be resolved late in 1977. Meanwhile, Medicaid abortions continue to be available.

### AFTER THE ABORTION

Immediately after an early outpatient abortion, you may feel a little dizzy, nauseated or faint. This should quickly pass while you rest during the usual two hours recovery time. You should then be checked to make sure everything is normal before going home. After a saline or prosta-glandin abortion, you will be required to stay in your hospital bed for up to twenty-four hours for observation. A hysterotomy puts a more severe strain on the system and requires several days convalescence.

It is normal to lose some blood for a few days and feel some cramping after the abortion. You will be advised to use sanitary pads to cope with the bleeding. To guard against infection, you should not use tampons. For at least two weeks you should avoid sexual intercourse, tub baths and swimming. It is also wise to avoid strenuous exercise of any kind for a few days. It is important to have a medical checkup about two weeks after the abortion; if all is well you can then resume your normal activities.

Most women have no complications after an abortion. However, if you feel ill, develop a high temperature, notice an unusual discharge from the vagina, bleed profusely or have any other reason for thinking that something is wrong, see your doctor or telephone the clinic or hospital where you had the abortion *immediately.* If you suddenly begin bleeding so excessively that a couple of pads cannot cope with it (which might mean a hemorrhage) go straight to the nearest hospital.

What about the emotional aftereffects of abortion? The commonest feeling is relief. It is also normal to feel rather sad. Feeling sad is different from feeling guilty. Many women feel no guilt, but some do. When this happens it helps to try to see why. Sometimes a woman has a bad time trying to get an abortion and has been made to feel ashamed by a doctor's hostile attitude. Sometimes a woman cannot reconcile her need for an abortion with what she has been brought up to believe is right. Sometimes a woman has not entirely resolved her ambivalence about abortion, or she has allowed herself to be pushed into it by someone else.

Quite often feeling guilty about having sex makes the abortion seems like a kind of punishment. Remember that it takes time for social attitudes, which affect us all, to change. Our society is still uneasy about sexual freedom and abortion. It is only comparatively recently that contraceptives have become available to all women, regardless of marital status, and before 1973 legal abortion was often very difficult to obtain. The sense of shame caused by having to go underground for both in those days, and the difficulty of talking openly about such matters, persists for many women today.

Fortunately, this is changing as the means to avoid unwanted preg-nancy becomes more easily available and as women are able to support each other emotionally by freely discussing their feelings and ideas. If you do happen to feel badly about your abortion, don't suppress your feelings. Try to understand them and deal with them. It may help a lot to discuss them with a friend who has also had an abortion, or to talk to a counselor.

## Abortion Rights Organizations

*Religious Coalition for Abortion Rights,* 100 Maryland Avenue N.E., Washington D.C. 20002 (tel: 202–543–7032) consists of national religious organizations committed to safeguarding the legal option of abortion and the right of individual conscience. It issues information on the legal, religious, ethical and moral aspects of the abortion debate. A free brochure of publications is available on request.

*American Civil Liberties Union Reproductive Freedom Project,* 22 East 40th Street, New York, N.Y. 10016 (tel: 212–725–1222) has been instrumental in upholding the Supreme Court decisions in court actions throughout the country and advises ACLU affiliates on issues such as the standing of hospitals which refuse to provide abortions.

## Publications

*Abortion Two: Making the Revolution* by Lawrence Lader (Boston: Beacon, 1974) traces the long struggle for abortion law reform up to the 1973 Supreme Court decision.

*Abortion: Law, Choice and Morality* by Daniel Callahan (New York: Macmillan, 1970) is a comprehensive study of the implications of abortion to society and the individual—written before abortion laws were liberalized in the United States but still valid in its sensitive discussion of the moral choices facing the individual.

*The Abortion Controversy,* edited by Betty Sarvis and Hyman Rodman (New York: Columbia University Press, 1974) reviews the legal, social, medical and moral problems involved in the continuing abortion debate.

*Abortion: A Woman's Guide* by Planned Parenthood of New York City (New York: Pocket Books, 1975) is a practical handbook to the modern clinic abortion, based on procedures at the Margaret Sanger Center in New York City.

*Legalized Abortion and the Public Health* (Washington D.C.: National Academy of Sciences, 1975), reports the Institute of Medicine study on the safety of abortion, including the physical and psychological risks compared with childbirth and contraception.

*Constitutional Aspects of the Right to Limit Childbearing* (Washington D.C.: U.S. Commission on Civil Rights, 1975) provides a valuable insight into the Supreme Court decisions and discusses the legal implications of proposed Constitutional amendments to extend legal protection to the fetus.

*Abortion Factbook* (New York: The Population Council) is an annual review of the demographic and health aspects of abortion in the United States and some other countries.

*Abortion Surveillance* (Washington D.C.: U.S. Department of Health, Education and Welfare) is an annual summary of American abortion statistics.

*Early Medical Complications of Legal Abortion* (New York: The Population Council, 1972) is the report of the Joint Program for the Study of Abortion which studied 73,000 legal abortions in the United States and provides the best information to date on health risks.

*Abortion Eve* by Chin Lyvely and Joyce Sutton (Nanny Goat Productions, P.O. Box 845, Laguna Beach, California 92652, 1973), a witty comic book offering practical information through the story line of five very different women faced with unwanted pregnancy.

*Family Planning Perspectives* (New York: The Alan Guttmacher Institute) a bimonthly review of research papers on all aspects of birth control, including up-to-date reports on abortion availability and health risks.

*Family Planning/Population Reporter* (Washington D.C.: The Alan Guttmacher Institute) a bimonthly review of state laws and policies which monitors all legal developments on abortion.

# 5

⚜

# *Pregnancy*

Having a child is a perfectly normal thing for any woman. Pregnancy is not an illness or a crime. It is a natural occurrence, whether you are married or not, and is nothing to be ashamed of. Yet this simple truth is belied by the fact that the conventions of our society still expect a woman to be supported by a man before and after her child is born.

For many women today, to be pregnant without the support of a man is a matter of choice: either they deliberately plan a child outside marriage or, having conceived accidentally, they make a conscious decision to continue the pregnancy. For others, the circumstances are quite different: their husbands die or desert them during pregnancy, or they are unable to obtain the abortion they would have preferred.

Whatever your own circumstances, it is essential to confront the realities of the situation. You need to work out how your pregnancy will affect your work or education and how you will support yourself financially before and after the birth of your child. You may need to find alternative housing if you can no longer go on living in your present home. Your health becomes top priority: ideally, you should obtain good prenatal care and preparation for childbirth to maximize your chances of having a trouble-free pregnancy and a healthy child. And not least, you may need to get your feelings into perspective if you are to cope with the emotional problems that often beset a pregnant woman.

You may think that any feelings of anxiety, doubt, depression, fear or guilt you experience *must* be because you are not married or would prefer not to be pregnant. But this is not necessarily true. Many women have doubts and fears of one sort or another during pregnancy, even when they are happily married and have planned to have a child. Many of your reactions may be entirely normal. It may help if you can identify these and separate them from the ones that *are* caused by your particular circumstances.

Many pregnant women easily get depressed, bursting into tears for no reason at all. They may be scared at the thought of the birth and blame their fears on their own inadequacies. Some women feel threatened by pregnancy and worry that when the child arrives they may dislike it or feel unable to cope. Or they may feel resentful at having been taken over so completely by this tiny unborn thing—as though their bodies had been hijacked and their lives sent in an entirely different direction. And often they feel guilty for these feelings because they are not what they think they *should* feel.

Of course, many women also feel happy and excited. Some become intensely interested in what is happening to their bodies, feeling great pleasure in their own fertility and maybe feeling sexier as well. Often women think that these feelings—the traditional, expected ones—are "normal," whereas negative feelings are "abnormal." In fact, *both* are normal insofar as many women experience them.

Whereas everyone tends to congratulate a married woman on having a child (whether she is sure she wants one or not), reactions to a single woman's pregnancy are usually not nearly so encouraging. This isn't always due to disapproval. Some people don't know how they're supposed to react or may assume that you are embarrassed and don't want to talk about it. Or they may be worried *for* you.

Your own attitude toward yourself is the key. It will help greatly if you can feel happy about the pregnancy and conscious of your right to enjoy it. If you feel reasonably confident and cheerful, the image you project is bound to influence other people's reactions to you. Try not to let anyone else make you feel guilty, ashamed or confused. The important thing is to be yourself, instead of acting out how other people expect you to feel.

Your feelings at first are likely to center on your relationship with the father of the coming baby. Naturally you may feel unhappy if he has rejected you when you most needed his support. On the other hand, a single woman's feelings for the man may lessen as she becomes more absorbed in her pregnancy. Quite often the physical changes bring about a relaxation of tension so that worries which seemed hugely important at the beginning may lessen or even disappear. It isn't uncommon for even a married woman to transfer the focus of her attention from her husband to her child as the birth approaches.

A woman who is widowed while she is pregnant can usually count on the unstinted sympathy of others. She may also find strength in herself.

One young woman, whose husband was killed in an accident during her first pregnancy, recalls her feelings: "After the immediate shock, my reaction was pure relief that I'd conceived in time, that I was going to have the child that would be forever a part of him. I felt irrationally angry at him too at times, as though he'd opted out deliberately. But the most unexpected development was finding that I *could* cope on my own; a sense of strength came from somewhere. I think a happy marriage can do that—it builds up your confidence and emotional resources, which count when you're put to the test."

A married woman who is deserted during pregnancy inevitably feels differently. One woman said: "It was the ultimate betrayal. He was the one who seemed to want a child most, yet he went off with his girlfriend within a month of knowing I was pregnant." The sense of rejection implied by such a desertion can dominate all other feelings.

Most pregnant women on their own experience moments of great loneliness; for the widow or deserted wife such feelings can be made especially acute by memories of happy times formerly shared with a husband. But dwelling on the past, though natural, can become counter-productive if taken to extremes. A deserted wife remembers: "For the first couple of months I rehearsed every conversation we'd had together, relived everything we'd ever done. I was obsessed with the thought that if I'd only done this or said that, he'd have stayed. I even convinced myself that he hadn't really wanted to go, that I'd driven him out. Pure fantasy. Finally, when I was on the point of cracking completely, I suddenly realized that all I was doing was wasting all my emotional energy on the past. I began to come alive again then. I owed him *nothing*, but my child. . . . She was two months off being born, and from that time on I concentrated all my energy on making a future for *us*."

## OBTAINING PRENATAL CARE

Prenatal care consists of a series of routine medical tests and checkups which determine if the pregnancy is progressing normally. If something isn't quite right, these tests will detect the problem early enough for remedial steps to be taken and, very often, make everything well again. For example, toxemia (the most dangerous common complication of later pregnancy, characterized by high blood pressure and fluid retention) can be controlled by medical treatment in time, but lack or delay of treatment can have serious consequences and on occasion can cause death.[1]

Ideally, prenatal checkups should begin no later than the fifteenth week of pregnancy (that is, fifteen weeks after your last menstrual period), but you should also have had a complete physical examination when your pregnancy was first confirmed. If possible, it is best to return about once a month until the twenty-eighth week, then every two weeks until the thirty-sixth week, and after that once a week until the baby is born.

You can obtain checkups from private doctors who offer prenatal care (not all do) or public hospitals and clinics. Which you settle for will probably be determined by your financial situation (see below), but it is worth repeating here some excellent advice offered in *Our Bodies, Ourselves,* the book put out by the Boston Women's Health Collective (see p. 72). They point out that if you are eligible for Medicaid, it may be worth seeking out a private doctor who will accept welfare patients for whatever fee Medicaid pays instead of going to a clinic; and conversely, if you are middle class but need to save money, it may be worth going to a clinic instead of a private doctor. "Terrible as it sounds," they say, "sociologists have found plenty of evidence that if you are white, college-educated and not noticeably ethnic, you will get the best possible care from your attendants in the clinic setting. . . . If you do not have most of these advantages, do whatever you can to get private care." They cite a recent study of maternal care throughout the United States as evidence that in many hospitals and clinics women who are wealthy, married and white tend to receive better treatment than women who are poor, black and unmarried.[2]

Certainly it is well worth shopping around among private doctors, hospitals and clinics in your area in order to compare the quality of care, fees, attitudes and distances to be traveled. A useful source of information are the women's centers which have been established throughout the country to refer women to providers of good health care. (The Women's Action Alliance (see p. 136) keeps a list of women's centers nationwide.)

Teaching hospitals usually give good care, so it is an excellent idea to contact one in your area. Your local government health department can also give information on programs in the area or make other recommendations on obtaining prenatal care.

It is imperative to check out precisely how you are covered for maternity care by your own health insurance policy (if you are working and have some coverage), your husband's policy (if you are a separated wife), your parents' policy (if you are a dependent minor), or by Medicaid (if you are on welfare or otherwise eligible by low income). If you are covered by none of these, or if such coverage is unlikely to cover all the costs of your pregnancy (which is usually the case), remember that there are private doctors and nonprofit hospitals which charge according to your ability to pay. Search them out.

### Assessing the quality of care you receive

Some women have nothing but praise for the medical staff who attend them during pregnancy and childbirth. But many have become increasingly critical of the predominantly male medical profession, complaining that doctors have transformed a natural, normal process into a complicated medical event. More specifically, they complain that doctors see pregnant women as bodies rather than human beings.

Certainly, the system can work in a very impersonal way. If you go to a clinic you may see different staff members at each visit, and when you enter the hospital for delivery there will be yet another collection of doctors and nurses who are strange to you. And it is often difficult to get questions answered. How, then, do you deal with this? The best way is to arm yourself with knowledge, and use that knowledge to become confident of your own rights as a health consumer so that you can more easily assess the kind of care you receive. Increase your knowledge of pregnancy and childbirth by reading and, if possible, by attending childbirth preparation classes (see pp. 74–76). It also helps to keep certain fundamental points in mind:

1. You have every right to know what is happening to your body and to ask for explanations of anything that puzzles, worries or simply interests you. A good doctor will cooperate without making you feel that you are wasting his or her time.
2. You have the right to know why certain tests and procedures are performed, to discuss in advance how necessary or desirable they are, what they involve and whether they carry any element of risk. The same applies to any drugs that may be prescribed.
3. You have the right to refuse any procedure that should be elective (such as drugs used to induce birth so that the delivery takes place at a time convenient to the obstetric staff).
4. You are entitled to a second medical opinion if you are not satisfied with a doctor's diagnosis or suggested treatment.
5. You have the right to know in advance what fees will be charged, how these are broken down (into prenatal visits, obstetric charges, hospitalization costs, etc.), and the relative cost of certain procedures (such as different pain-killing methods used during delivery).

6. You have the right to be treated as an adult capable of making your own decisions and, if you are unmarried or very young, to be considered no differently from any other pregnant woman. A good doctor may inquire how you are coping (some go out of their way to refer women with socio-economic problems to useful sources of help), but making moral judgments is not a part of the doctor's job.

Another factor to be considered is where your baby will be born. Most American women give birth in hospitals because that is the way medical tradition in this country has developed. But in recent years many women have begun to look with favor on the practice of home births attended by midwives with a doctor on call.

As with other controversies, it is important to retain your common sense on this question. If midwifery or home obstetric services are available to you, there is no reason why you should not give birth at home if you wish, providing that you are healthy, your pregnancy has been normal, you are of an age when complications are not likely to occur, and there are proper back-up arrangements to speed you to the hospital if an emergency should crop up at the last minute. But it is more sensible to give birth in the hospital if some problem is anticipated during delivery, or if you are not in good health, or if you are under twenty or over thirty-five (when complications are more likely) or if your home conditions are unsuitable. A hospital is often recommended for a first birth, although many women have been safely delivered of their first babies at home.

You can find out more about midwifery services in your area from your local government department of health or any women's center. Information on home delivery is also available from:

*Maternity Service Association,* 48 East 92nd Street, New York, N.Y. 10028 (tel: 212–369–7300), which has been active in the cause of home births since 1900. In 1975 it opened a childbearing center which offers all-round pregnancy care and midwife deliveries for about $750.

*American College of Nurse-Midwives* (same address and telephone number as for Maternity Service Association), which sets standards for the training of nurse-midwives and certifies graduates through a national examination.

*The Birth Center,* 208 Escaloma Drive, Santa Cruz, California 95060, which was started in 1971 by a group of women childbirth teachers who provided prenatal care, home deliveries and training for fathers to deliver their own children—until 1974 when they were raided and closed down on the ground that the midwives were "practising medicine" without a licence. During the three-year period, the center's midwives attended nearly 300 women, including 231 home deliveries, with only one lost baby, stillborn before the onset of labor—a death rate nine times lower than the national mortality rate. The center continues, however, to provide information and support to women who want to give birth at home.

### Figuring out when your baby will arrive

The doctor or midwife will work out the estimated date of delivery (often abbreviated to EDD—or EDC, estimated date of confinement), but this is also easy to calculate for yourself. You simply count 280 days from the first day of your last normal menstrual period. Or, to use a quicker method, take away three calendar months from that day and add on seven days. For example, if the first day of your last period was September 12, go back three months to June 12 and add on seven days —so your EDD would be June 19. This is only an estimate, of course; babies are often early or late in arriving.

## FINDING OUT ABOUT PREGNANCY AND CHILDBIRTH

To a large extent a healthy pregnancy and normal delivery depend on self-help—how well you look after yourself. So there are a great many things you need to know. What food should you be eating so that your nutritional intake meets the extra demands of pregnancy? What exercise should you be doing? Which drugs are dangerous, and why do you need to avoid smoking and alcohol? What about sex and other energetic activities? How much rest will you need? How do you know that everything is normal? How will you know when the baby is ready to arrive? The answers to these questions are all the more vital if, for one reason or another, you are unable to receive adequate prenatal medical care.

One of the best companions you can have is a good book (or ideally several) which gives you all the necessary information in plain, simple language. The following publications can give you a good working knowledge of pregnancy and childbirth and, in some cases, a broader perspective on the issues than you might otherwise receive from your doctor or clinic.

*Our Bodies, Ourselves* by the Boston Women's Health Collective (New York: Simon & Schuster, 1972) is a book written exclusively by women for women on all aspects of being a woman—from sex and birth control to abortion, pregnancy and childbirth. This classic work challenges many assumptions about women held by the medical profession, suggests ways of insisting on good health care and offers proposals for change. Its practical information is well-researched and includes a long bibliography of recommended literature on pregnancy and childbirth.

*The Experience of Childbirth* by Sheila Kitzinger (New York: Penguin, 1972) is a detailed guide to pregnancy, childbirth and the postnatal period sensitively written by a British childbirth teacher. It explains one approach to natural childbirth and includes a positive chapter on home delivery.

*Immaculate Deception: A New Look At Women and Childbirth in America* by Suzanne Arms (San Francisco: San Francisco Book Co., 1975) is the best-documented book to date on how American women have been "deceived" into thinking that birth is a dangerous, pathological event, made safe only by medical intervention and the drug-technology approach of hospitals. The author argues forcefully against hospitalization for normal births and in favor of natural deliveries at home supervised by midwives. Ms. Arms has impeccably marshalled her evidence from primitive cultures and modern European countries as well as from the United States, and at times her account of American hospital birth procedures is frightening. Even if you remain unconvinced about the virtues of home births, this book is worth reading for the perspective it gives on the medical approach to childbirth.

*Maternity Nursing* by Elsie Fitzpatrick et al. (Philadelphia: Lippincott, 1971) is a textbook for nurses especially recommended by the Boston Women's Health Collective for its comprehensive information on physiological and emotional changes in pregnancy.

*Birth* by Caterine Milinaire (First Things First, 2334 Ontario Road NW, Washington D.C. 20009) is a lavishly illustrated handbook on health care in pregnancy, alternative methods of childbirth, normal physiological processes and complications. It includes many accounts, from men as well as women, on different childbirth experiences.

*Smoking and Pregnancy,* U.S. Department of Health, Education and Welfare (U.S. Government Printing Office, Washington D.C.) is a reprint of the Surgeon General's 1971 report on the effects of smoking on health. It brings together the experimental evidence which proves that smoking during pregnancy increases the risk of low birthweight, prematurity, miscarriage and infant deaths.

This also seems a good place to recommend two novels which, far more engagingly than any factual book, give remarkable insights into the complex reactions of their very different heroines, both of whom become pregnant accidentally and give birth outside marriage. In *The Millstone* by Margáret Drabble, (New York: Morrow, 1965), young academic Rosamund becomes pregnant during her first sexual experience with a man who never learns he is responsible, fails in her amateurish attempts to abort herself and begins to face up to the realities of her predicament as she emerges from a doctor's office she had picked out at random on a London street. Drabble shows, with sensitivity and wit, how Rosamund survives the unconscious cruelties of the medical system and social attitudes, achieving maturity and a new kind of independence.

In *Jane* (New York: Avon, 1975), the heroine of the title is, like its author Dee Wells, an American journalist working in London. Jane has no idea before the birth of her son which of her three lovers—an English lord, a black American lawyer or a young professional thief—is the father. This is not only one of the funniest books ever written by a woman; Dee Wells makes the circumstances of each love affair, and its denouement, absolutely believable and convinces us that Jane is a real woman, prey to the conflicts of the situation but true to herself and able to give and receive love on many different levels.

## Childbirth preparation classes

The purpose of prepared childbirth is to teach you what to expect before, during and after delivery, and the techniques that will enable you more easily to control the process so that you receive maximum enjoyment out of it. Childbirth preparation classes consist of a series of lectures and demonstrations by trained childbirth teachers, who use different methods and have different preferences. But the classes generally include:

1. Basic information about your body, how it changes during pregnancy, how the fetus develops in the uterus, and the three stages of labor.
2. Instruction on different methods and techniques for "natural" childbirth—that is, easier delivery made possible not by drugs but by learning how to relax and control your muscles and breathing during labor. Sometimes only one technique is taught, but ideally you should have a choice.
3. Instruction to someone (husband, lover, friend, relative) who shares the preparation practice with you and acts as coach during labor. Sometimes a trained labor companion can be provided.

4. Instruction on exercises that tone your muscles before the birth and help you regain your figure afterwards.
5. Advice on nutrition, sex during pregnancy, layettes, breast feeding, and how to care for your infant in the postpartum period.
6. A visit to a hospital delivery room or, if you are to give birth at home, suggestions on what arrangements you should make to prepare the room in which the delivery will take place.

Childbirth preparation classes are held in every major city and many smaller communities, sometimes in hospitals. Ideally, classes should be small so that the teacher can cope with individual needs, but many are oversubscribed. Most are quite expensive, and it pays to shop around and compare prices. The following organizations can provide information on preparatory childbirth classes in your area:

*American Society for Psychoprophylaxis in Obstetrics,* 1523 L Street N.W., Washington D.C. 20005 (tel: 202–783–7050), was started in 1960 by Marjorie Karmel who introduced the Lamaze method of natural childbirth to the United States. It trains doctors, childbirth teachers and parents and can put you in touch with local Lamaze instructors.

*International Childbirth Education Association,* Box 20852 Milwaukee, Wisconsin 53220 (tel: 414–476–0130), provides information for preparing for childbirth with "minimal obstetric intervention in uncomplicated births."

If you are fortunate enough to have in your area a woman's clinic which offers all-round health care, this includes childbirth preparation as a normal part of the nonprofit service. One of the longest established of these is *Womancare of Feminist Women's Health Center,* 1050 Garnet, San Diego, California 92109 (tel: 714–488–7591), which offers a comprehensive maternal service, including Lamaze preparation, home deliveries with a doctor on the team, prenatal and postpartum care. Other clinics offering childbirth preparation that are known to be operating at the time of writing are the *Delta Women's Clinic* in New Orleans and the *Emma Goldman Clinic* in Iowa City (addresses on p. 58) and the *Maternity Service Association* childbearing center in New York City (see p. 71). Any women's centers in your area can also give you information on any newer local women's clinics.

If you plan to breastfeed your baby and want to know more about it, the following organization can be useful: *La Leche League International,* 9616 Minneapolis Avenue, Franklin Park, Illinois 60131 (tel: 312–455–7730).

There are also many publications on the different childbirth techniques, which, if you cannot manage classes, provide a certain amount of instruction that you can follow yourself:

*Childbirth Without Fear* by Grantly Dick-Read (New York: Harper & Row, 1972) was written by the British doctor who originated the concept of "natural" childbirth.

*Thank You, Doctor Lamaze* by Marjorie Karmel (New York: Doubleday, 1959) is a personal account of childbirth using the Lamaze method.

*Six Practical Lessons for an Easier Birth* by Elisabeth Bing (New York: Bantam Books, 1969) takes the Lamaze method step by step and is particularly useful for women who cannot receive personal instruction.

*Common Sense in Child Rearing* by Erna Wright (New York: Hart, 1973) is another excellent home manual on the Lamaze method written by a British midwife.

*Commonsense Childbirth* by Lester D. Hazell (New York: Tower, 1972) is recommended by the Boston Women's Health Collective as the "best over-all book" conveying the experience of giving birth.

*Prenatal Yoga and Natural Childbirth* by Jeannine O'Brien Medvin (Albion, Calif.: Freestone Pub. Co., 1975) describes the yoga method that helped the author through pregnancy and natural childbirth.

## EMPLOYMENT DURING PREGNANCY

Discriminatory practices against women in employment have always been based on the expectation that women will give up work when they become pregnant—an expectation fulfilled in many cases simply because women were given no other choice. Fortunately, this is changing as more women enter and claim the right to remain in the labor force, and as antidiscrimination laws gradually encourage or force employers to give equal opportunities to women regardless of their biologic role. However, these opportunities are still not available to all and it is therefore essential to know your rights as a pregnant working woman.

### Can you lose your job because of pregnancy?

You shouldn't. Guidelines laid down by the Equal Employment Opportunity Commission (EEOC) make it clear that an employer can neither fire you nor turn down your application for a job simply because you are pregnant. To do so is a violation of Title VII of the 1964 Civil Rights Act.[3] However, firms employing fewer than fifteen people are usually exempt, and the law is not always observed by other employers. Although unmarried women are protected legally on exactly the same basis as married women, there have been several recent examples of unwed pregnant teachers losing their jobs. In one consequent legal action, an Illinois court held that the "suspension and discharge for "immorality" of a public school teacher who became pregnant while unmarried was improper sex discrimination where no similar penalty was enforced against male teachers with respect to unmarried pregnancies."[4] Most court decisions have gone the same way.

### Can you return to the same job after your baby is born?

The right to be reinstated in the same job with no loss of seniority or fringe benefits after absence due to childbearing is still not fully guaranteed by law. It usually depends on your employer's policy on maternity leave. However, some protection is provided by Title VII. The EEOC guidelines state:

> Written and unwritten employment policies and practices involving matters such as the commencement and duration of leave, the availability of extensions, the accrual of seniority and other benefits and privileges, reinstatement, and payment under any health or temporary disability insurance or sick leave plan, formal or informal, shall be applied to disability due to pregnancy or childbirth on the same terms and conditions as they are applied to other temporary disabilities.[5]

This means that if your employment agreement guarantees reinstatement in the same job after absences caused by other physical disabilities, you have the right to be reinstated after childbearing as well. You would also be able to take legal action against your employer if you were denied that right. But if there is no such agreement, you are dependent on the goodwill of your employer to get the same job back. Another snag is that any agreement will guarantee reinstatement only if the employee returns within a specified period of time, which may be too short in the case of pregnancy and childbirth (see below). However, the outlook is very much better if you work for a company contracted by the federal government (to build roads, supply stationery, etc.). Such companies are bound by regulations laid down by the Office of Federal Contract Compliance. The 1975 guidelines of the OFCC require that you must be reinstated in your original job or to a position of similar status and pay without loss of service credits following childbirth, provided that you have notified your employer of your intent to return within a reasonable time.[6]

*How long can you stay away from work for childbearing?* This too depends on your employment agreement. You are definitely entitled to the same length of time granted to employees on sick leave for other disabilities. But sick leave covers only the time when you are unable to work; you can't claim it simply because you are pregnant. Moreover, the period granted for sick leave may be too short to cover the time you need, particularly if you develop the kind of complications that can send you to bed for several months. You would be entitled to an extension of sick leave if other employees were allowed extensions for other disabling conditions; if not, the EEOC suggests that in order to bring any legal pressure on the company you would have to prove that more women than men lose their jobs because leave periods are too short. Some employers allow women to maximize the period of paid maternity leave by accumulating annual leave and combining it with sick leave and leave without pay. Very few offer generous maternity leave on full pay. If you work for a company contracted by the federal government, OFCC guidelines require that, if your employer has no leave policy, childbearing must be considered a justification for a leave of absence for a reasonable period of time.

*Can you be obliged to give up work for a specified period?* No. It is now illegal for any employer to insist that you give up your job by a specified month in your pregnancy and stay away until a specified time after the birth. In 1974 the U.S. Supreme Court ruled as unconstitutional regulations that forced public school teachers to leave their jobs halfway through pregnancy and prohibited their return until three months after the birth.[7] The Court observed from medical evidence that "the ability of any particular pregnant woman to continue at work past any fixed time in her pregnancy is very much an individual matter." This decision should affect similar practices in other jobs. Under Title VII, according to the EEOC, an employer has no right to exclude any woman from employment because of pregnancy if she is able to work, although many still try.

## EDUCATION

If you are a student, you should continue your education through pregnancy if you possibly can—particularly if you are not married and plan to keep your baby. Even if you marry, you need to complete your education. Your future independence depends on your ability to earn money for yourself and all the more so if, like many teen-age brides, your marriage ends in divorce.

What, then, are your rights to continue your education during pregnancy if you are in high school or college? The most important law governing those rights is Title IX of the Educational Amendments of 1972, which bans sex discrimination by all educational institutions receiving federal aid. In 1975 new regulations for enforcing Title IX dealt specifically with pregnancy, stating that:

> A recipient shall not discriminate against any student or exclude any student from its education program or activity, including any class or extra-curricular activity, on the basis of such student's pregnancy, childbirth, false pregnancy, miscarriage, abortion or recovery therefrom, unless:
> (1) the student requests voluntarily to participate in a different program or activity; or
> (2) the student's physician certifies to the recipient that such different participation is necessary for her physical, mental or emotional well being."[8](The "recipient" means *every* institution offering lower or higher education, public or private, which receives Federal money in the form of grants, loans or contracts—in other words, virtually all educational establishments in the United States.)

If you wish to continue at your present school and the school tries to prevent this, you have the right to take legal action against the school under Title IX. How to go about this is explained on p. 138. The reasons often given by school authorities for barring pregnant students do not bear close scrutiny. Pregnant teen-agers are physically able to cope with schoolwork and psychologically may be better off among their own friends. And there is no reason for thinking that pregnancy makes a student more of a "bad influence" on her peers than she might otherwise be. As Luella Klein has remarked in an article on this subject[9]: "Pregnancy is not contagious. Girls don't get girls pregnant."

Alternatively, there may be a special educational program for pregnant students in your area. In 1975 there were over three hundred such programs in the United States, mostly in major cities, and their numbers are expanding. Many of these programs offer instruction in parenting and health care as well as normal schoolwork. There are experts who believe that to segregate pregnant students in this way is not advisable, but as long as prejudice persists in some schools, making pregnant students uncomfortable or unhappy, these programs offer a means of continuing your education in ways adapted to your needs. You can find out more about any programs available in your area from your present school administrator or from your local department of education. Useful information is also available from the National Alliance Concerned with School-Age Parents, 7315 Wisconsin Avenue, Suite 211–W, Washington D.C. 20014 (tel: 301–654–2335).

One special program is worth mentioning here for its approach in helping young pregnant women from sixteen to twenty-one who have dropped out of school and are unable to get further education or meaningful employment. This is the comprehensive maternity program established at San Francisco General Hospital in 1969. The program includes prenatal care, childbirth preparation classes, delivery, instruction in parenthood and vocational guidance leading to employment in local companies.[10]

What if you are in college? Higher educational institutions tend to be less stuffy about pregnancy, and any form of discrimination can be challenged under Title IX. The many on-campus women's centers that have been set up in recent years also provide useful sources of help in fighting discrimination. However, you may find it more difficult to be accepted by institutions of higher education if you are pregnant.

## MONEY

American women have no national protection against loss of earnings during maternity but are dependent on a fragmented system made up of an individual employer's policies on maternity leave, disability insurance, unemployment benefits, and uneven welfare provisions in different states. It is important to know what money will be available to you from these sources, particularly if you will have no financial support from a man, or help from your family, or savings to draw on.

*Paid maternity leave* Very few employers grant special cash benefits for maternity or allow women employees maternity leave on full pay, as distinct from benefits paid out under disability insurance plans. If you are one of the lucky ones, your employment agreement will specify the conditions—for example, how long you have to work for this employer before becoming eligible.

*Group disability insurance plans*  Disability insurance is intended to protect workers against loss of earnings if they become ill or injured. Under EEOC guidelines, this protection must extend to women unable to work because of normal late pregnancy and childbirth, as well as medical complications arising from both.[11] Many employers now comply with these requirements, but some have contended that as pregnancy is a "voluntary" condition, it cannot be regarded in the same light as sickness or accident. This argument was unexpectedly upheld by the U.S. Supreme Court in December 1976. The ruling, unless overturned by a newly proposed federal law, is likely to mean even more discrimination in the future against pregnant working women.

*Individual disability insurance*  Many employers have no group disability insurance plans, and women (including the self-employed) who try to obtain individual coverage often find that they are refused, or have to pay twice as much as a man, or that their policies specifically exclude disabilities arising from "female disorders." These discriminatory practices perpetrated by the insurance industry are often based on outdated assumptions that women are supported by men, working temporarily for "pin money," and are generally "poor risks." Yet statistics show that women are absent from work no more frequently than men,[12] and that nearly 90 percent of women in the labor force are single, divorced, separated, widowed or living with husbands earning low wages.[13] As Barbara Shacks of the American Civil Liberties Union has commented: "For twenty million women, health care costs and loss of earnings could mean financial disaster."[14] The insurance industry is only gradually changing its attitudes toward women, quite often as a result of being challenged by women. In 1972, for example, the local chapter of the National Organization of Women, by threatening a class-action suit, forced a change in the wording of the California insurance code which allowed insurance companies to refuse payments for disabilities arising from "war, suicide, hallucinatory drugs, and organs peculiar to females."[15]

*Unemployment insurance*

Each state administers its own program of unemployment insurance. To be eligible for benefits, you must have worked long enough to meet your state's regulations, must be available for work and must not refuse the offer of a suitable job. If you lose your job during pregnancy for any reason, you cannot be denied benefits to which you are otherwise entitled on the ground that you are pregnant and unable to work. In November 1975, the U.S. Supreme Court ruled as unconstitutional Utah's unemployment compensation law, which denied benefit to women between twelve weeks before and six weeks after childbirth. The Court declared: "It cannot be doubted that a substantial number of women are fully capable of working well into their last trimester of pregnancy and of resuming employment shortly after childbirth."[16] However, this ruling did not grant women the right to unemployment benefit during the time they *cannot* work. Even if you remain eligible because no suitable job has been offered, you can be denied a week's benefit if you do not report in person to the local unemployment insurance office as required.

*Welfare* A pregnant woman who is not covered by disability or unemployment insurance and has no other means of support clearly needs financial assistance during the period when she cannot work. Eligibility for assistance depends on the requirements of different state and local welfare programs.

*Aid to Families with Dependent Children* AFDC is a weekly benefit paid to mothers on behalf of children whose fathers are not supporting them (explained in more detail on pp. 126–30). HEW allows states the option of paying benefits for unborn children as well. Until 1975 about half the states did this. But in March 1975, when one test case finally reached the U.S. Supreme Court, the Court ruled that the unborn are *not* "dependent children" within the meaning of the Social Security Act.[17] This ruling did not deny any state the option of continuing to pay AFDC for unborn children, but it provides the perfect excuse for any state that wishes to cut back on this part of its welfare program. To find out whether your state provides AFDC for the unborn, contact the state agency which administers welfare (usually listed under "Department of Social Services" in the telephone directory). If it does, you can claim benefit from your local welfare office in the usual way (see p. 126). If not, remember that you can claim it as soon as your child is born, although it is best to apply sooner to avoid delay in receiving your money.

*General assistance* This is intended for people in need who fall outside the eligibility requirements of federally funded welfare programs, so it may be claimed by pregnant women who cannot obtain AFDC. General assistance is administered solely by the states or local government welfare agencies. Payments are usually less than in federal programs and quite often eligibility requirements are so tight as to discourage all but the most desperately poor. For example, you might have to show that absolutely no money is available from any other source, such as members of your family or the father of your coming child. For more information, contact your state or city department of social welfare.

*Help from other sources*

*The food stamp program* offers a way of buying more food than you actually pay for, which may help meet the extra nutritional needs of pregnancy. Eligibility requirements, and how to apply, are explained on p. 130.

*Charitable organizations* sometimes offer small cash grants or other forms of help to people in need, particularly unwed expectant mothers. These include church welfare bodies (see p. 26), adoption agencies (see p. 92), groups concerned with alternatives to abortion, such as Birthright (see p. 25), and special programs for unwed mothers (contact your state or local department of social service for information).

*"Black market" adoption arrangements* are dubious practices discussed in more detail on p. 93. But they are relevant here for the simple reason that pregnant women are often persuaded to sign over their coming child to adoptive parents in return for all the expenses of pregnancy and childbirth. Such parents are often willing to pay a woman up to about $10,000 to cover her rent, living costs, the best private medical care and legal costs, as well as a lot more money to the doctor or lawyer who arranges the deal. Such a practice may be attractive to a woman who is absolutely certain that she does not want to keep her child. But if you want to keep your options open, try not to get involved. The very extent of this practice in the United States is an appalling measure of how inadequately the system serves the needs of women who are pregnant and on their own.

## HOUSING

Pregnancy does not always present housing problems in the same way that being a single mother with a child might (see p.131–32). But pregnant women on their own sometimes find they can no longer remain in their present homes: they may be unable to pay the rent, wish to get away from their families or simply want to move elsewhere to avoid embarrassment. Most women in this situation can turn to friends. If this is not practicable, there are three other possibilities:

*Maternity Homes* Maternity homes were very common in the days when unmarried pregnant women had little option but to disappear for a few months until their babies were born and then adopted. Today, attitudes have changed and fewer unmarried women feel the need for concealment. The homes that survive vary a great deal: conditions may be modern or old, cheerful or depressing, geared to the new, more liberal approach to unmarried mothers' needs or still clinging to outdated ideas. On the whole, they are more easygoing and sympathetic places than they used to be. At the very least, they provide shelter, food and arrangements for delivery and health care. Some are exclusively for school-age expectant mothers, offering educational classes and instruction in parenting. Many go to enormous lengths to protect the confidence of women who wish to keep their pregnancy secret; they often have unlisted telephone numbers and provide addresses in other towns where letters can be sent to you. Most offer adoption services, but it is important to remember that *no one* can force you to give your child up for adoption if you would prefer to bring it up yourself (see p. 92).

*Cost* Different homes have varying charges and policies on how payment is made. In most cases, fees are scaled to your ability to pay, and you should not be asked for more than you can afford. Sometimes payments can be spread over a period of time, so that you can pay out of your earnings when you return to work.

*Finding a maternity home* Most homes are run by religious welfare organizations, some by social agencies and other by voluntary agencies within the community. You can contact them through these organizations locally (listed in the telephone directory under the various church denominations), or your local or state social service agency can put you in touch. The Child Welfare League of America publishes a directory listing their member agencies, many of which provide assistance in locating maternity homes (see p. 137).

*Living in a Family* Voluntary organizations and social agencies can sometimes put you in touch with families who are willing to have pregnant women living with them in the later stages of pregnancy and for a short time after the birth. In this arrangement you live as a member of the family but pay board. You can find out more about this alternative from the religious welfare organizations mentioned above, any adoption agency (see p. 92) and perhaps your local department of social services.

*Residential jobs* In this arrangement a pregnant woman lives with a family and receives room, board and a small salary in exchange for light household work and/or baby-sitting services. This can be a very useful way of tiding you over; you get to live in comfortable surroundings and have some money of your own. If your relationship with the family is good, you avoid isolation and can feel you are among people who care. (It does not always turn out so well, and you should be on your guard against exploitation. Some people regard pregnant women on their own as a cheap solution to the "servant problem.") Residential jobs of this type can be found through religious welfare organizations (see p. 26), adoption agencies (p. 92), community help services and hot lines (p. 26), advertisements in newspapers, or by asking around (doctors are sometimes a good source of information).

## IF YOU WISH TO KEEP YOUR
## PREGNANCY SECRET

The great majority of single women these days are able to be open about their pregnancies and do not need to go into hiding—which is why this section is something of an afterthought to this chapter instead of being, as it would have been twenty years ago, up front. But some women still feel they have to keep their pregnancies secret from their families, their friends or the communities they live in. If you are considering dropping out of sight until after your child is born, it is best to ask yourself whether this is really necessary or a good idea.

If it is your family you are worried about, are you sure they would be unwilling to help you or that the news would be more than they could bear? Most families rise to the occasion and cope with all kinds of crisis. Many parents would be far more shocked to know that their daughters were trying to get through pregnancy on their own. Even if they aren't very sympathetic, it still might be better to have them around than no one at all. Isolation is probably the worst problem that any pregnant woman can face.

There is also the important question of what you will do when your baby arrives. You may intend to have the child adopted so that you can return to your normal way of life without anyone knowing about it. But you should be prepared to face the possibility that you may change your mind and want to keep your child.

If you decide to leave home, it may help to keep the following points in mind:

*If possible, go and stay with someone you know,* or in a place where you have a sympathetic friend or relative.

*Contact someone who can give you professional help* if you run into any problems over accommodation, money or loneliness. Likely sources are among those listed on pp. 24–27.

*Make sure you get proper medical care* The women with the greatest risk of medical complications are those who receive no prenatal care because they are trying to keep their pregnancies secret. This is particularly common among pregnant teen-agers who, apart from being physically most in need of medical care, are often afraid to approach a doctor in case he informs their parents about the pregnancy.

*Let your family know you are all right* It would be unfair to leave home without a word and never let your parents know what has happened to you. Even if you get on with them very badly, you should at least let them know you are alive and well. If you cannot bring yourself to get in touch personally, you can use a recently established service called "Operation Peace of Mind," which offers help to the 500,000 young people who run away from home each year. The number is toll-free: 1–800–231–6946. A volunteer takes your call and phones a member of your family to let them know you are alive and well. You don't have to say where you are, and your call will not be traced. The volunteer will also act as go-between for messages between yourself and your family if you wish, and put you in touch with sources of help if you need it, wherever you happen to be.

# 6

❧

# Adoption and Fostering

If you are not ready to accept the full responsibilities of being a parent, or feel that there is no hope of providing a reasonable standard of living for your child, then adoption is probably in the child's best interests. And if other people make you feel guilty about this decision, that is probably because they have no idea of the difficulties you face or because they share the romantic view that all women have a desire and talent for bringing up children, which is not necessarily true. It is important to bear this in mind if you are already resolved on having your child adopted, because the pressures on you to keep the infant may be strong. On the other hand, the pressures may be all the other way: you want to keep your child, but the people closest to you are persuading you against it, raising serious doubts in your own mind about how you could manage as a single parent.

Although in recent years most unmarried mothers have kept their children, there have been some unhappy results. The Child Welfare League of America reports that some mothers, unable finally to cope, have relinquished their children for adoption at age two, three or even older—when adoption is far more traumatic for a child.

The next chapter should give you some idea of what it means to bring up a child alone. This chapter looks at the factors to consider when making up your mind about adoption and the legal processes involved if you finally decide on that course of action. It also considers fostering, which means having your child cared for by someone else until you are able to take full charge yourself. The last section concerns a quite different question—that of an unmarried woman who wishes to become a single parent by adopting a child.

## ADOPTION: WEIGHING THE PROS AND CONS

Perhaps the only thing you know for sure about adoption is that it means giving up all your parental rights and allowing your child to be brought up in a strange family. The implications of this can be difficult to confront, but it may help to gain a perspective on the problem to know what other mothers in the same position have experienced.

Some mothers choose adoption because they feel strongly that a child should have two parents and a potentially secure future. Some painfully come to the conclusion that adoption is best because they have no immediate hope of providing a suitable home for a child. Some feel they cannot cope emotionally with parenthood at this time in their lives and think it is fairer to a child to be brought up by someone who really wants one.

But not all single mothers are convinced that adoption will give their children a better life. They point out that the adoptive parents could die, fall ill or get divorced. It is true that divorce, in particular, is a risk of the times and adoptive parents are not immune. So a mother sometimes argues that if there is any chance of her child ending up in a single-parent family she would prefer it to be her own.

### How will my child feel about being adopted?

Many adopted children grow up feeling only a mild, natural curiosity about their natural parents, accepting their adoptive families as the "real" ones. But some adopted children, now adults, have testified to their feelings of resentment and even anger against their own mothers for giving them away. Some say that in adolescence they experienced feelings of disorientation, wanting to know more of their origins and becoming intensely frustrated when their inquiries drew a blank.

A great deal depends on the attitudes of the adoptive parents. Adoption agencies nowadays usually advise parents to tell children they are adopted at an early age and answer their questions honestly about their natural mothers. A few personal details of what the mother looked like, what her interests were and perhaps what kind of work she did are considered sufficient to satisfy the child's curiosity. A gentle explanation of why she could not bring up the child herself may also be advised.

Recently, however, some groups of adults who were adopted as children have organized to declare their right to know their origins and to contact their natural parents. At present the laws of every state forbid this: once the adoption decree becomes final, the records (including the child's original birth certificate) are sealed and may be opened only at the direction of a court order. Nevertheless, some people have searched persistently and a few have succeeded in contacting their natural parents. The outcome can lead to a happy reunion—or to the utmost consternation and disappointment.

## How would I feel if I had my child adopted?

This would depend very much on why you decided on adoption and how sure you were that you had done the right thing. You might well feel that you were denying your own maternal instincts if you had already developed strong feelings toward the child. You would almost certainly feel upset. It is natural to grieve—particularly if, in other circumstances, you would have dearly loved to have kept your child.

The saddest situation is when a woman is pressured into adoption by other people's attitudes or by lack of money. Too often a woman is forced to agree to adoption early in pregnancy in return for having her living costs and medical bills paid. Her right to a free choice is denied if she cannot support herself during maternity.

Would you regret the decision later? Some mothers don't. Some do, especially when their circumstances change and they can no longer see so clearly the difficulties that influenced their decision at the time. Adoption workers sometimes say that it helps to think of adoption as giving something *to* your child rather than as giving the child away. There's a lot in that advice, though it's probably easier said than done.

## What other mothers have said

Here are the comments of a mother who felt she had made the right choice in having her child adopted, followed by those of a mother who felt she had made the wrong one.

JEAN: I decided on adoption almost from the beginning. I couldn't face the idea of abortion. But there wasn't any possibility of keeping the baby. I couldn't stay here with him [in her parents' two-bedroom apartment] and I couldn't afford to find a place of my own—well, nothing you could bear to live in. I would have had to keep on working, and day care is nonexistent. I didn't see how I would be able to get by except by scrimping and scraping, and I wasn't prepared to do that. I also felt strongly that the child needed a father as well—for emotional reasons rather than practical ones.

I loved being pregnant. As it got nearer the time I kept day-dreaming about how lovely it would be to keep the baby. I enjoyed the birth, which was quite easy. The baby was a boy—I still think he was the most beautiful baby in the world. I was very happy looking after him in the hospital. That was the closest I came to deciding to keep him.

The nurses kept on saying "Isn't he lovely? Look how much he loves you. How can you bear to give him away?" I got very upset and emotional and told my mother I wanted to keep him. I let the other mothers in the hospital think I was keeping him. It was the only way to get any peace. But then I thought more about it and came back to my original decision. I was glad I'd looked after him in the hospital, but I decided to place him in a foster home when I came out in case I got more upset and changed my mind again. When I came home I felt empty, crying my eyes out and wondering whether I'd done the right thing. I thought about him all the time, though getting back to work helped.

The final adoption went through about four months ago. I'm glad it's settled, and I know I've done the right thing. I've given him the best start I can. He'll have a much more comfortable and secure life than if he were with me, and he's with people who love him. They had photos taken of him with his new sister, and they rang up the adoption agency to ask if I'd like them. People are very surprised that I'm proud to show those pictures around. But I *am* proud. You can see from them that he's happy.

SUE: I was 17 when I got pregnant and in those days (1967) no one even talked about abortion. My parents were terribly upset, and it was just taken for granted that I'd have the child adopted. They didn't talk about my pregnancy much and hardly ever referred to "the baby." I think I was very confused so I didn't really try to find out about getting a home of my own and keeping the baby; I knew my parents wouldn't tolerate me keeping it at home.

My daughter was adorable, but my mother kept on saying I mustn't get too attached to her. I think it would have been better not to see her, but in the hospital they say you've got to, and that's that. I kept on looking at the other mothers and envying them because they were so happy.

I wish now I'd refused to part with her, but it seemed impossible at the time, with my parents feeling the way they did. The adoption woman said she would have a good home and that it was natural to feel upset about giving her up. Well of course it was natural. I didn't want to give her up. Afterwards I just cried all the time and felt miserable for months. I felt I'd done a terrible thing. My baby does have a good home, I'm sure, and I like to think that she's happy. But it had a terrible effect on me at first and I kept on looking on the worst side, wondering whether she was all right.

Of course, I don't feel so badly about it now. I thought it would get better when I got married and had another child, and I suppose that did help a lot. But you can never replace a child. When I look at. my son sometimes I think of his sister and wonder what she's doing and what she's like.

## ARRANGING TO HAVE YOUR CHILD ADOPTED

Adoptions can be arranged either through licensed adoption agencies or privately. It is important to know the differences between the two.

### Adoption agencies

This is the most usual way of finding a suitable family to adopt a child. It is generally accepted that going through an agency is safer—in terms of the child's future—than making an independent adoption. Three states—Connecticut, Delaware and Illinois—insist that all adoptions be handled by licensed agencies.

You may be worried that, once in touch with an agency, pressure will be put on you to have your child adopted before you have fully made up your mind. This can happen. But on the whole agencies are very careful to make sure that a mother has explored all the possibilities. Some have adapted themselves sufficiently to changing attitudes to give a comprehensive service to unmarried mothers who keep their children as well as those who have them adopted. Most agencies will not allow mothers to give their formal consent to adoption until after the child is born and they have had time to reconsider the decision.

The most important service provided by any agency is its experience in screening would-be adoptive parents. Nowadays agencies are less concerned about satisfying the needs of childless couples than they are about making sure that a child goes to the right home. They are therefore careful to assess the prospective parents not only on their material circumstances but on their motives for adopting a child, the maturity of their outlook, the strength of their marriage and the attitudes they are likely to develop toward an adopted child later on.

In recent years, as the shortage of the kind of infants most in demand (newborn, healthy, white) has grown acute, agencies have also broadened their service. They now make real efforts to place children once considered unsuitable for adoption—children who are older, emotionally disturbed, physically or mentally handicapped or of mixed race. Prospective parents are deliberately selected, as far as possible, from people whose qualities of understanding and patience enable them to make a loving home for such children.

Remember that if an agency gives *you* good service, this is your best possible guarantee that it will work in the best interests of your child if you do go ahead with adoption. It is good practice for an agency to offer help with practical problems during pregnancy. Normally it cannot give financial support, but it should be able to put you in touch with other sources of help if you need it. The agency caseworker should discuss the possibilities of keeping your child and help you arrive at your own decision without applying any pressure. She should be prepared for the fact that you may change your mind—perhaps change it several times —and have sympathy with your doubts.

Beware, however, of an agency that tries to push you into adoption or urges you to make up your mind quickly, seems uninterested in your personal problems during pregnancy or succeeds only in making you feel confused and upset. If you receive bad treatment, or have doubts about what you are told, take advice from the Child Welfare League of America (address p. 137) which sets national standards on adoption.

*Finding an adoption agency* Some agencies are state- or city-controlled. Most are run by voluntary groups, usually church organizations. The church agencies (usually, but not always, geared to infants of their own faith) can be found in the telephone directory under the name of the church. City or state social services departments keep a list of local licensed agencies. The Child Welfare League can also provide a list.

## Independent adoptions

These are nonagency adoptions in which the natural mother makes her own arrangements directly with the adoptive parents. Sometimes it is a family she knows; more often another person (maybe a doctor, nurse or lawyer) acts as go-between to bring the two parties together.

Independent adoptions are legal in most states (except Connecticut, Delaware and Illinois) on the ground that a mother has the right to approve the family her child goes to. But usually such adoptions do not work out quite like that. Because the law allows the adoptive parents to pay for all the mother's living expenses and medical bills—and because a lawyer who acts as go-between has the right to be paid for his services —the system is open to abuse. For this reason, adoption experts and others concerned about the welfare of adopted children regard independent adoptions as a "gray area" in which too many things can go wrong.

The people who handle independent adoptions are careful to make sure that all the legal formalities are complied with. Most states also require that the adoptive parents be investigated by a state agency as a check on their suitability to look after a child. But such checks are often not nearly so thorough as the investigations carried out by a licensed adoption agency. The fact that prospective parents often pay large sums of money to secure a child—anything from $3,000 to $20,000, out of which the go-between takes a cut—adds to the suspicion that such adoptions, though sometimes successful, are not always carried out in the best interests of the child.

From the natural mother's point of view, financial support during pregnancy and childbirth is obviously a powerful incentive if she has no other means of support. But it is also a powerful pressure on her not to change her mind about keeping the child, which should be her right.

*Black market adoptions* These are independent adoptions in which all the legal formalities are bypassed. The children are literally sold—a practice illegal in every state—to adoptive parents for anything up to $25,000. There are no checks on the suitability of the prospective parents, who may already have been turned down by a reputable adoption agency. Black market adoptions are undesirable for the same reason that they are illegal: the child's interests are not protected at all.

## The legal process

Though adoption practices are governed by state laws which vary in their requirements, the basic legal process for adoption is the same:

1. The natural parents must give their consent, freeing the child for adoption.
2. The couple (or in some cases a single person) wishing to adopt the child must make the necessary formal application.
3. The suitability of the would-be adoptive parents must be investigated by a licenced adoption agency or, in the case of independent adoptions, by a state agency if required by law.
4. A court hearing is held to make sure that the necessary consents have been obtained and that the investigation of the adoptive parents has proved satisfactory. Once satisfied on these points, the court issues an "interlocutory decree" which allows the child to be placed with the adoptive parents.
5. The child stays with the adoptive parents for the waiting period

required by law before the adoption becomes final (usually six months to a year), unless either they or the natural parents change their minds.

6. The court issues a final decree, making the child the legal responsibility of the adoptive parents and terminating all rights of the natural parents.

*Whose consent is necessary?* The natural mother's consent is essential before the adoption process can begin. Her consent can be waived only in certain special circumstances according to state law—for example, if she has abandoned the child, is mentally incompetent, or has been declared an unfit parent.

The child's consent is also required by some states if she or he is over a certain age (10, 12, 14, depending on the state).

The natural father's consent is a more complicated issue. Some state laws specifically require the father's consent if he has acknowledged the child as his own or if his paternity has been established by a court. However, in 1972 a ruling by the U.S. Supreme Court in *Stanley v. Illinois* in effect gave natural fathers throughout the country the right to claim custody of their illegitimate children. The Stanley case concerned a father who had lived with the mother of his children for years and who, after her death, claimed custody of them—a right denied him by the law then effective in Illinois. But the decision made the laws on adoption consents ambiguous. Whether the consent of the father is now required—or, if he cannot be found, whether the adoption can be indefinitely delayed—seems to depend on how individual judges interpret the Supreme Court ruling. But a mother can expect to be asked to obtain the father's consent, and adoption agencies are likely to want to involve him in the adoption decision. This means that a father is in a far stronger position than previously if he wishes to contest the adoption of his child and claim custody for himself. A few fathers have now done this, although it is ultimately always up to the court to decide whether this is in the best interests of the child.

*Relinquishment* A mother is said to have "relinquished" her child when she signs the formal consent papers freeing the child for adoption. This may be done at any time, although a reputable adoption agency prefers not to accept a complete consent before a week or two after the child is born.

A mother has the right to change her mind and take back her child at any time before she signs the consent form. After that it becomes more complicated. During the "interlocutory period" when the child is living with the adoptive parents, the natural mother still has rights over the child in most states but must apply to the court if she wants the child returned to her. Once a court grants a final adoption decree, she no longer has any rights and cannot get the child back.

Some states, however, allow for the rights of a natural parent to be terminated *before* the child is made available for adoption. This is regarded as the best way of insuring that the growing bonds between the child and adoptive parents cannot be interrupted by a natural mother who changes her mind. Under this system, adoption agencies probably do all they can to insure that the mother knows what she is doing and will not regret her decision. But it does underline a golden rule when considering adoption: don't sign anything until you are sure.

## IF YOU WISH TO ADOPT A CHILD AS A SINGLE PARENT

There is irony in the fact that, while some single mothers are unable to keep their natural children, other unmarried women are able to adopt children and become single parents as a matter of deliberate choice. The fact that they are now sometimes allowed to do so reflects a remarkable change of attitude on the part of adoption workers in recent years.

No state adoption law specifically excludes an unmarried person from adopting a child, but for many years it was taken for granted that only married couples were "suitable." Then, in 1967, the Child Welfare League of America announced that several adoption agencies were prepared to consider single adoptive parents for children who—because they were older, emotionally disturbed, handicapped, or interracial—could not readily be placed in two-parent homes. The thinking behind this step was that it was better for a child to be cared for by a single parent than to continue in an institution with no family at all.

Not all adoption workers agree. Some cling to conventional ideas about "ideal" adoptive parents. Others argue, more reasonably, that the single-parent role is itself difficult, and the strain may prove too much in attempting to cope with a child with special needs. This, of course, is also the question that the single adoptive parent must confront. She, even more than a natural mother, has to examine honestly how she will manage. The difference, however, is that she also has to convince an adoption agency.

But it is already clear that some single-parent adoptions are working better than anyone expected. And it may be that in the future adoptive parents will more often be selected because their personal qualities make them appear right for a particular child (special needs or not) than on the basis of their marital status.

If you are single and wish to adopt a child, the Child Welfare League of America can advise you on how to go about it. If your local adoption agencies are against the idea, you can inquire about an organization called ARENA (Adoption Resource Exchange of North America), set up by the League to match children with adoptive parents on a nation-wide scale so that neither is restricted to placements in their own state. *The Single Parent Experience* by Carole Klein, which contains some excellent interviews with single parents who did adopt and who speak candidly about the joys and the problems they encountered, is well worth the reading if you are considering this seriously (see p. 136).

## FOSTERING

Fostering is quite different from adoption. It means having your child looked after by someone else but keeping your right to take the child back at any time you choose. This may seem an ideal solution if at present you cannot provide a home for a child but cannot bear the thought of adoption. It has also allowed some mothers a useful breathing space both to consider adoption more fully and to find ways of keeping their children. However, public attention has increasingly focused on the major drawbacks of long-term fostering and the problems it can create for all concerned—the child, the foster family and the natural mother.

It is important to recognize these problems if you consider fostering. Your relationship with the foster mother may become very strained. You may disagree on how the child should be brought up. You may worry that your child's affections will be divided and that he or she will gradually come to look on the foster mother as the real mother. The foster mother may feel she is doing a better job in caring for the child than you could: she may not fully understand why you can't look after him yourself. If it goes on for years, she may naturally come to think of the child as her own and the child may naturally become very close to her. It is bad for a child to be emotionally pulled between the two of you; he may well become confused and upset. The child may really suffer if you take little interest in him over several years and then claim him back. This is how those lacerating "tug of love" cases you read about in the newspapers actually happen.

Such cases have led to a change in thinking on the part of those who are concerned about the welfare of children. Traditionally, the law has emphasized the rights of natural parents to their own children, and social workers have generally accepted the principle that it is best for children to be reunited with their biological parents except in cases of abandonment or clear neglect and ill-treatment. Now it is believed that the rights of natural parents should be limited, that more legal rights should be given to children and foster parents, and that the courts should be given more discretion to act in the interests of a fostered child.

Many single mothers, on the other hand, argue that children are very often left in foster homes not out of a lack of interest but because of their parents' inadequate resources. They maintain that society has the wrong priorities if it allows foster parents to be paid out of public funds to look after children when lack of money is the main reason why mothers cannot provide an adequate home themselves.

Perhaps one of the best summaries of the dangers and conflicts of fostering came from a mother who wrote of her own dilemma when responding to the 1972 British survey carried out by Mothers In Action. She said:

"After the fostering was arranged, I suffered much anguish and misgivings as the foster parents, though lavishing affection upon my daughter, became very possessive and succeeded to some extent in alienating her from me by preventing my visiting her on friendly pretexts, and by teaching her to regard me as an aunt rather than her mother.

"After a bitter struggle and argument I was able to secure her release at the age of two years. During this time I received very little sympathy from the social worker who seemed to feel that I had been an inadequate mother and unwilling to seek a home for my daughter and myself. I felt bitter and heartbroken as I had really tried hard to find a home for us both, with no success.

"On reflection, I feel now that such a long-term fostering was bad for both my daughter and myself. If I was now in the same position I would shout louder and louder at official doors to ensure that my daughter could be accommodated with me and that the period of fostering was kept to a minimum. I am glad to be able to say that my daughter is now a happy and contented child, enjoying as near to normal a home life as is possible. In my view, fostering must be minimal if the child is to remain well-balanced. Therefore natural parents must be quickly helped to re-establish themselves in order that children do not suffer irreparable mental damage."

These words emphasize the dilemma that many mothers face. But they also clearly reveal how a child may suffer in an ambiguous situation. The answer, as this mother said, may well be to "shout louder and louder at official doors" so that women who genuinely wish to provide for their children are given a proper chance to do so. That goal comes steadily nearer as women achieve greater opportunities for financial independence. But for many single mothers the reality at present remains bleak. Under these circumstances it is necessary to be as honest as you can when considering fostering and adoption—confronting not only what you would ideally prefer for yourself but what, in the long run, would be best for your child.

# 7

## Bringing Up a Child on Your Own

The single-parent family is a rapidly growing phenomenon of American life. In 1970 there were 3.5 million families with children under eighteen headed by one parent (usually the mother)—an increase of 25 percent since 1960.[1] In 1975 more than 11 million children (or one in five) were being raised by single parents (compared to one in seven in 1970) but, since many of the parents remarry after a period of time, it has been estimated that at least one-third and perhaps close to one-half of all children spend a part of their childhood in single-parent families.[2]

This development does not mean that marriage is on the way out so much as that ideas about marriage have changed. The generation who have become parents since 1960 have fewer children, no longer equate sex with procreation and, if their high expectations of finding happiness through marriage do not work out, are more likely to end the partnership and try again. For women in particular, the pursuit of "identity" and "self-fulfillment" beyond marriage and motherhood, the opportunities that have enabled them to break out of their traditional roles, together with the ideology of women's liberation, have all combined to persuade them that they can, even should, make it on their own. For the first time in history, women are as likely as men to be the instigators of divorce or separation.

Although marital breakups (which now occur in more than half of all American marriages) have been the most important factor in swelling the ranks of single-parent families, other trends have also contributed: unwed mothers are now more apt to keep their children instead of having them adopted; single men and women have begun to adopt children; homosexual men and women, previously attempting to conform in conventional marriages, are now "coming out" and taking their children with them.

Single parents have two main worries. The first is economic survival:

how can single parents maintain an adequate standard of living when the absence of one parent nearly always means a large drop in the family's income? The second is the impact of this type of family structure on the emotional and social development of the children.

The economic issue is fairly clearcut. Family life today is geared to an economic partnership in which a man and a woman divide between them the duties of earning money, running a home, bringing up children. This system works reasonably well until one person is absent—then the flaws stand out only too clearly. Because mothers are expected to have husbands to support them, women's earnings are on the whole too low to support families at a level most couples would regard as reasonable. Because it is still often assumed that mothers do not need to work, proper child-care services are grossly inadequate. (Because fathers are expected to have wives at home running their households and looking after their children single fathers' earnings too are not usually enough to hire an employee to do such a comprehensive job for them.) The result is that most single parents are forced onto the poverty line or must accept a drastic reduction in their standard of living.

The enormous gap between society's assumptions about "the all-American family" and the harsh reality of the way many single-parent families, especially those headed by women, actually live is clearly reflected in the statistics. In 1974 the median earnings of women who headed families was about $4,500 a year—less than half that of male family heads.[3] Between 1963 and 1975, a period of unparalleled prosperity, the number of women with dependent children who were on welfare rose from 800,000 to over 3 million, in spite of the 1967 amendment requiring AFDC mothers to work.[4] In 1975 there were an estimated 6 million preschool children whose mothers were working—and only about 1 million spaces available in licensed child-care programs.[5]

There are, of course, signs that this is changing, but they are happening too slowly, and mothers are concerned about the effects on their children *now*. Poverty is considered a major cause of child deprivation, associated as it is with poor housing, poor nutrition, poor health care, poor schooling and poor substitute child care. Even relative poverty restricts choice in these areas, and lack of money brings tensions that can put more of a strain on family relationships than anything else.

Yet even relatively affluent single parents worry about how their family status might affect their children's development. And this is a far more complicated issue. Do children really need two parents? How are they influenced by parental split-ups, bereavement, or by not knowing their fathers at all? How are they affected by new emotional and sexual relationships entered into by their parents, including remarriage? Will their own chances of success as marriage partners and parents in later life be damaged by their childhood experiences in a one-parent family —or will those experiences give them a healthier, broader outlook?

This chapter looks first at what is known about the development of children in single-parent families, the child's needs and the steps to take to avoid or lessen any adverse effects. It then concentrates on the practical information that is useful to know when weighing decisions about work, money and housing. It finally suggests a "survival strategy" that will enable a single parent to contact sources of help rapidly if she gets into difficulties.

## CHILDREN IN SINGLE-PARENT FAMILIES

It can be alarming, when you are a single parent, to read reports suggesting that children from "broken homes" generally do less well at school, get into trouble with the police more frequently and are more prone to behavioral problems than children in two-parent families. But it is important to know the evidence on which these reports are based. Most studies have examined only small groups of children at a particular point in time, while any meaningful attempt to assess the impact of different kinds of family environment must necessarily examine a very large group over a considerable period of time. To date, only one investigation has done this: the National Child Development Study, carried out in Britain by the National Children's Bureau, which traced the development of 17,000 children, all born the same week in March 1958. The children were assessed at birth and at ages 7, 11 and, so far, 16. The most recent report on the information gained from this study was published in 1976 and dealt with one-parent families.[6] Its conclusions are interesting and worth summarizing here because, although based on British families, they bear out the findings of some well-designed, if small, American studies.

*Poverty* "Compared with children living in unbroken homes, *all* groups which lacked a parent tended to suffer from a disadvantage in terms of their material environment and standard of living." This disadvantage was far more marked in fatherless than in motherless families. Families headed by unmarried, divorced or separated mothers tended to suffer economic hardship more than those headed by widows.

*School performance* The progress of widows' children differed little from that of children in two-parent families, but the performance of other fatherless children was somewhat poorer. This was found to be "strongly associated with disadvantaging factors in their background and environment, such as low income and financial hardship, poor housing, low social class and so on." The absence of a father appeared to affect many children's skills in math, whereas the absence of a mother more often affected their verbal skills.

*Social adjustment* One-parent children were found to be slightly less well-adjusted than those in two-parent families in terms of anxiety, lack of concentration, settling in at school, etc. But the differences were small and "suggested that the absence of a parent had not in itself had the overwhelmingly detrimental effect so often attributed to it."

*Children's aspirations* There was no evidence that the one-parent children had lower aspirations of the kind of jobs they would eventually do, although more of the boys intended to leave school earlier. When asked to write a description of the kind of lives they thought they would be leading at age twenty-five, the fatherless children (particularly the illegitimate) were less likely to mention marriage or having children of their own.

*Family health* There was little evidence that one-parent children suffered poorer health than those in two-parent families. Single mothers, however, were more prone to illness, particularly psychiatric illness where the marriages had ended in divorce or separation. The report comments: "When one considers the burdensome responsibilities facing lone parents, and the increased anxiety and problems which such illness is bound to produce, it seems likely that the effects may well be far-reaching and severe, threatening the material, physical and emotional welfare of both parents and children."

The report emphasizes that not all one-parent children do worse than their peers; some do better. "In fact, the relatively small magnitude of the *average* difference between the various groups suggests that a great many lone parents had been highly successful in bringing up their children singlehanded."

The most striking conclusion of the study is that it appears to be the economic difficulties associated with single-parent families rather than the absence of a parent that most affects a child's development. When economic circumstances were taken into account (by comparing one- and two-parent families with similar incomes) the differences between the children's social adjustment and school performance were small and often disappeared altogether. This finding, together with the fact that single-parent families headed by women suffered more economic disadvantages than those headed by men, bears out the conclusion of a 1970 American study: "Many of the difficulties faced by mothers and children in female-headed households are not inherent to that family structure. The difficulties in part stem from the expectations of others about what is a normal family, from the socially limited alternatives deemed appropriate for women, and the specificity of sex roles."[7]

One important exception to this general rule, however, emerged when the British study compared different kinds of fatherless families. Once allowance had been made for economic disadvantages, the children of both widows and unmarried mothers showed few adverse effects. But this was not so true of the children of divorced or separated mothers. The report comments: "The period of stress and conflict which was likely to have preceded the final breakdown in the family may well have been the key factor in the rather poorer development shown among these fatherless children even after other disadvantaging factors had been taken into account." Another explanation (since these children were not actually fatherless in the same way as the children of widows or most unmarried mothers) may be that continuing tension between divorced or separated parents can affect the children even after the final split.

## If your child knows his/her father

The death of a father or the breakup of a marriage inevitably affects children emotionally. In some cases, when parental conflict has already had a disturbing impact, a separation can make things easier. More often, though, there is a period of shock, expressed in depression, bad behavior, inability to concentrate, poor work at school, and sometimes in physical symptoms like headaches and asthma. These effects frequently fade after a time. Bereaved children, in particular, seem to recover quite quickly. But children whose fathers are alive and living separately require careful handling.

It is most important, first of all, that the mother make every effort to reassure the child that the father's absence is the result of something personal between him and her, and is in no way a rejection of the child. The father should be able to help here if he genuinely involves himself with the child. But if he visits only occasionally, or stops coming after a time, the child may come to feel personally at fault. One mother, faced with this, said: "I tried to explain that while Daddy was great fun when he was around, he didn't like staying in one place all the time. I said some Daddies were like that."

Many mothers feel resentful if the children associate their fathers with treats and outings, while they are left to cope with the day-to-day routine and discipline. It can be especially galling to see the children given presents they themselves cannot afford, particularly if the fathers are not contributing enough toward the more basic needs. If the father remarries, a mother may feel an even greater sense of rejection, or be unable to suppress her jealousy if her children get on well with the new wife. In this situation it may be tempting to even up the score by complaining about the father, but it is best to let the children make up their own minds about their fathers as they grow up and try not to confuse them with the complications of the relationship between their parents.

Some mothers prefer the children not to see their fathers at all—either out of spite or from a genuine fear that the relationship will be too disruptive for the children's good. But, except in extreme cases where women have good reason to fear violence from their former husbands or the possibility that the father will "kidnap" his children and remove them entirely from the mother's care, it is doubtful whether denying access is a good idea. After a family break-up, children have a real need to know that they are important to *both* parents.

It is important to consider the father's point of view too. Whatever the circumstances of the break-up, it can be hard on a father to live apart from his children, to have to make appointments to see them, to try to communicate with them and keep a real relationship going in the space of maybe only a few hours a week. A father too may be confronted with the question of just why he left or was left—a question that may be even harder to answer if the parents are trying to keep up a "civilized" front for the children's sake—and how, if he no longer loves their mother, can they be sure that he still loves them.

Gradually, divorced or separated parents work out their own ways of minimizing the impact of marital breakdown on the children. Some see cause for optimism in the development of the new "extended family" —the variety of relationships brought about by divorce and remarriage —provided that the original parents keep open the lines of communication with their children. This means, for example, letting the children know that they are free to contact the absent parent who, in turn, will always welcome being contacted. In *Part-Time Father* (New York: Vanguard, 1975), a book for divorced men, authors Edith Atkin and Estelle Rubin observe that each parent likes to feel that the children love him or her "best." They advise: "The child needs both parents. He also needs to feel that each parent recognizes his right to care about the other."

### If your child does not know his/her father

Children who have never known their fathers sooner or later begin to be concerned about this, so it is important to reassure your child that he or she did have a father at one time just like other children, and to answer questions naturally as they arise. For widows this is usually no problem. If you are unmarried and your memories of the man are unhappy or bitter, you should still say something—if only a noncommittal description of what he looked like and what his job was. It will be no help to your child to know that on looking back you couldn't stand the man or, perhaps, knew him for only a very short time.

At some stage, you will probably be asked why Daddy is not around. Most children can accept, even if they do not fully understand, the concept of death from a relatively early age. But what if you were deserted before the child was born? At first, simple explanations like "many children have fathers who don't live with them" may be enough, as long as they are delivered in a normal, matter-of-fact manner. Later on, you will be able to judge whether your child is ready—or even wants—to hear more, and how much you are prepared to tell. What matters again is that you make it clear that parents do not always want to live together, but that this does not imply rejection of the child. One unmarried mother said: "I explained to my daughter that, as her father had never seen her, he could not be expected to love her as I did. This did not explain why he had never wanted to see her, but she seemed to accept it and never showed any resentment."

Although fatherless children are not subject to the tensions of conflict between their parents, their mothers often worry about the effect of having no father. However, even in two-parent families, a young child may have little contact with its father: one investigation of American middle-class families, by attaching microphones to the babies' clothing during their first year of life, found that these infants heard their fathers' voices for an average of only 37.7 *seconds* a day.[8] Nevertheless, as children grow older they probably do need a relationship with a man.

Many mothers rely on friends and relatives to provide a male perspective in their children's lives. Another useful source is Big Brothers—a national organization that encourages adult men, single or married, to become friends of fatherless children (see p. 137).

If you marry, remarry, or live with another man, he will inevitably become the father figure in your children's life. Most advisers, however, think that children have the right to be told about their real fathers and helped to understand that their relationship with other men, though they may love them as fathers, is different. Many mothers find that it helps prevent confusion if the children are encouraged to call other men by their first names instead of "Daddy." It also helps if you can avoid a situation in which the child comes to think of a new man in your life as a father until you are sure that the relationship will be permanent.

## PROBLEMS OF THE SINGLE PARENT

### If you get into difficulties

There may be times when you feel you're not doing a very good job of being a mother. You may wonder (if you are unmarried) whether you did the right thing in trying to bring up your child single-handedly or (if divorced or separated) whether you and your husband should have stayed together, at whatever personal cost, for the sake of the children. But it is important to keep a sense of proportion. All mothers feel unable to cope at times and lose patience when their children are exasperating. But when you're on your own, and trying to make up to your child for having only one parent, you may feel guiltier about it than you would otherwise.

Occasionally tension can build up to such a pitch that you may find yourself fighting down the urge to hurt your child in some way. You have heard of parents who abuse their children and you are terrified you may do the same. ("Sunday is child-abuse day," said one mother, only half humorously.) What can you do?

First, it helps to try to work out why you have got into this state. Usually it happens because a mother feels trapped and has no other outlet for her frustration. This is why it is so important to have some life of your own (see p. 109). Sometimes it is the result of trying to do too much. If you are working, running your home without help, and trying to be both mother and father to your children at the same time, you are bound to be under strain, and you should find a way of cutting down on something to give yourself more time to relax.

You should also talk to someone about how you feel. Talking it out releases tension, and you feel better just for getting it off your chest. Some women can turn to their friends at times like this. Others can't or don't want to. But there are others who can help—for example, the many centers and hot lines that have been set up to help parents in trouble (see pp. 134–40).

### If your child gets into difficulties

Whatever material comforts are lacking, a child is unlikely to grow up deprived if given plenty of love and care. Love gives children more security than anything else. Taking an interest in their progress and encouraging their efforts is vital. It will also help if you don't let your own problems get you down too much.

The most frequently noted problem of young children in single-parent families is the fear that the remaining parent will die or leave them. After a marriage break-up or bereavement they often go through a period of clinging, becoming upset if left for even a short time. This phase usually passes quite quickly, but in the meantime you have to be extra patient, extra loving, to reassure the child that you will be staying around.

Children frequently run into problems of one kind or another as they grow up, and signs of this often come out at school. The kinds of behavior that can give cause for concern include: withdrawal, depression, bedwetting, aggressiveness, sullenness, not making friends, not wanting to go to school, playing truant, lack of interest in work, lying, stealing, cheating and so on. These things may appear in any child. What you have to decide is whether it is a passing phase or a sign of some deeper emotional trouble. You may be able to find out by talking to your child or discussing it with his or her teacher.

If you become really worried, it is best to get professional help. Your state or local department of health or child welfare can tell you what facilities exist in your area to help children with emotional problems. A family crisis center or hotline may also be a sympathetic place to turn to and a useful source of information.

### How to build confidence

Single parenthood is, above all, an exercise in self-sufficiency. It calls for qualities of determination and resilience that few of us think we possess until put to the test. Many single mothers find out for the first time just how self-sufficient they can be.

This can take time, of course. But you will find your confidence growing rapidly if you make plans to organize your life so that you know you are managing to the best of your ability, and if you develop an image of yourself as an independent woman with a mind of your own, the right to your own decisions and the determination to develop as a person. Your attitude toward *yourself* is the key to avoiding many of the emotional problems that single mothers often suffer.

When you first become a single parent, you may find it very difficult to adjust to the fact that your identity has suddenly changed. Right after the breakup of a marriage or the death of a husband, there is bound to be a period of dislocation. Whatever the circumstances, you have passed through an invisible barrier into a new kind of life; at best you feel on unfamiliar ground, at worst, in shock and terrified that you cannot manage alone.

It isn't just the pressure of the practical problems that suddenly crowd in, nor the impact of the personal crisis that made you a single parent: there is also the self-image of being a woman who no longer has a man. We live in a society that, for a complexity of historical reasons well-documented by the women's movement, often makes women feel inadequate and insecure by emphasizing their economic and emotional dependence on men. It is a society that places great value on personal happiness achieved through sexual relationships, that persuades women that their ideal goal is marriage and that they can acquire more status through their husbands than by their own achievements. There is no real reason, however, to feel that you are less of a woman—or less of a mother—if you are on your own. You may well miss the emotional support of a man. You may be very conscious of the responsibility of bringing up children alone. But there is a lot of difference between wanting a man to fulfill your needs for affection, love and sex and to share the normal ups and downs of family life, and feeling that without a man you are nothing.

Fortunately, the consciousness-raising of the women's movement has helped many women to question the conditioning process and to explore their feelings in a new way, starting from their own real-life experiences instead of from inherited and accepted beliefs. Perhaps consciousness-raising sessions for single parents would be equally useful in assessing to what extent their feelings are conditioned by the mythical ideal of the two-parent family, rather than by the varied realities of different kinds of family life.

*If you are unmarried* A special word must be added for the unmarried mother. Some prejudice against mothers who are not married still remains. How you handle this depends on how you see yourself, how sensitive you are to what other people think and whether, in fact, you meet any unpleasant or prejudiced attitudes. There is no reason why you should not have a strong sense of your right to be a single mother openly and proudly, without feeling the need to call yourself Mrs. or to buy yourself a fake wedding ring. On the other hand, there is equally no reason why you should not wear a ring and present yourself as a widow or a divorced or separated wife, if you think this will make things easier for you or your child in the community where you live. Some women can afford to defy the conventions; others find it expedient to go along with them, no matter how hypocritical they may seem.

## A LIFE OF YOUR OWN

You owe it to your child to stay as cheerful and relaxed as you possibly can. You also owe it to yourself. You need to express yourself as a woman as well as a mother, and to feel that you count as a person in your own right.

At the very least, you need adult company, breaks in routine, and some fun. Becoming isolated is the worst trap a single mother can fall into. Though, unfortunately, it is all too easy for them to do so. Some deliberately cut themselves off from other people. Divorced, separated or widowed mothers often feel uncomfortable in the "couples" scene they were once part of, or lose former friends who had been closer to their husbands than to themselves. Young unmarried mothers often lose their friends if they become absorbed in their new babies and are no longer quite so interested in the things they did before. Sometimes it seems a lot easier to stay in than to go to all the trouble of finding a baby sitter; going out may also seem a waste of precious money if things are tight.

You may become isolated because of your housing situation. For example, you may move to an area where you know no one, or may be in an apartment where you have never known the neighbors and now see no one all day. If this is the case, it might be worth considering sharing a home with another mother, or moving into a communal group (see p. 133). Some mothers believe it is important for a child to have varied relationships with different people rather than depending on one parent for everything.

But it is also possible to feel lonely if you are living with other people —for example, with your parents. Sometimes a mother is made to feel selfish and guilty if she goes out and enjoys herself. If you live with relatives, you may find it particularly hard to convince them that you need some time for yourself, in the company of people your own age. They may feel you are evading your responsibilities as a mother or, if you are an unmarried teen-ager, they may be worried that you will get pregnant again. But whatever the obstacles, you must find at least a little time to get out.

There are other reasons for not letting your life center on your child the *whole* time. You cannot risk building up resentment against the child for having tied you down. It needs you very much now, but as it grows older it will make fewer demands on your time and attention. You do not want to wake up one day feeling that life has passed you by and left you with nothing much to do.

What it takes to make you feel you are functioning as a person in your own right will depend on your own personality and what you want out of life. It may mean working or completing your education. This involves considering the possibilities of working and finding someone to care for your child properly while you are out (see pp. 116–21). If you don't want a regular job, you might become active in politics or the women's movement or voluntary work; organizations always need helpers. You might develop an interest in art or music or a sport, or learn a new skill. Obviously, all these things have to be planned around the needs of your child. Conflicts may well occur, but there are many opportunities to create a satisfying life for yourself.

### New relationships with men

Most mothers alone, with the exception of lesbian mothers, embark on new relationships with men sooner or later. In many ways the process of meeting men, perhaps falling in love and getting married, is exactly the same whether you have children or not. But there may also be special conflicts and problems.

Your previous relationship with your child's father may affect the way you act toward other men. You may shy away from any new relationships if you felt badly let down before. You may rush from man to man, perhaps needing to prove to yourself that you are still attractive. Or you may be more relaxed about it, believing that what happened in the past is an important, if not entirely happy, part of your experience. There is no need to feel that if one relationship didn't work out, you won't be more successful with another. A woman often needs to develop herself through several relationships, gathering experience and insight about herself from both happy and distressing times.

It may not be easy to be a mother and a "girlfriend" at the same time. You will have to arrange for someone to baby-sit every time you date. There may be times when you have to turn down invitations because your child is sick or needs you there for some other reason. You may find it hard to get out if you haven't much money. However, as explained in previous pages, it is important to try to keep a little money aside for this.

If the high remarriage rates of divorced mothers are anything to judge by, children do not seem to be much of an obstacle to forming new relationships, but they can put some men off. Mothers have very different experiences here. "As soon as they know you've got a baby at home, they think you must be dying to get married," said one unwed mother. Another observed: "It's not the boys so much as their mothers; they don't want their sons involved with a girl who's got a child." Others say it attracts too many men with dubious motives: "Either they assume you're promiscuous, or they think you're starved for sex. It's a no-win situation." "I always seem to collect men with hang-ups—I don't know whether it's just me or whether they think that with all my problems I'll be more sympathetic to theirs." Others find men are natural and outgoing about it: "There are a lot of very maternal men around who adore children," said one mother. "I sometimes feel my man thinks more of my kids than he does of me." And there are many divorced men around who miss daily contact with their own children: "I was very suspicious of his motives at first. I didn't want him seeing my kids as substitutes for his own. But I now think I was overreacting; he's a beautiful guy who loves children, period."

Some men can accept and enjoy children as part of the person their mother is; sometimes the strong demonstrative affection between a mother and child can be very attractive to a man. Others may feel awkward if they have had no close contact with children before. A man may be jealous of the demands a child can make on the mother's time and attention—just as a husband sometimes is, or he may try to interfere with the way a mother is bringing up her children. If the relationship grows serious, you will usually be able to tell whether the man can accept and love the child or whether he will always feel threatened by this constant reminder of a previous relationship.

Some children enjoy meeting their mother's men friends. Others see the men as rivals. One mother said: "My son obviously felt so terribly threatened by it at one stage that I found it almost impossible to have a man in the place at all. It was embarrassing too—he'd scream that he was going to cut their heads off. Very Freudian! Sometimes he'd accept it and seem pleased that someone was taking his Mommy out. But if a man stayed there too long, it seemed to cut too much into my son's relationship with me."

You can work out what seems good and bad for your child only by trial and error. Children have to learn that they are not the sole objects of their mother's attention and interest, but it is important to recognise that it may not take much for a young child to feel insecure. Look for warning signs: if your child gets upset when a man appears, it may be better to avoid direct confrontations for a time and meet him away from home. Remember that it may take a lot of patience to reassure children that your affection for someone else is not a rejection of them. The man will have to be patient too. If serious conflicts occur, you will have to decide whether things are likely to work themselves out or whether it is best to forget the man.

However, if your child develops a strong attachment to a particular man, you may worry about the consequences if you later split up. Some mothers are so concerned about this possibility that they avoid a serious relationship with a man altogether. On the one hand, it may be very good for your child to have a close relationship with a man, particularly if there has never been any contact with his or her own father. On the other hand, it isn't always easy to judge whether the relationship will last —and the mother of a child who has already suffered parental separation may be especially anxious to avoid a second emotional upheaval. This has to be dealt with in advance. It may be best to encourage children to know and like as many people of both sexes as possible, so that they do not become too attached to any one person. Even if a certain man becomes the central person in both your lives, it will be better to let your child think of him as a friend rather than someone closer.

## MARRIAGE

It is probably always wise to question one's desire to marry, or remarry, and all the more when you have been bringing up children alone. Some mothers marry because they think their practical problems will be eased, and some because they have always felt emotionally dependent on men and are unable to come to terms with life until they have found another man to rely on. Sometimes the failure of one marriage drives a woman into another on the rebound, or as a kind of therapy for her self-esteem. (This may explain why a far higher proportion of divorced mothers than widowed mothers of the same age get married again within five years.) Such motives tend to be a shaky basis for good marriages and can often cause another break-up. This is not to say that remarriage itself is a risk: it often works out far more successfully than the first marriage. But many mothers who have remarried happily are convinced that it is *because* they developed self-sufficiency during their period alone and came to feel secure in themselves that their second partnerships proved so much better than the first. As one mother put it: "To need a man because you love him is far healthier than to love him because you need him."

If you contemplate getting married, you will naturally be concerned about the effect on your children. It is undoubtedly best to prepare them gradually, accustoming them to your new relationship slowly so that they come to accept your future husband in their own time; it is *sudden* changes that make children feel threatened. Even so, some children take the news badly. They need to know that your marriage will not cause a great upheaval in their lives, that your personal happiness includes them, and that this new man will not cut into their relationship with their real father, if they still see him. A great deal depends, of course, on the attitude of the man you want to marry. If he genuinely likes the children for their own sake and is not merely prepared to "take them on" for your sake, the outlook is much brighter. Children sense such distinctions very quickly.

## WORK AND EDUCATION

Ideally, all mothers should be able to choose between working and staying home to care for their children. This would not only allow women to achieve self-fulfillment in the way they (rather than other people) think appropriate, but would be a recognition by society that the care of children can be, like any other job, valued and satisfying. To provide such a choice, however, would mean paying women as much as they could earn elsewhere to look after their own children—a measure that, though supported by the women's movement, is unlikely to attract governmental favor for a very long time to come.

At present, only those single mothers who are relatively rich can afford not to work as a matter of preference. Welfare also offers an element of choice which should not be disregarded: if you are eligible for AFDC (see p. 126), you do have the right, under federal law, to claim benefit *without* registering for work or training while you have a dependent child under six years of age—or even beyond that if no other child-care arrangements can be made. But relying on welfare means living on virtually the lowest income possible. Most single mothers, therefore, are obliged to work to maintain a decent standard of living in spite of all the difficulties that this often involves.

*Should you work when your children are young?* This question has been endlessly debated by child psychologists and educators, mothers who work and mothers who don't. But the argument has nearly always centered on middle-class working wives—that is, mothers who are thought not to need to work because they have husbands to support them. A single mother is in a completely different position. If you are the breadwinner, your child's welfare depends on the standard of living *you* can provide.

There is no doubt that a single mother's best asset is a well-paid job. Money not only provides a reasonable standard of living but brings independence and freedom of choice. But mothers whose jobs are not well paid often find that they are no better off than they would be on welfare once the expenses of working have been met (see p. 116). For this reason it is usually an advantage to complete your education if you are still in school (see pp. 79–80) or get trained for a better paid job (see p. 123) if you can.

There is no evidence that children become emotionally disturbed or grow up delinquent just because they spend their early days in someone else's care while their mothers are out at work. The widespread belief that a mother's absence can have a detrimental effect on children derives from a misunderstanding of the theories on maternal deprivation (that is, children who are deprived of mothering for long periods of time) advanced by British psychiatrist John Bowlby twenty-five years ago. Bowlby's theory that every infant, to grow into a normal adult, needs a continuous relationship with a warm, loving mother-figure (*not* necessarily the natural mother) has, in any case, been seriously questioned recently—but it had absolutely nothing to do with a mother's temporary absence at work during the day. The important thing is how much love and attention you give your children when you are together. And—just as vital—how well they are cared for by whoever looks after them in your place.

If you are happy, a lot of your sense of well-being is bound to rub off on your child. Some mothers are happiest at home. Others need the daily mental stimulation and social contact that work can provide. There is no "right" way or "wrong" way. You may feel conflicts whatever you do, but in the end it depends on finding the right balance between what is important for you and what is important for your child.

A compromise may be possible if your child is very young. Financial considerations may not be so important for the first year or two of a child's life, so you may prefer to stay home during this time (by claiming AFDC or relying on child support or help from relatives or a combination of resources) to enjoy a close relationship with your child and (if this is your first) to get used to being a mother. Then you will have a little time to decide the best thing to do.

*Is it practical to work?* At present, single mothers are the victims of a system that actively discourages mothers from working. Licensed child-care facilities are actually far less adequate in the United States today than at the end of World War II. In 1945 there were 1,500,000 places in day centers provided under the Lanham Act of 1941.[9] By 1975 the number of mothers in the labor force had increased tenfold to around 14 million—yet by then there were no more than 1 million places available. Once the wartime need for women workers passed, the day centers were closed because it was thought that mothers should stay home and look after their children. This official view was reinforced throughout the fifties and early sixties by Bowlby's misinterpreted theories on mother-care. The result is that today there is a colossal gap between demand and supply. There are now more than 27 million children under age eighteen whose mothers are in the labor force; of these more than 6 million are under age six and over 4 million are being brought up by single mothers.[10] In other words, the 1 million licensed places available actually meet the needs of only one in six preschool children whose mothers *already* work. The rest, plus those of school age who also require care after school and during holidays, have to be left in a variety of unlicensed arrangements, good and bad.

The other drawback of child care, from the working mother's point of view, is the expense. Unless you are lucky enough to have a relative who will look after your child free, or can enroll the child in one of the few programs which charge according to your ability to pay, you are likely to find the cost considerable: in private programs $20 a week is about average and more than $50 not uncommon.

No mother would begrudge spending money on good care. But the problem, for single mothers in particular, is that in many cases the cost of child care combined with low or even medium earnings may not make a job financially worthwhile. If you suspect this might be true in your own case, it is worth listing all your work-related expenses—child care, carfare, lunches, income tax, clothes for work—in order to see whether the money you have left over is more than you would receive on welfare. If it is *less*, then welfare is a realistic alternative—unless you can find a job that pays more, or if you can cut down on your expenses, or unless you prefer to work for its own sake.

## DAY CARE FOR CHILDREN UNDER SIX

The essence of quality care for young children is an environment that not only meets their physical needs but encourages their emotional and social development through the stimulation of play and relationships with people who are warm, caring and sensitive to their needs. Mothers have very different ideas about how this can best be achieved: some favor the direct "mother substitute" who looks after the children in their own home; some prefer a communal center where children can experience more varied activities and relationships; still others would welcome facilities where they work. However, for most mothers at the present, choice is restricted to what is available and what they can afford.

### Nonprofit day centers
These may be public programs funded by the government (such as Head Start) or they may be run by philanthropic organizations or, in a few cases, women's groups.

*Advantages* Fees are usually low and geared to the mother's ability to pay; some are free. There is usually a good ratio of staff to children, the equipment and facilities are often excellent, and the standard of physical care high. Some can justly claim to be truly child-oriented, providing the sensitivity and stimulation that children need. Public programs are more likely than any others to admit very young children (under three, sometimes from a few weeks old), to offer more flexible hours, and to provide some preschool education as well as play (as in Head Start). Priority is often given to the children of single mothers.

*Disadvantages* There are too few places, waiting lists are often long, and mothers are sometimes told they have to get a job before applying

—whereas they can't get a job until they are sure of a place for their children. Public programs are seen as accommodating primarily "disadvantaged" children in poor areas, which can cause patronizing attitudes and the tendency to regard all children as "problem" children. Though offering good physical care on the whole, some regiment the children too much, offering little scope for creativity. Parental involvement, which might improve matters, is often discouraged.

### Profit-making day centers

These may be attached to private schools or run by a variety of business interests. They include "franchise" systems, in which a franchise company sells a day-care "package" to investors in much the same way that restaurant franchises are sold: standardized techniques, including cost control, are worked out by the company and those who buy the system expect a good return on their investment.

*Advantages* They provide the greatest number of day-care places, often the only ones in middle-class areas. The standard of physical care and facilities is often high. Some offer good creative and educational opportunities for children.

*Disadvantages* The average cost is around $20 a week, but may be much higher. Hours may be too inflexible to meet the needs of some working mothers, and most centers will not admit children under three years old. They are often criticized for being more concerned with profits than with children. Though this is not true of all centers, it *was* the private operators who most opposed the standards and high staffing ratios proposed by the federal government. It has been claimed that centers cannot be run profitably except at the expense of quality. The franchise system (often known as "Kentucky Fried Children") is suspected of being exploitative, in regarding day care as a "product" and allowing the consumer no control over what goes on.

### Family day care

This means paying a woman to look after your child, usually with a group of other children, in her own home.

*Advantages* It may cost less (some are subsidized), be closer to home, offer more flexible hours and admit children at younger ages than the average day center. A woman who gives your child individual attention and enjoys a good relationship with both of you is worth her weight in gold. A true "mother substitute" would care for your child in much the same way as you would at home.

*Disadvantages* Many women who provide this care are themselves underpaid, overworked and isolated. They cannot offer the varied activities or educational opportunities of a day center, and too often children receive nothing more stimulating than nonstop television. If the child is left uncuddled and unattended for long hours, there is a real danger of emotional disturbance. Most homes are not licensed, and there have been instances of physical neglect. Nor can you rely on family day care to the degree you can a day center: the woman may fall ill or change her plans and have to suspend or break off the arrangement at short notice. Her ideas on how a child should be trained and treated may be different from yours, which may exasperate you or confuse your child. You are also dependent on her own whims and prejudices: she may refuse to take nonwhite, handicapped or sickly children, or any others she objects to. Mothers are sometimes asked to make other arrangements on the ground that their children are "naughty" or "uncontrollable" or a "bad influence" on others.

### Work-related day care
A small but growing number of companies, hospitals and educational establishments provide day care on their own premises for their employees' children. Some schools and colleges offer a similar service to students' children. Some employers also provide a "voucher system" which guarantees their staff a certain number of places at nearby public or private day-care centers.

*Advantages* Mothers can take their children to work with them, instead of having to make a detour to deposit them elsewhere, and are on hand to see their children during off-duty periods during the day. The service is either free or on a sliding scale related to earnings. Standards vary but are usually as good as the average private center.

*Disadvantages* Day-care facilities that go with the job are few and far between. Employers that offer this service are usually in need of women workers and may see it as an incentive to women who would not otherwise tolerate low wages and poor conditions. If standards are not what they might be, it is more difficult to complain to an employer than to an independent proprietor who has no control over your livelihood.

### Privately hired care
This means paying someone to come to your home each day, or live in, to look after the children in their own surroundings.

*Advantages* The children do not have to move out of their own environment, which may especially benefit very young infants. It is also reassuring to know that the same person will be there to care for them when you really need them, such as when they are ill, or when you go out socially. A person who can build a loving relationship with the child over a long period of time, and can be absolutely relied on, is of the greatest possible value to a working mother.

*Disadvantages* Only mothers in the highest paid jobs, or with other means, can afford this arrangement. The other big drawback is finding someone you can trust who will stay a long time. Children become attached to a person who looks after them individually day after day and may feel insecure if they have to get used to someone new every so often.

## Playgroups

The purpose of playgroups is to allow young children to express themselves and learn to cooperate with others through play. The "staff" usually consists of mothers, fathers or anyone interested in helping out; sometimes a trained supervisor is on hand. Playgroups are useless for full-time working mothers because the hours are too short and a mother is expected to help run activities at least one day a week. But they may fit in with your needs if you work part-time. They can also give you a break from your child for a few hours a week if you don't work at all.

## DAY CARE FOR SCHOOL-AGE CHILDREN

The greatest problem for a working mother is what to do with a child after school hours and during the school holidays. It has been estimated that two-thirds of children in need of day care are at school. At the Congressional hearings on American families in 1973, psychologist Dr. Edward Zigler of Yale University said: "Because of our slowness in developing day-care models for school-age children . . . we are now witnessing the national tragedy of over one million latchkey children, cared for by no one, with probably an equal number being cared for by siblings who are themselves too young to assume such responsibilities."

This is all the more ironic since it is frequently assumed that when children start school, their mothers are "free" to work. Such thinking is implicit in AFDC regulations that require mothers on welfare to register for work or training as soon as their youngest dependent child is six years old. Yet organized programs are few and far between. Some day-care centers admit children older than six after school hours; some schools organize after-school and holiday activities for the children of working mothers. But most often mothers are left to make their own arrangements: relying on relatives, neighbors and family day-care homes, or giving children their own keys to let themselves into the house as soon as they are old enough. Some mothers join the system when they've given up trying to beat it—and find jobs in schools. Another idea is to set up housekeeping with another single mother who would prefer to stay home and look after all the children.

### Finding day care

Your state, city or county department of social service, child welfare, or child development can give you information on licensed day-care facilities in your area. Local voluntary organizations, such as Community Chest, and women's groups are also useful sources of information. If all else fails, however, you may have to go round knocking on doors, or advertise, to find an individual who is willing to offer unlicensed care— and then rely on your judgment as to whether you can leave your child there with reasonable confidence.

### Setting up your own day-care center

Many mothers are so concerned about the day-care shortage and the effects of unsatisfactory arrangements on their children, that they are getting together to run child centers of their own. This takes a great deal of determination, time and energy and there are many technical pitfalls to be overcome. But it has been done successfully. Excellent advice on how to go about it is given in *The Day Care Book* by Vicki Breibart and others (New York: Knopf, 1975). Pamphlets and guidebooks are also available from the Children's Defense Fund (see p. 137).

### Tax deductions for child care and household help

Thanks mainly to the fight waged by a New York widow, Elizabeth Barrett, with the Internal Revenue Service, the Revenue Act of 1971 allowed deductions in federal income taxes to be made for "employment-related expenses," including day care for children both within and outside the home. However, the allowable deductions cover only a fraction of the real costs of day care, and as they are taken as a personal expense only taxpayers who use the itemized tax return (the "long form") are eligible. Since then there have been several proposals, including one passed by the House Ways and Means Committee in September 1975, to permit child care to be considered a *business* expense, which would extend the benefit to many more parents, particularly those on low incomes. Check with a tax lawyer, the IRS or the Women's Bureau of the Department of Labor in Washington D.C. for up-to-date information on eligibility and how much can be deducted.

## TYPES OF WORK AVAILABLE

The kind of work you do will depend mainly on what you are trained for and what choices are available, but some types of work are more practical than others when you have a child to consider.

### Full-time work

As we have seen, day care is the most critical problem when working full time, but there are other considerations, too. For example, your choice of job may be affected, or restricted, by where your child is looked after during the day. If you have to pick the child up by a specified time (often the case with day-care centers), you may have to find a job that is less well-paid but at least close-by, or settle for a job that is less interesting but not so demanding on your time and energy. The industrial and commercial world is not geared to the needs of working mothers. Women are generally expected to work on the same terms as men, particularly where equal pay has been introduced. It can be argued that this is right. But at times of crisis—for example, when your child is ill —you may jeopardize your job by staying away. As your child is bound to be sick sometimes, it is essential to arrange with your employer to be able to take time off, or to have someone who is available to tend the child in your absence. It is ideal if you have a whole network of friends, neighbors and relatives who can be called on in emergencies.

### Part-time work

It may be more convenient to work part-time while your child is young even if this means a cut in your standard of living. Welfare regulations allow a mother to earn up to a certain amount (after work-related expenses are deducted) before the AFDC benefit is reduced. However, the opportunities for part-time work are limited except, usually, for menial jobs.

### Free-lance work

If you can work as a free-lancer (that is, working for several people as a self-employed person) you may be able to organize the amount of time you spend with your child more easily. Free-lance work can be precarious, and in some jobs you may have to wait some time before getting paid. However, some enterprising mothers have put their skills to good use in this way. One mother, for example, uses an old car and her training as a hairdresser to provide a hairdressing-at-home service for housebound women. Another offers her services as a cook to other busy working mothers, spending several hours each day in a different home cooking a supply of food for the family freezer. Both these women take their children to work with them.

### Working at home

There are few women who can earn enough for a family to live on by working at home. Some industries employ outside workers and some professional women can carry on at least part of their work at home. But in general this work would be regarded as a part-time rather than full-time occupation.

### Residential jobs

A residential, or live-in job, means that you receive bed and board for yourself and your child, plus a small salary, in return for carrying out certain duties—usually domestic work in a family. This has its advantages: you can work and be with your child at the same time and you get a home (and possibly a higher standard of living than you could manage on your own). But there are big drawbacks too. There is the possibility of being exploited as cheap labor; low wages mean that it is difficult to save anything toward a home of your own; and the fact that the home is tied to the job can intensify a sense of insecurity. You may also find it difficult to combine your domestic duties with the demands of your child: young children constantly want attention and you may worry about falling behind with your work and losing both home and job. Afraid that your child will damage the family possessions, you may be stricter than you want to be. This type of arrangement, though it can work out well in some cases, is best used only as a stop-gap when there is no alternative.

### Discrimination against working mothers

Title VII of the Civil Rights Act of 1964 prohibits discrimination in employment based on sex—and that includes discrimination against women who are mothers. Nevertheless, many mothers remain convinced that they fail to be hired for some jobs because they have children, and with reason. "In the interview he asked me who would look after my kid and what would I do when the kid got sick," is a typical remark. Many employers cling to the belief that absenteeism among mothers is high, in spite of overwhelming evidence to the contrary. Some single mothers contend that they are less likely to take time off than married mothers. "When it's your bread and butter, you don't stay home every time your kid coughs," said a divorcée.

Another form of discrimination that occasionally surfaces is against unmarried mothers. In 1973, for example, a U.S. District Court in Mississippi heard the case of two women who had brought action against the policy of a school district not to employ any parent of an illegitimate child. The court ruled that this policy was unconstitutional because it amounted to sex discrimination, given that it "would in fact be applied mainly to mothers because detection of such fathers is difficult."[11] This decision was reaffirmed by the U.S. Court of Appeals for the Fifth Circuit in 1975, but when the case finally reached the U.S. Supreme Court in 1976, the Court announced that on technical grounds it would not decide the appeal.[12]

If you *are* discriminated against in any way, it is important to remember that you can take legal action against an employer. It is only in this way that the law can be enforced against recalcitrant employers, reducing the likelihood of sex discrimination in the future. You can file a complaint by writing to the Equal Employment Opportunity Commission, 2401 E Street NW, Washington D.C. Ask for a discrimination charge form. Fill out the form, giving details of the alleged discrimination against you, and have it notarized. The EEOC will inform the employer of the complaint, including a warning that it is illegal to take any retaliation against you. An EEOC official will investigate the charge and attempt to negotiate. If the complaint is thought to be valid, and negotiation fails, the EEOC can take action against the employer on your behalf by filing suit in the U.S. district court. If the EEOC takes no action within 180 days after you have filed your complaint, you can file suit yourself. In this case, it is wise to get advice from the American Civil Liberties Union or a lawyer experienced in sex discrimination cases.

## Vocational training opportunities

There are several ways to be trained for skilled occupations that do not require a college degree. You can enroll in a variety of courses in secondary and adult education schools, or apprenticeship and on-the-job training programs; there are government-aided programs available under the

Manpower Development and Training Act, and home-study courses which can be especially useful to women obliged to stay at home with small children. If you are on welfare, there is the Work Incentive Program (WIN) which has got a bad name because mothers with children over six are required to enroll in it, whether they want to work or not; and because adequate jobs are not always available in the end. But it may be a useful way of developing new skills at no cost, since an allowance is made to cover the cost of lunches and carfare and day care is provided. For more information on job training of all kinds, write to the Women's Bureau, U.S. Department of Labor, Washington D.C. 20210, or your nearest state Office of Economic Opportunity.

## MONEY

Most single mothers, contrary to popular belief, *do* work, and still, in many cases, that is not enough. This section, therefore, looks at all the additional sources of income you may be able to claim.

### Child support

Under the laws of every state, all minor children are entitled to support from their fathers whether born inside or outside marriage, but not all children actually get it: in 1972, according to a study carried out by the University of Michigan, 47 percent of divorced mothers and 73 percent of separated mothers received *no* child support or alimony income at all; of those who did, the median annual payments amounted to $1,350. The figures are likely to be even lower for mothers who are not married. The Child Support Enforcement Program, which became effective in 1975, set up a new bureaucratic machinery to recover support from recalcitrant fathers; this is available to any mother, but those on welfare are compelled to use it as a condition for receiving AFDC (see p. 127). Under this program, the Parent Locater Service can be used to trace fathers who have moved to other states.

How much a father should pay can be decided either by a voluntary agreement or by a court. The court should settle the matter by considering your needs and the father's financial resources. It is not absolutely necessary to hire a lawyer to represent you, but it would be wise to do so if you think the father will be legally represented or may try to mislead the court as to how much he earns. (If you have very little money, you may be entitled to legal aid—see p. 138) Do not be surprised, however, if the amount awarded is lower than you need; a father who lives apart from his family cannot provide as much as if he lived with them, and judges are often reluctant to order payments which, if too high, simply won't be paid.

Once a support order has been made, payment should begin at once —either directly to you or (as is possible in some states) through the court. If the father stops paying after a time, or gets into arrears, the court has the power of enforcement—ultimately by imposing fines or, in some states, by attaching his earnings (which means that his employer must deduct the support payment from his paycheck in advance and send it via the court to you), or by imprisonment. This can be successful, although the hassle involved can make women give up trying to enforce payment after a time. A father can generally evade paying support if he is determined enough, and judges often hesitate to impose the final penalty, imprisonment, unless the man is easily able to pay and seems to be in deliberate contempt of court by not doing so. Moreover, a father in prison is no advantage: the child still gets no support.

For more detailed information on the process and pitfalls of obtaining child support (plus alimony, property division and custody), see *Women in Transition, A Feminist Handbook on Separation and Divorce* (see p. 135).

## Alimony

Alimony (payment for the support of divorced or separated wives) is usually decided together with child support and is subject to the same limitations. Whether you get alimony at all depends on whether you want it, whether your ex-husband is willing to give it to you, and what the judge finally decides. Under the old divorce laws (still effective in some states) alimony was often awarded according to whether the wife was the "innocent" or "guilty" party. Now, with the introduction of "no fault" divorce, settlement is more often made according to the circumstances of both husband and wife.

## Establishing paternity

If you are unmarried and the man denies he is the father of your child, you have to file suit to establish his paternity before you can petition for child support. You may also wish to do this to insure your child's right to inherit from the father. States have different laws regarding paternity suits, and some have time limits after which you can no longer file, so it is wise to get legal advice as soon after the child is born as possible —not only to find out what your state law requires, but to increase your chance of success.

You must produce evidence to support your claim—such as a witness who can tell the court of hearing the man admit to being the father or to having sexual intercourse with you at the time the child was conceived, or letters the man has written you, or proof that he has already contributed money to support the child. Without evidence, there is little hope of winning the case. The court will almost certainly order both you and the alleged father to take blood tests. These are based on the fact that parents with combinations of certain blood groups cannot possibly have children belonging to other blood groups. The tests are of limited value: they may prove a man could *not* be the father of a particular child, but cannot prove definitely that he is. However, they sometimes persuade a father to admit paternity—and sometimes give *him* confidence that he really is the father.

You can also expect to be cross-examined in court on your sexual relationship with the alleged father, and with other men too. This can be a humiliating experience; as in rape cases, the woman who brings a legitimate action can receive tougher treatment than the man she has accused. Naturally enough, this inhibits many unmarried mothers from filing suit and allows many fathers to evade their responsibility to help support their natural children. Yet recent welfare legislation *forces* such mothers who need AFDC to file paternity suits and endure the consequences in court.

### Social security

If you are a widow, you may be eligible for survivors' insurance benefit (SI). This depends on your late husband's social security insurance record. If eligible, the amount you receive will be no less than 82½ percent of the benefit your husband would have received if he had lived to draw retirement benefit. As a mother, you may also receive 75 percent of the basic benefit for each of your husband's children until they reach eighteen or complete their education. For more information, contact your local social security office.

### Aid to Families with Dependent Children (AFDC)

AFDC is the largest program in the welfare system. Its purpose is to provide a basic income for needy families with dependent children where the father is dead, absent, incapacitated or (in 25 states) unemployed. This money is not charity. It is a legal *right*. It is important to remember this if you, like three million other single mothers, are forced to depend on welfare to survive, or if you are badly in need of assistance but hate the idea of accepting "handouts."(Note: The information below is for mothers on their own and does not include AFDC regulations for families where the father is present but unemployed, or for children being raised by someone other than the mother.)

*Who can claim AFDC?* You can claim AFDC if:

(a) you have one or more dependent children under eighteen (or under twenty-one if in school full-time) and living with you; *or,* in those states which grant aid to unborn children, you are pregnant; *and*

(b) your assets and income from all sources (including child support, alimony, etc.) fall below the limit set by the law of your state; *and*

(c) the father of your child(ren) is dead, disabled or not living with you; *and*

(d) you are willing to cooperate in seeking support from the father where possible, and to assign your support rights to the state.

*How to apply* Make an appointment with your nearest welfare office. (get the number from your local department of social services.) When you go for your interview take with you as many documents as you can that will help establish your eligibility and need—for example, your children's birth certificates (or a letter from a doctor confirming your pregnancy); some proof of death if the father of your child is dead; any pay stubs or support orders that indicate your income; rent or mortgage receipts; utility, telephone and medical bills. You will also need your social security number.

*The application form* You will be given an application form which must be filled out and signed before your claim can be considered. It is important to put a line through any question that does not apply to you and write "unknown" if you don't know the answer to a question; this avoids delay in processing the application. It is also wise to get two copies of the completed form, date stamped by the office, so that you have a record of exactly what you wrote on the original, in case of problems later on.

*The interview* An eligibility worker will interview you, help fill out the application and inform you of the eligibility requirements in your state. The interviewer is entitled to ask questions relating to eligibility (for example, details of your income and assets, the whereabouts of the father of your child) but is *not* entitled to ask irrelevant questions such as your child's grades in school or anything about your sex life.

*Verification* Under federal law the welfare department can check out all the facts given in your application. This includes visiting your home to verify the address and to check up that the father of your children is not there, that the children you are claiming for are living with you, etc. You should be notified of the home visit in advance, but it may be made without warning.

*The decision* You should hear whether your claim has been granted within a week or two. Under federal law, the welfare department must let you know within forty-five days. The decision must be given in writing and, if it refuses you aid, the reasons must be explained in full. If you feel you have been refused unfairly, you have the right to a fair hearing. If you have not heard anything within forty-five days, contact the office immediately and, if possible, get a welfare advocate (see p. 130) to support you.

*Emergency payments* If you haven't enough money even to wait a day or two, or a sudden disaster (like a stolen pocketbook or a house fire) has left you with no cash at all, call the welfare office and explain the emergency. The office has the power to make emergency payments immediately, but you will probably have to be very persistent to get it. The best way is to go to the office with your children (and preferably a welfare advocate) and sit it out there until you get a check.

*The basis on which you claim* As a single mother in need, you can claim AFDC on the basis that your children are deprived of the full support and care of their father. But you can *also* claim on the basis of your own illness or incapacity. If you are going to a doctor, or are in need of medical assistance for any physical or emotional illness or incapacity, it is very important to claim on this basis, because you will receive a lot more help (such as extra money for special diet, or maybe a homemaker service to help you at home) and you will not be required to register for work or training.

You will need substantial medical evidence from an approved doctor or psychiatrist to support your claim. The welfare agency will probably also require an independent opinion from a doctor whom they appoint. It helps if you can get a welfare advocate to assist you, particularly if the doctor appointed by the welfare agency disagrees with the opinion given by your own doctor.

*Registering for work or training* You must register with your state employment service, or for training in the Work Incentive Program (WIN) or other employment, Manpower or training program, in order to be eligible for AFDC *unless:*

(a) you have one or more dependent children under age six; *or*
(b) your youngest child is over six but no other child-care arrangements can be made; *or*
(c) you are ill or incapacitated; *or*
(d) you must care for ill or incapacitated members of your household; *or*
(e) you are under seventeen.

This requirement has been heavily criticized on the ground that it denies women (other than those who can claim one of the exemptions listed above) the right to care for their children full-time if they choose. *Work in America,* the report of a special task force to the Secretary of HEW in December 1972, commented: "When we say to an AFDC mother, for example, 'You must go to work or take job training to be eligible for public assistance,' we are in effect telling her that, from society's point of view, she is not now working, that keeping house and raising children are not socially useful, at least not as useful as 'a job.' But we are able to make this judgment of the AFDC mother who stays home and raises her children only because we make this same judgment of all housewives."

*Help with welfare problems* The sheer complexity of the welfare system makes it very difficult for anyone on AFDC to understand their rights. Rules are laid down at three different levels: federal, state and local. Sometimes a right conferred by federal law is infringed by local policy, and although HEW has the power to withhold federal funds from a noncompliant agency, it has never yet done so. Welfare officers can misinterpret regulations, make mistakes or be obstructive over perfectly legitimate claims. So where can you go for accurate information and help?

*Published information* You can find out the regulations that apply in your state from the welfare manual, the bulletins that announce changes in policy, and the administrative letters that contain interpretations of state welfare law. These should be available at your local welfare office. The *Handbook of Public Assistance Administration,* which outlines federal policy, is available from the Social and Rehabilitation Services office of the Department of Health, Education and Welfare, Washington D.C. More useful as a handbook for advocates is an up-to-date guide on rights, the *Summary of the Aid to Families with Dependent Children Program,* written by Catherine Day-Jermany, a leading welfare rights advocate who was once herself on welfare. It is published by the Legal Services Corporation, Office of Program Support, room 637, 733 15th Street N.W., Washington D.C. 20005. *Common Wealth,* the newsletter of NOW's task force on women and poverty, contains news and analyses of welfare issues. It is available from Mary-Jo Binder, 1824 Redwood Terrace N.W., Washington D.C. 20012.

*People who can help* Welfare rights workers or advocates can give you information on your rights, check that you are receiving the correct grant, assist in your dealings with the welfare department, and if necessary represent you at a fair hearing. An advocate may be a lawyer with a special interest in welfare, but is more often a "paralegal"—that is, someone who has acquired knowledge of the law by working on behalf of welfare recipients. You can contact such people through your local Legal Services Program, community help organizations, welfare rights groups, or women's groups. The National Paralegal Institute Inc., suite 600, 2000 P Street N.W., Washington D.C. 20036 (tel: 202–872– 0655), may also be able to put you in touch with a paralegal advocate. The National Welfare Rights Organization had ceased to function as a national coordinating body at the time of writing but some local groups still operate. NWRO acts as a legal watchdog and litigates against welfare policies which adversely affect AFDC recipients. It works through the Center on Social Welfare Policy and Law, 95 Madison Avenue, New York, N.Y. 10016 (tel: 212–679–3709).

### Food stamps

Food stamps are a helpful way to reduce living costs. The best source of information on them is the *Guide to the Food Stamp Program* issued by the Food Research and Action Center, 2011 I Street N.W., Washington D.C. 20006 (tel: 202–452–8250). The guide is priced at $1.00 but is free for low-income individuals. It explains how the program works, how to figure whether you are eligible, how to get free food stamps on the spot in an emergency, and your right to a fair hearing if you think you have been wrongly denied stamps. The guide is regularly updated as the rules change and acts as a useful consumer watchdog on attempts to cut back the food stamp program. It is worth reading this guide before you apply for stamps from the welfare office (if you are on welfare) or from the local food stamp office (listed in the telephone directory under your local social services department).

## Credit

You may find it very much more difficult to obtain credit (for an automobile, mortgage, charge account or personal loan) than if you were still married. Divorce, separation or widowhood instantly wipes out the credit rating you enjoyed with your former husband because creditors assume that during marriage a woman is dependent on her husband and they usually allow credit only in his name. Women who depend mainly on alimony or child support are usually denied credit automatically because it is assumed (often reasonably) that this is not a reliable source of income.

To obtain any kind of credit, it helps if you are unmarried (or managed to keep your own name through marriage) and have established a credit rating in your own right. It also helps if you have a regular, well-paid job. But discrimination against women in this field is so rife that even a good job may not be regarded as sufficient security and you may have to agree to have your contract countersigned by a male guarantor to be considered at all.

The best guide through all the pitfalls that can occur is *Women and Credit*, a handbook compiled by the National Organization for Women, available from the national headquarters: NOW, National Action Center, 425 13th Street NW, Washington D.C. 20005 (tel: 202-638-6054). Some women have also taken action to change the system directly. In 1973 the first Feminist Federal Credit Union opened in Detroit; in 1975 the First Women's Bank opened in New York—the first feminist bank in the country.

## HOUSING

It is not possible here to discuss the intricacies of property division after separation or divorce; you will find good advice on that in *Women in Transition* (see p. 135) and NOW's legal kit on marriage and divorce (see p. 139). But you should be prepared to face the fact that you may find it difficult as a single mother to find suitable housing if you have to move. The 1975 amendments to Title VIII of the Fair Housing Act of 1968 prohibit sex discrimination against tenants in housing where the landlord does not live on the premises. But it does not specify marital status, and many landlords, like many mortgage lenders, suspect that mothers on their own are unable to support themselves, and discrimination, in practice, is still strong.

You should also think carefully about what kind of living arrangements are best suited to your needs if you have the choice.

### Living alone

Many women who have suffered the strain of marital breakup welcome the chance to live alone with their children. An unmarried mother may feel the same way if she has been through a crisis with her family. Even a widow may feel, a little guiltily, that here for the first time in years is an opportunity to live her life in her own way.

Most women tend to hang onto their own home if they can, deciding that the disadvantages of living alone may not be as bad as the drawbacks of living with someone else. But if loneliness, household expenses and day-to-day management begin to bear down too heavily, you should at least consider the alternatives.

### Living with your parents

A great many single mothers live with their parents—sometimes out of choice, sometimes because there is nowhere else to go. How well it works out depends on what kind of family feeling exists, and whether there is adequate room. Although there is a lot of sentimental nostalgia about the vanishing extended family, it usually requires tact and understanding on both sides to succeed.

If your parents can give you emotional comfort and financial support, it may make it easier for you to live with them and work or complete your education. If you are an unmarried teen-ager, your mother may help you care for your child and be a useful source of advice. Children may benefit from a close relationship with their grandparents, particularly their grandfathers if there is no other close male influence in their life.

On the other hand, your family may find it hard to adjust to your changed status. Because they may still see you as a child, it may be difficult to make your own decisions, or to express your own ideas about how you want your child brought up without offending them. They on their part may find it unsettling to have small children in the house again.

### Sharing a home

Sharing a home with someone other than parents or relatives can involve several different arrangements. You can invite a friend to live in your home; set up a new home with another single mother or with someone without children; or live communally in a group. The advantages are obvious. It cuts costs and helps prevent loneliness; it may solve baby-sitting problems; your children, particularly an only child, may benefit from close relationships with other people.

*Sharing with one person* Sometimes a happy sharing set-up works out naturally; more often you have to work at it. It is best to establish in advance what is expected in sharing expenses and household tasks. Conflicts are bound to arise sometimes; it usually helps to talk them out instead of saying nothing and feeling resentful. If you are sharing with another mother, there is also the problem of conflicts between the children. Mothers who have done this say that it seems to work best when the children are *not* the same age and when the house or apartment can allow each mother enough privacy.

*Group living* Many people are now experimenting with living together in groups. Some do so out of a desire to improve the quality of family life, others get together out of a shared philosophy or a common craft or trade. Either way, it is an attempt to solve the problems created by the nuclear family system—and some groups have considerable success. A woman in particular can enjoy more time to herself when the responsibility for cooking, cleaning, laundry and child care is shared equally with others. But group living can also require greater self-discipline and tolerance than living with one person; it can be very difficult to adjust when you have lived your whole life in a nuclear family. For the group to survive, it may have to fix standards of cleanliness and responsibilities which may come to seem like institutionalized rules. There may be more intimacy and less privacy than you can cope with. Children may be unsettled if the members of the group change too often. Group living can be a liberating experience if it contains the right people who can really communicate with each other while developing and respecting individuality; it can be unbearable if it achieves the opposite.

*Getting in touch* Bulletin boards, women's centers, community action groups, food co-ops, advertisements in newspapers are all ways of finding an individual or group to share with. It is best to discuss the possibilities and the problems thoroughly before you take the plunge.

## A STRATEGY FOR SURVIVAL:
## SOURCES OF HELP

Throughout this chapter, the emphasis has been on *your* self-sufficiency, *your* outlook on life, *your* ability to organize things so that your family can survive. But you are not Superwoman. There will be times when you hit problems that you can't handle alone, when suddenly you're in need of help and don't know whom to ask. Ideally, you should be able to pick up the phone, dial a number, state the problem, and instantly get connected to the right source of help. Unfortunately, there is no such system and probably never will be.

It is, however, an excellent idea to create your own system. Don't wait until problems crop up. Sit down and compile a list of every conceivable kind of help you might need—from emergency plumbing to suicide prevention. Don't skip something unpleasant, like child-abuse prevention or welfare, because you are convinced you will never need it. You never know—and it is precisely that kind of help that you have to get fastest if a crisis does arise. Once you've got the list, find out and write down the appropriate local telephone numbers. It will save you a lot of time if you should run into really bad trouble.

This survival strategy will probably be only a beginning. Ferreting out sources of help and information may spark off curiosity in what is going on in your community, who is doing what and why. You will find yourself automatically writing down new services or organizations announced on bulletin boards and in newspapers. Soon you'll be calling them up to find out more, and perhaps joining in. You will almost certainly discover several unmet needs; you wonder why no one is doing anything, and before you know it everyone else is saying the same thing. From that point, it is not too big a step to get together to fill the gap. That is how almost every self-help system—from baby-sitting clubs to women's liberation—actually began.

The following sources of information and help can be used not only as a basis for compiling your list, but to raise consciousness on how far self-help can go.

*Parents Without Partners,* 7901 Woodmont Avenue, Bethesda, Maryland 20014 (tel: 301–654–8850) is the oldest and largest organization of single-parent groups in the United States. It has chapters throughout the country and a somewhat old-fashioned image of helping single parents mix socially with a view to marrying again rather than helping them find identity through the single-parent experience. Recently, however, the coordinating committee has been rethinking the PWP role and considering a more modern approach—practical self-help and the promotion of single parents' rights.

*MOMMA*, founded in 1972 in California by two divorced mothers, Karol Hope and Lisa Connolly, was the first American organization of any substance to apply feminist techniques of information-sharing and consciousness-raising to the single parent experience. Two years later MOMMA was producing an excellent newsletter and there were fifty chapters throughout the country, offering housing referrals, counseling services and support. By 1975, however, many groups had foundered under the strain of members trying to work, bring up their children, help each other and keep the group going. But MOMMA showed what could be done. For up-to-date news contact MOMMA c/o Jeannette Townsend, 2030 E. 4th Street, Suite 240, Santa Ana, California 92705. Or contact the Women's Action Alliance (see p. 136).

*Women in Transition*, 3700 Chestnut Street, Philadelphia, Pennsylvania 19104 (tel: 215–382–7016) is a highly successful group for women who are contemplating or going through the process of separation or divorce. It has published an invaluable survival manual (see below) and can offer information and assistance to women in other parts of the country who wish to start a similar group. Locally, it provides legal help, support and counseling.

*The Single Parent Resource Center*, 3896 24th Street, San Francisco, California 94114 (tel: 415–821–7058) is a unique organization staffed by volunteers. It runs regular workshops on all aspects of the single parent experience, holds drop-in "rap" sessions and is an important local source of practical information and help. It is affiliated with the Childcare Switchboard which helps mothers find day care in the San Francisco area. At the time of writing the Center had published the first issue of its journal, *One Parent Family* which can be obtained by sending $1.00 to the address above.

## Publications

*Women in Transition: A Feminist Handbook on Separation and Divorce* (New York: Scribner's, 1975) is exactly what the title promises. Written from first-hand experience by the Philadelphia group noted above, it is both a sensitive and practical guide to single parenthood, which in many ways is just as useful for the unmarried or widowed mother as for the divorced or separated.

*The Single Parent Experience* by Carole Klein (New York: Avon Books, 1975) focuses on the new trend to become a single parent as a matter of choice. It is not intended as a practical guide, but as a testimony to the varied experiences (the joys and the problems) of parents who seek new life-styles in a rapidly changing society. It is particularly enlightening on single parents (male and female) who are homosexual and/or adopting children on their own.

*Widow* by Lynn Caine (New York: Bantam, 1975) is a best-selling personal account of widowhood with common-sense advice on how to handle grief and carry on functioning after the trauma of bereavement.

## Self-help for women

The women's movement, though it rarely promotes the cause of mothers alone as a separate political issue, is concerned with anything that discriminates against women in general. It has been the inspiration for many women to get together to set up their own help and information programs.

*National Organization for Women* (NOW) is the main national body promoting women's rights, with 800 chapters throughout the country. It has formed many task forces for coordinating action in areas of sex discrimination—for example on child care, poverty, rape, sexuality, employment and education, etc. Task force newsletters are an important source of up-to-date information and comment. For details on publications and NOW membership, contact the national headquarters (see p. 131).

*Women's Action Alliance,* 370 Lexington Avenue, New York, N.Y. 10017 (tel: 212–532–8330) is a nonprofit educational organization which provides resource materials for all women. Publications include *How to Organize a Multi-Service Women's Center.* It is also the best central clearing house for up-to-date information on women's groups and services throughout the country. Write for a brochure of current materials.

## Publications

*Women's Rights Almanac,* edited by Nancy Gager (New York: Harper & Row, 1975) is a unique reference manual containing sources of help and information state by state, together with penetrating analyses of women's issues.

*The New Woman's Survival Sourcebook,* edited by Susan Rennie and Kirsten Grimstad (New York: Knopf, 1975) is an invaluable compilation of organizations, publications and campaigns of direct interest to women. It also contains information on other useful directories for women in their own areas; its perspective is critical and feminist.

*A Practical Guide to the Women's Movement,* edited by Deena Peterson and published by the Women's Action Alliance, is another useful compilation of feminist organizations and literature.

*Ms Magazine,* a monthly available nationwide, is a good source of news on women's rights and various kinds of self-help.

### Self-help in the community
There are innumerable self-help and action groups organized at the community or neighborhood level, offering various kinds of assistance. Local information is available through bulletin boards, public information centers and the department of social services.

### Help for children
*The Child Welfare League of America Inc.,* 67 Irving Place, New York, N.Y. 10003 (tel: 212–254–7410) has four hundred affiliated agencies throughout North America and promotes the care and interests of children. Its library is a treasure trove of literature on children and families. A list of its own child-care publications is available on request.

*The Children's Defense Fund,* 1520 New Hampshire Ave. N.W., Washington D.C. 20036 (tel: 202–483–1470) is a nonprofit organization of lawyers, federal policy monitors, researchers and community liaison people dedicated to advocacy on behalf of children. It has undertaken first-class research. A list of publications is available on request.

*The Children's Foundation,* 1028 Connecticut Avenue N.W., Washington D.C. 20036 (tel: 202–296–4451) is expert on all food programs and can offer help on getting these properly implemented in local communities. It also publishes a food rights handbook and newsletter.

*National Center for Comprehensive Emergency Services to Children,* 321 Metro Howard Office Building, 25 Middleton Street, Nashville, Tennessee 37210 (tel: 615–259–5371) gives help in setting up centers for children in emergencies who may be the victims of child abuse, family breakdown or parental illness. The aim is to avoid the problems posed by fragmented services. If there is a CES program in your area, it can give emergency help on a 24-hour basis.

*Big Brothers* (local chapters listed in the telephone directory) are groups of men, usually from religious organizations, whose concern is to befriend fatherless boys and their families. As MOMMA resources guide comments: "Some big-brother organizations are run with the attitude that all households headed by women are 'broken' and only the attention of men can repair them. Others are truly helping groups of men who can offer fun activities and true assistance in lessening the stresses of single motherhood."

There are several state agencies and voluntary organizations in your area that provide services for children. It's worth finding out who does what. State programs for children are listed under the Office of Child Development, the Department of Children's Welfare, Social Services or Health.

## Publications

*American Families, Trends and Pressures.* Hearings before the Subcommittee on Children and Youth, September 1973, (U.S. Government Printing Office, Washington D.C. 1974). Provides a mass of expert testimony on the often grim realities of family life in American society, with detailed proposals for change to improve conditions for children. Several references to single-parent families.

## Help with legal problems

Single mothers are often in need of legal services—to file for divorce, child support, alimony or establish paternity; to help with welfare problems or to fight discrimination in employment, education or housing. But the law is expensive. You should therefore find out what legal assistance in your area is available free or at a lower cost than usual.

*Public programs* These are free legal services (listed in the telephone book under "Legal Aid," "Community Legal Services," etc.) available to people whose income is below or near the level of the maximum welfare grant in that area. There are not nearly enough of them, and you may have to wait a long time for help that is not "urgent"—for example, if you want a divorce. If your case is urgent (you have been summoned to appear in court) explain the emergency when you call for an appointment.

*Community law centers* These are usually nonprofit voluntary organizations that provide legal services according to a client's ability to pay. Some workers are paralegals with a good working knowledge of a particular aspect of law (such as welfare or housing) and can give advice though they cannot represent you in court.

*Women's groups* are often a good source of information on legal services locally or they can put you in touch with a sympathetic lawyer. If you don't know of any groups near you, call the nearest chapter of NOW; there is one in every state.

*Legal Services Administration,* 733 15th Street N.W., Washington D.C. 20005 (tel: 202-376-5100) publishes a directory of many legal services programs throughout the country, for people at the poverty level.

*National Legal Aid and Defender Association,* 2100 M Street N.W., Washington D.C. 20037 (tel: 202-452-0620) also publishes a directory of legal services programs.

You will have a much greater chance of obtaining good free legal assistance if your case is not a routine domestic matter but involves sex discrimination. There are now many programs litigating class actions—that is, cases that, if successful, will improve the conditions of all women in similar situations and not simply benefit the woman who initiated the action. Any state or city commission on the status of women is a good place to seek advice. The main organizations working in this area are:

*American Civil Liberties Union,* 22 East 40 Street, New York, N.Y. 10016 (tel: 212-725-1222) has chapters in every state. It has also published the handbook *Rights of Women.*

*Human Rights for Women Inc.,* 1128 National Press Building, Washington D.C. 20004 (tel: 202-737-1059) provides free legal help to women bringing action against sex discrimination.

*NOW Legal Defense and Education Fund,* 9 West 57th Street, New York, N.Y. 10019 (tel: 212-688-1751) will give assistance in precedent-setting cases.

*Publications*

*The Rights of Women* by Susan Deller Ross, the ACLU handbook (New York: Avon Books, 1973).

*NOW Marriage and Divorce Task Force Legal Kit,* from Elizabeth Spalding, Hill Road, Greenwich, Connecticut 06830.

*Women's Rights Law Reporter,* 180 University Avenue, Newark, New Jersey 07102, a quarterly covering developments in the laws relating to women.

## Help with emotional problems

*Suicide prevention* services (listed in phone directory under "Suicide") operate in nearly all areas. They offer a sympathetic ear, friendship and understanding to people who are in despair. They are usually staffed by voluntary helpers, many of whom have been in trouble themselves. They can put you in touch with professional help if necessary but will not press you to give your name or address on the telephone if you don't want to. Most offer a 24-hour service.

*Parents Anonymous,* 2810 Artesia, Redondo Beach, California 90278 (tel: 1–800–421–0353; toll free) has chapters in many parts of the country which offer weekly meetings and emergency help for parents who think they might, or already do, abuse their children. (By this, they mean emotional, as well as physical, abuse or neglect.) The emphasis is on changing your ideas about children and yourself; like Alcoholics Anonymous there is no pressure to talk about your feelings until you want to.

*Feminist counseling and therapy referral* services are listed in the phone book (usually under "Women" or "Counseling"). They offer a feminist alternative to community mental health programs (listed under community names or local government) or family service agencies (listed under community names and religious or other voluntary organizations).

*Publications.*

*Women and Madness* by Phyllis Chesler (New York: Avon, 1973), the first book to bring a feminist perspective to bear on women's emotional and mental problems, provides an indictment of the psychiatric treatment of women on assumptions formed by specious male perspectives.

*Guidelines for Women Seeking Psychotherapy* (from Cleveland Women's Counseling, 2420 South Taylor, Box 20279, Cleveland Heights, Ohio 44118 (tel: 216–321–8585) provides excellent advice on how to shop around for a therapist and how to evaluate the service you receive.

# 8

*Contraception*

## HOW EASY IS IT TO GET PREGNANT?

All it takes for a woman to conceive a child is for one sperm (out of the 300 million sperm cells contained in the semen ejaculated from a man's penis) to swim up from a woman's vagina and fertilize one egg. Of course, an egg is not always lying in the oviduct (Fallopian tube) ready to be fertilized; this occurs once a month during ovulation. But at present it is not known how long sperm can survive in a woman's body and remain capable of fertilizing an egg, nor how long an egg remains capable of being fertilized.

This point cannot be emphasized too strongly, because it is frequently stated (even in gynecological textbooks) that an egg can survive for only about twenty-four hours and sperm up to seventy-two hours—which implies a relatively short period of fertility in the middle of the month between menstrual periods. But according to a leading American expert on rhythm, Professor Luigi Mastroianni, Jr., they are assumptions "without scientific validity."[1] So every time a woman has sex without contraception she is taking a risk.

How great is that risk? If you have sex only once during a month (what the statisticians like to call a "single random act of unprotected sexual intercourse") the estimated risk is as low as 2 to 4 percent in general.[2] It is much higher if you have sex frequently. A sexually active woman's chance of getting pregnant during a month is one in seven if she is in her teens, one in five is she is between 20 and 35, one in eight between 35 and 40, and just under one in ten between 40 and 45. Over the course of a year, if no contraception is used at all, the chances of becoming pregnant are as high as 85 to 90 percent.

## METHODS OF CONTRACEPTION

The perfect contraceptive has not yet been devised. The best one can do is to make an informed choice about the methods now available, recognizing that each has advantages and drawbacks. The facts that follow are based mainly on the Population Reports issued periodically by the Department of Medical and Public Affairs at George Washington University, Washington D.C. The information on health risks has been based, wherever possible, on independent research *not* funded or sponsored by manufacturing companies.

The probable failure rates of different methods are expressed below in two ways. The first, based on the calculations of leading authorities, is given per Hundred Woman Years (HWY)—that is, the *theoretical* number of women out of every one hundred who are expected to get pregnant if they use a particular method properly for a year. The second is a calculation of how many will *actually* get pregnant regardless of how they use the method. This derives from a study carried out by Norman B. Ryder, Professor of Sociology at Princeton University, which allowed for human error: it showed that whatever method was used, failure rates were higher among couples who were only trying to space or delay pregnancies than among those who intend to prevent them.[3]

## The pill (oral contraceptive)

The pill was the first, and is still the only, contraceptive that enables a woman to control her fertility by swallowing a drug in tablet form. After five years of being tested on women volunteers in Boston, Los Angeles and Puerto Rico, it became generally available to American women in 1960. Although rightly hailed as an historic breakthrough in birth control, enthusiasm for the pill has diminished as continued research has revealed certain risks to health. The pill is, nevertheless, the most effective and one of the most convenient means of preventing pregnancy currently available. Since 1960 an estimated 150 million women throughout the world have used it. Today, some 50 million are taking it, 10 million of whom are in the United States where it is now the most popular method of contraception.

*How it works* The commonest kind of pill contains synthetic hormones called estrogens and progestogens, which are similar to those produced naturally by a woman's body during her normal cycle; this is called the "combined" pill. It prevents conception in three ways: by stopping the release of the egg from the ovaries; by thickening the liquid in the neck of the womb so that it is more difficult for sperm to pass through into the womb; and by changing the lining of the womb so that it cannot receive a fertilized egg. The combined pill is effective because, if one of the reactions fails to occur, another will do the trick.

*Failure rate* Virtually nil—providing you follow the instructions and take the pills faithfully. No more than one out of a thousand women using the pill for a year should become pregnant, but when human error is taken into account, the rate is higher. Ryder found that six women in every hundred became pregnant within a year while on the pill, not only because they occasionally forgot to take it but because, if side-effects prompted them to abandon it suddenly, they did not always begin another method of contraception right away.

*Causes of failure* Pregnancy can sometimes occur if you miss two or three pills, if you don't use another contraceptive during the first two weeks when you go on the pill for the first time, or, more rarely, if you change brands and use no other protection during the first two weeks on the new pill. There is also some evidence that barbiturates, anti-epileptic drugs and the antibiotic rifampicin (used to treat tuberculosis) can make the pill less efficient. And on at least one occasion a brand of pills was found to be defective: in 1975 the Ortho Pharmaceutical Company withdrew its low-estrogen pill Modicon when its effectiveness was found to be reduced by exposure to light.

*Going on the pill* The pill must be prescribed by a doctor who should first give you an internal examination and make several checks: he should ask about your medical history (to find out whether you have a tendency toward any condition which would make it best for you not to take the pill) weigh you, test your urine (to check for diabetes) and your blood pressure, examine your breasts (for lumps) and take a Pap smear (to check for cervical cancer). All this is vital in making sure that you are healthy enough to take the pill, and to help the doctor decide which brand would suit you best. Never borrow pills from anyone else, or let a doctor write a prescription without a thorough examination. This initial exam and regular checkups afterwards are your most reassuring safeguards.

*Starting the pill* You start your first course of pills on the fifth day after your period begins. It is wise to use another method of contraception as well for the first two weeks; after that, you are fully protected by the pill alone.

*Starting the pill after pregnancy* You can start taking the pills on the fifth day after an abortion. After childbirth, you can start after four weeks because ovulation may begin again around that time, whether your periods have returned or not. However, if you are breast-feeding your baby, you should not take the pill. It may cause the milk to dry up or reduce in volume and may also lessen its nutritional value. Even more seriously, there are indications that estrogen may be passed on through the milk to the infant. Estrogen is suspected of inhibiting bone growth and possibly of causing jaundice in newborns. There is some disagreement among doctors over whether low-dosage pills are likely to cause these effects, but no mother with a newborn child would want to take chances.

*Periods* Each month you will probably have a period during the week you stop taking the pills. There may be less bleeding than before, and it may last a shorter time. Sometimes the blood is darker rather than bright red. If you used to have irregular and/or painful periods, you are likely to find that they now become regular and painless. Doctors sometimes prescribe the pill as a cure for painfully heavy periods as well as for contraception. A very few women have heavier periods on the pill, but this can usually be cured by a change of brand. Quite often, there is also a marked reduction in premenstrual tension. Another benefit, according to the long-term study carried out by the British Royal College of General Practitioners,[4] is that the pill, by reducing menstrual blood loss, can give "highly significant" protection against anemia.

*If you miss a period* Missed periods (amenorrhea) are quite common when on the pill. You are unlikely to be pregnant if you have taken the pills regularly, but if you have missed two pills or more it would be wise to have a pregnancy test. Some women miss periods for months on end, particularly if they have been on the pill for several years. There is no firm evidence at present that the menstrual cycle could stop functioning altogether, and thus cause sterility, if suppressed too long. According to one report, "in very rare instances, a premature menopause appears to have been precipitated by the use of the pill"[5] but this has happened mostly in women who had a history of menstrual irregularities before they started taking it. Some doctors advise women with persistent amenorrhea to change to a pill with a higher dose of estrogen (since it is progestogen that is responsible for suppressing periods), but too much estrogen may increase a tendency to the more serious blood-clotting disorders. Other doctors advise coming off the pill for a while to make sure that the woman's periods return to normal; usually periods return very quickly or within a year. Occasionally, however, they do not. In this case a woman can be given clomiphene citrate therapy which is reportedly often effective in restoring menstruation.

*Planned pregnancy* There is no evidence that the pill might affect your ability to become pregnant when you decide to have a child. At one time it was thought that women were more fertile than usual immediately after going off the pill, but this theory is now discounted. Instead, the Royal College study has confirmed that there may be a slight delay in the return of fertility. In its study, the Royal College also reported on 2,291 couples who came off the pill deliberately to have a child: 85 percent of those women who had never been pregnant before, and 93 percent of those who had already had a child, conceived within two years of stopping the pill. The effect of the hormones in the pill is thought to disappear from the system very quickly once the pill is discontinued. However, there is evidence that if a woman becomes pregnant *soon* after going off the pill, the embryo is more susceptible to triploidy, an abnormality of the chromosomes (which determine the sexual and inherited characteristics of the child).[6] Embryos with this abnormality virtually always miscarry in early pregnancy, and it was the microscopic analyses of miscarriages that revealed the link between triploidy and recent use of the pill. It is therefore recommended that women use another method of contraception for three months or so before trying for a baby.

*Side effects* Some women have no apparent side effects; some feel even healthier on the pill; others are so troubled by the effects that they stop taking it; and many, though not altogether happy, put up with minor effects for the sake of the pill's convenience and reliability.

According to the Royal College study, about 40 percent of the women who stop taking the pill do so because of side effects, and about 15 percent because of anxiety about possible effects. Some doctors think that women may develop effects from the pill psychosomatically—they read or hear about them, so they get them. This is far too simplistic a view. Nevertheless, if we have a generalized fear of the pill we tend to blame it for every twinge of pain we develop. So it is important to be aware of all the known side effects, including those that have been suggested and discounted.

*Nausea and vomiting* A feeling of queasiness, sometimes accompanied by vomiting, is quite common, especially during the first cycle of pills. It is similar to morning sickness in early pregnancy (though usually not as severe) and has the same cause—an increase in estrogen. If it persists it will probably help to change to a pill with a lower dose. It also seems to help if you take the pills at night instead of in the morning. Usually, however, this side effect quickly disappears.

*Breasts* The pill can make the breasts fuller and larger. Sometimes the breasts feel tender or sore, though this usually passes after a few months of use. Both effects are more pronounced on pills with higher estrogen doses.

*Skin* The pill can improve the complexion. Dermatologists, noting that it reduces sebum production, have sometimes used it to treat severe cases of acne. On the other hand, the pill can also increase the risk of developing certain skin disorders such as chloasma (a change in pigmentation resembling huge freckles) and eczema. The Royal College study found that this happens only infrequently—seventy per 100,000 pill-users in each case—but twice as often as among nonusers. Most skin disorders associated with the pill disappear when it is discontinued, but chloasma persists. If chloasma develops in a woman taking the pill, she is likely to get it when she is pregnant as well, and vice versa. (Some nutrition experts believe that chloasma and eczema are caused by vitamin deficiencies—see pp. 153–54) A few women on the pill also experience allergic rashes.

*Hair* A certain amount of hair loss is common in women of childbearing age, and the Royal College study found no increased hair loss among women on the pill. A high level of natural progesterone in the body is normally associated with hairiness, however, so it is possible that pills with low estrogen and more progestogen may slightly increase body hair.

*Eyes* There is no evidence that the pill can cause an increase in eye disease or irregularities of sight, although some women report that their vision became affected while on the pill, and there have been suggestions that the increased sensitivity of the eye might make it more difficult to wear contact lenses. However, you should see a doctor immediately if you develop blurred vision or a blood clot in the eye.

*Weight gain* This does not happen to all women, but it is one of the main reasons some choose to go off the pill. There are three reasons why it may occur: an increase in appetite, a build-up of protein in the muscular tissue (both progestogen-related effects), or fluid retention caused by estrogen-dominant pills. Any of these effects may be cured by switching brands. A woman who is already very heavy, however, is not advised to take the pill.

*Break-through bleeding* Any vaginal bleeding between periods should be investigated by a doctor, whether you are on the pill or not, but a little spotting or staining from the vagina between periods is a fairly common minor side effect. It happens more frequently on low estrogen pills and may be cured by switching to a brand with a higher dose; or an extra pill a day can be taken while the bleeding lasts. If you miss two or three pills, you may also begin to bleed. This is a sure sign you are no longer protected. Otherwise, bleeding does not usually mean that the pill has stopped working.

*Headaches and dizziness* It is difficult to establish how often these symptoms are actually caused by the pill because they occur so frequently among nonusers too. It is also difficult to tell when they should be taken seriously or disregarded. Sometimes women with a tendency to migraine find that the pill makes it worse; some find the opposite. A sudden and severe headache or a sudden fit of intense dizziness may mean hypertension or a thromboembolic disorder and could be very serious. If this happens see a doctor at once.

*Fluid retention* This condition (known medically as edema) occurs when water builds up in the body tissues. It is an estrogen-related effect (also occurring in pregnancy) and can cause weight gain, headaches, leg cramps and pains. Switching to a lower-estrogen dose often cures it. Nutrition experts believe that it can also be corrected by an increased intake of potassium in the diet. Women who suffer from epilepsy, asthma and migraine can be particularly affected by fluid retention and should therefore take the pill only under close medical supervision.

*Leg cramps or pains* As noted above, these are most often caused by fluid retention and can be cured or alleviated by changing to a pill with less estrogen. Very occasionally such cramps or pains may be early warning signs of thromboembolic disorders such as phlebitis (see p. 149). Any severe or persistent pain should be investigated by a doctor.

*Fatigue* Women on the pill quite often complain of lack of energy, feeling tired or exhausted. Once again, it is difficult to blame the pill entirely because other factors may be responsible. Nevertheless, it may contribute; the symptoms are similar to those in pregnancy which are caused by higher levels of progesterone. Like other pill symptoms which mimic pregnancy, these may disappear after a few months use. If not, switching to an estrogen-dominant pill may help. Very occasionally, fatigue may be a symptom of hypertension (see p. 152). More often, it is a sign of low blood sugar (see p. 154).

*Depression* Whether the pill can cause depression, or increase depression in women who already have a tendency toward it, remains unclear. Most women who get depressed cannot themselves decide whether it is because of the pill or something else. The Royal College study reported an apparent slight increase in mild depression among women on the pill but suggested that this occurred at most in twenty-two cases out of 100,000 a year. But another thorough, on-going study carried out by the Kaiser Permanente Medical Center, Walnut Creek, California,[7] found no difference in depression or mental health between women currently on the pill, women who formerly took it, and women who had never taken it.

*Changed sexual desire* Most women find that they have more desire and enthusiasm for sex when they go on the pill—probably because they have no fear of pregnancy. Others report no change at all. But quite a lot of women have begun to complain about loss of sex drive, a reduction of vaginal lubricating juices, decreased vaginal or clitoral sensitivity and fewer orgasms. The Royal College study has also reported a fourfold increase over the past few years in the number of women who complain about this loss of libido. It is not known whether this is because more women are now talking about the pill, or because the effect is more pronounced with the lower-estrogen pills that most women are taking nowadays, or because libido can be affected by the length of time a woman stays on the pill.

*Increased blood pressure* Blood pressure that is slightly higher than usual is a fairly common side effect of the pill and becomes more likely the longer the pill is used. The Kaiser Permanente study found that women on the pill were more than six times more likely to develop higher blood pressure than nonusers, whereas the Royal College study found the chances to be just over two and one half times as great. But these higher levels usually fall back to normal within three months of stopping the pill. As no increase in blood pressure seems to occur in women using progestogen-only pills, estrogen is thought to be responsible. But it is still not clear whether the very slight increases experienced by most women have any harmful, or potentially harmful, effect. In a very few women, the rise is sufficiently high to create severe hypertension. When this happens, a woman should come off the pill—and she should not take it at all if she is thought to be susceptible to severe hypertension.

*Varicose veins* Veins are said to become "varicose" when a spot on the wall of the vein weakens and swells under pressure from the surge of blood beneath. Excessive weight and standing for long periods can cause this to happen; sometimes the tendency is inherited. Women predisposed to varicose veins may develop them in pregnancy, when increased progesterone in the system causes the muscle of the vein to relax and swell. The same thing can happen on the pill. In most cases, the varicosity is slight, but such veins need watching. Women with very distended varicose veins are usually advised not to take the pill.

*Delayed or premature menopause* An early well-publicized speculation about the pill was whether it could delay menopause so that women in their sixties or seventies could become pregnant. This idea has now been totally discounted. At the other extreme is speculation on whether the pill can bring on menopause earlier than normal. This now seems doubtful, but there is no firm evidence either way, although there have been a few instances of women whose periods never returned after taking the pill. Bearing this in mind, women with irregular periods—particularly young teen-agers whose periods have not yet settled into an established pattern—should consider using an alternative method of contraception.

*Potential Dangers*

*Blood-clotting disorders* Blood-clotting disorders (thromboembolism) are still rare in women, but research has shown that the risk of developing them is about five to ten times greater among pill-users than among nonusers. There are several different types:

*Phlebitis* This happens when a blood clot attaches itself to the blood vessel wall, causing inflammation, pain and tenderness. It is relatively common and not dangerous. Nevertheless, any woman who develops phlebitis is advised to come off the pill. The pill increases the risk by about 50 percent, from about 200 to 300 cases per 100,000 women each year.

*Deep-vein thrombosis* This is very rare but very serious. The pill increases the risk five or six times, from about twenty to 110 per 100,000 women each year. Of these about three will die if the blood clot works its way into the lungs or brain.

*Cerebrovascular disease* This means a stroke, usually rare in young women, which can cause paralysis and sometimes death. The Royal College study found that the pill increases the risk four times, from ten to forty per 100,000 women each year, whereas the Collaborative Group for the Study of Strokes in Young Women[8] found that women on the pill run nine times the risk of thrombotic stroke and twice the risk of hemorrhagic stroke. These risks are greater if women are also heavy smokers or suffer from high blood pressure.

The link between the pill and blood-clotting disorders was first established by British research[9] in 1968. This showed that out of every 100,000 on the pill, one or two women under thirty-five and three or four women over thirty-five would die each year from thromboembolism. This and later studies also found that the risk of deep-vein thrombosis is reduced by about 25 percent if the estrogen level in the pill is reduced to fifty micrograms. These "low-dose" pills quickly became available in the United States and Britain, and today the majority of women on the pill use them. It is therefore probable that the risk of both serious and minor blood-clotting disorders is now lower than it used to be. Nevertheless, women with a history of blood-clotting problems should not take the pill.

*Heart attack* Heart attacks (myocardial infarction) are usually rare in women of childbearing age. But in May 1975 it was announced that two British studies[10-11] had found an increase in both fatal and nonfatal heart attacks among women on the pill.

Both these studies were on small groups of women, but they indicated that the risk of nonfatal heart attacks for women aged thirty to thirty-nine using the pill (projected at 5.6 per 100,000) was more than twice as high as for nonusers (2.1 per 100,000). And the risk of death from heart attack in this age group showed a similar increase (5.4 compared with 1.9 per 100,000). For older women aged forty to forty-four, the nonfatal rate was over five times as high (56.9 per 100,000 pill-users; 9.9 per 100,000 nonusers), and the death rate only slightly less (54.7 compared to 11.7 per 100,000). When the same British researchers continued their investigation with a larger group of women,[12] they found the death rate from heart attacks among women over forty on the pill to be considerably lower—24.5 per 100,000. This is still high.

The pill is not the only thing that can increase the risk of heart attacks. So can cigarette smoking, high blood pressure, diabetes, a high level of cholesterol (which hardens the arteries) in the blood, and obesity. The investigators found that women with only one risk factor were more than four times as likely to have heart attacks as women with no risk factors at all. But those with two factors had ten times the risk. And those with three or more had *seventy-eight times the risk*. More research is needed to confirm these findings, but doctors are taking them very seriously. Planned Parenthood, for example, now requires women over forty to sign consent forms, acknowledging awareness of the risks, before prescribing the pill.

*Cancer and tumors* Whether or not the pill causes cancer is the big unanswered question. In 1969 an American report[13] warned that: cancer may lie dormant for twenty to thirty years before being detected; estrogen activity in animals and humans has been linked to cancer; and cancer of the breast has never been noted in young girls before the age of puberty or in older women whose ovaries have been removed—neither of whom produce estrogen. Since then, numerous studies have attempted to find a link between cancer and oral contraceptives.

To date, the evidence is contradictory and disturbing. No positive indications have been found so far that the usual combined pill, or pills that contain only progestogens, increase the risk of any kind of cancer. However, very recently a link has been established between cancer of the endometrium (lining of the uterus) and certain estrogen compounds used to treat menopausal women. A similar link has been established with sequential pills, a type of oral contraceptive, now discontinued, with a high estrogen content. Some women on the pill have developed liver tumors. The fact that all these discoveries were made in a short period—toward the end of 1975—has increased fears that the pill may have a "time bomb" effect, the first signs of which are only now beginning to emerge. Far more research is needed. Meantime, here is a summary of what is known about the pill in relation to cancer and benign tumors.

*Breast cancer* No evidence has been found to link breast cancer with the pill.

*Benign breast tumors* These lumps in the breast are not malignant and therefore not life-threatening. Several studies have reported a slight *decrease* in the occurrence of these lumps among women on the pill.

*Cervical cancer* There is no evidence that the risk of cervical cancer is increased by the pill; and the disease has, in fact, declined in the United States since the pill was introduced. But it is wise, while taking the pill, to have a Pap smear test, which detects it in its very early stages.

*Endometrial cancer* This cancer, which develops in the lining of the uterus, is very rare in women under forty. Only one study,[14] published in November 1975, has so far examined cases of women who developed it while taking the pill. A significant number of these women had been taking sequential pills, which contained nearly twice as much estrogen as combined pills. The study found no link between endometrial cancer and the combined pill. In early 1976 all sequentials were withdrawn from the market.

*Hypertension (high blood pressure)* The pill commonly causes a slight increase in blood pressure, which is not thought to be harmful. However, a few women develop severe hypertension. The symptoms are headaches, dizziness, fatigue, nervousness, sleeplessness, palpitations and possibly nosebleeds. Women who experience these symptoms should not take the pill or, if they are already doing so, should stop. It is also wise to have your blood pressure tested regularly when on the pill.

*Diabetes* Diabetes is suffered by people whose bodies do not produce enough insulin to metabolize the glucose (sugar) levels in their blood. It is known that the pill can cause slight changes in glucose tolerance and insulin metabolism—not enough, probably, to affect healthy people. But it can worsen the condition of women who already have diabetes and possibly bring on the disease in those who are predisposed to it. However, pregnancy can worsen it even more.

*Liver disorders* The pill can affect excretory functions slightly, though this is probably of no consequence in healthy women, but it should not be used by women who already have diseases of the liver, such as hepatitis. It is possible that the pill increases the risk of jaundice in those women who are likely to develop the disease during pregnancy. So anyone who has already had jaundice in pregnancy should not take the pill. Several cases of liver tumor have recently been reported in women taking the pill; these are usually not cancerous, but even benign tumors can be dangerous.

*Gallbladder disease* The pill has been found to increase the risk of inflammation of the gallbladder (cholecystitis) and gallstones (cholelithiasis). The Boston study[15] found the risk twice as high in pill-takers as nonusers—an increase from 79 to 158 cases per 100,000 women in a year. The Royal College study found a similar increase and reported that the disease was associated with the length of pill-taking and the progestogen content of the pill.

*Vaginal infections* The pill can increase susceptibility to vaginal infections and discharge and infections of the urinary tract. This doesn't always happen, but the rise in the sugar content of vaginal secretions caused by the pill makes the vagina an ideal incubator for yeast infections such as *candida albicans* (monilia or thrush). The Royal College study showed that women on the pill are twice as likely to develop this as nonusers. It also showed a 50 percent increase in urinary tract infections (such as cystitis) and vaginal discharge. Frequent sexual intercourse can also cause these infections to flare up, and so can pregnancy. A woman on the pill is more susceptible the longer she stays on it. All these complaints can be treated, but if a condition persists you may have to come off the pill to find relief.

*Venereal disease* The pill can help spread VD in two ways. First, fewer men have used condoms (the only contraceptive that gives some protection against the sexually transmitted diseases) since the pill was introduced. Second, the pill makes women more susceptible to VD by increasing the sugar content of the vaginal juices.

*Chicken pox* This illness, rare in adults, usually strikes children once and does not occur again. But the Royal College study reported increased cases of chicken pox among women on the pill. It is not known why this happens, but a possible explanation is that the pill affects the normal adult immunity in some way.

*Changing brands* In the early 1960s, all brands of the pill contained high doses of estrogen because it was not then known precisely how much was necessary to give 100 percent protection against pregnancy. In 1968 British research discovered that no more than fifty micrograms of estrogen was necessary, and that higher doses substantially increased the risk of blood-clotting disorders. Today there are a number of low-dose brands approved by the Food and Drug Administration, which offer several different combinations of estrogen and progestogen doses.

*Temporarily coming off the pill* Some doctors advise "taking a break" from the pill every two or three years. This dates from the early days of pill-taking when doctors were uncertain about the long-term effects. Today there are doubts whether this is worthwhile. In general it is thought that the risk of getting pregnant while off the pill is far greater than any advantages that may be gained.

*Staying healthy while on the pill* The importance of nutrition in relation to pill-taking is only just beginning to be recognized. Some side effects are thought to be caused by vitamin deficiencies and may be corrected by changes in diet.

*Folic acid deficiency* This can cause chloasma, a discoloration of the skin pigment. Folic acid is one of the B vitamins found in whole-grain breads and cereals, wheat germ, lean meats (especially liver), brewers' yeast, green leafy vegetables, milk and dried beans. One nutritionist recommends taking five milligrams of folic acid in tablet form after each meal if chloasma develops.

*Vitamin B*$_6$ *deficiency* A lack of B$_6$ (pyridoxine) can cause headaches, nausea, fluid retention and eczema (which can develop in and around the vagina as well as on the face and hands). If these conditions develop, they may be helped by taking vitamin B$_6$ in tablet form (fifty milligrams at each meal). They may be prevented by a good supply from natural sources of the B vitamins listed above. A particularly rich source of B$_6$ is brewers' yeast, which can be added to milk and/or orange juice.

*Low blood sugar* This causes tiredness, apathy, depression. Paradoxical as it sounds, the condition is caused by too *much* sugar in the diet. Most Americans consume far too much sugar. Milk, fresh fruit and vegetables give us all the natural sugar we need for energy.

*High cholesterol levels* Cholesterol is found in animal fats (meat, butter, cheese, egg yolks). Too much cholesterol in the bloodstream hardens the arteries and can eventually cause blockages, leading to strokes and heart attacks. Cholesterol intake can be reduced by using polyunsaturated oils and margarines to eat and cook with.

*Vitamin E deficiency* Some nutritionists believe that both pregnancy and oral contraceptives greatly increase the body's need for vitamin E. They claim that a lack of this vitamin contributes to varicose veins and blood-clotting disorders, as well as to infertility, miscarriage, premature births and liver, kidney and muscular disorders. These claims are controversial, for the role of vitamin E in the metabolic process is not fully understood. The best natural sources of vitamin E are fresh wheat germ, cold-pressed vegetable oils, and nuts. Smaller quantities are found in eggs, dried beans, and fresh greens. Vitamin E can also be taken in capsule form.

*Potassium and sodium* Potassium deficiency is associated with heart attacks, and too much sodium (salt), with high blood pressure. In American diets, five times more sodium is consumed than is necessary because it is used as a preservative in many foods. Excessive consumption of salt also causes a serious loss of potassium from the body. The best natural sources of potassium are green leafy vegetables (especially spinach), seafood, whole grains, fruits and nuts.

*Vitamin C* This is the body's greatest fighter against infection and toxicity of all kinds. Nutritionists therefore believe that it may be especially needed by people who take drugs (including oral contraceptives). Vitamin C is particularly helpful to women who suffer from cystitis. The best natural sources of vitamin C are unsweetened orange, grapefruit and lemon juices, green or red peppers, parsley, broccoli and most fruits and vegetables. Extra quantities can be taken in tablet form.

*The "progestogen-only" pill (mini-pill)* This is a new kind of contraceptive pill which contains no estrogen. It does not stop ovulation, but works by thickening the liquid in the cervical canal so that it is more difficult for sperm to reach the egg. It has a higher failure rate (estimated at 2 to 4 HWY) than the combined pill.

The mini-pill must be taken every day without a break. Three British studies[16] have recently reported an "unusually high" rate of ectopic pregnancies among women who conceive while taking it.

### The Intra-Uterine Device (IUD)

The next most effective contraceptive after the combined pill is the IUD (sometimes known as the coil or loop). Primitive versions of the IUD have been used for centuries. The modern device dates from the early twentieth century. By the 1930s the German Graefenberg Ring, made of silver, and the Japanese Ota Ring, made of gold, had become fairly popular, but they quickly fell out of favor because of the danger of serious infections. It was not until the late 1950s that interest in IUDs revived.

Today IUDs are generally considered relatively effective and safe, although all carry a risk of pregnancy, and a common problem—the body's expulsion of the device from the uterus—has not been completely solved. IUDs sometimes cause unpleasant side-effects and have been known on occasion to cause serious complications and even, rarely, death. So, like the pill, they remain controversial.

### How IUDs work

*Inert IUDs* Ordinary IUDs are called "inert" to distinguish them from the newer copper and hormone-releasing devices which work chemically. An inert IUD is simply a small flexible piece of plastic which is inserted into the uterus. It is not known exactly why this prevents pregnancy. The most widely accepted theory is that IUDs in some way prevent a fertilized egg from implanting itself properly into the wall of the uterus, perhaps because an IUD constantly irritates the uterine lining, causing an inflammatory cell reaction. It is also thought that the lining reacts by producing quantities of macrophages (large white blood cells whose function is to drive out any foreign body) to force the IUD out but which, instead, devour the egg and/or sperm in the uterus.

*Copper IUDs* This newer type of IUD has thin copper wire wound round the plastic stem. The copper works chemically to help prevent pregnancy. Again, no one understands why, but the process is certainly more complex than in inert devices.

*Hormone-releasing IUDs* This most recent version is a sort of cross between the pill and IUD. The synthetic hormone progestogen in the pill is known to alter the lining of the uterus so that an egg cannot implant itself properly. In theory the same effect should be achieved if progestogen is placed directly in the uterus and released slowly over a period of time. Smaller amounts of the hormone are needed than in the pill (therefore possibly reducing side effects) and the whole body is not affected.

*Failure rates*

*Inert IUDs* Studies show pregnancy rates ranging from zero to 5.6 per 100 women in the first year of use. However, failure is more likely the first year after insertion and declines with each succeeding year that the IUD stays in place. For example, in one major study[17] it was found that with a commonly used device, the Lippes Loop D, the pregnancy rate was 3.2 per 100 users in the first year after insertion, 2.1 in the second year, 1.3 in the third year and 0.9 after six years.

*Copper IUDs* A variation of between zero and 3 per 100 women in the first year of use. The steadily reducing pregnancy rate in succeeding years noted for inert devices is not so marked for copper IUDs.

*Hormone-releasing IUDs* Research carried out by an American manufacturer reported a rate of 1 per 100 women who had previously had children in the first year of use, and 1.4 per 100 women who had never had children.[18] However, more independent evaluations are needed to substantiate these findings.

*Causes of failure* One reason women get pregnant while using the IUD is that it may become dislodged or fall out. Expulsion rates occur most frequently in women who have not borne children, and the shape of the device makes a difference. Of the three commonest types, the Copper-T has the lowest expulsion rate, the Copper-7 the next lowest and the Lippes Loop the highest.

But some women become pregnant with the device in place. The chances of this happening are small and can be reduced even further if contraceptive foam (see p. 171) is also used during sexual intercourse. Some women use foam in the ten days around the middle of their cycle when ovulation is most likely to occur. Planned Parenthood clinics also often advise women to use an additional means of contraception during the first three months after an IUD is inserted since there is a slightly higher risk of expulsion at this time.

*Types of IUD* Over the years many different types of IUD have come and gone. It is important to know which have been found both effective and relatively safe over a long period.

*Lippes Loop and Saf-T-Coil* These have been used longer than any others in the United States and are regarded as having a good safety record. The Loop, developed by Dr. Jack Lippes of Buffalo, New York, is especially popular and used as a standard by which all new IUDs are judged. However, a common drawback of both devices is that they are easily expelled by women who have not had children.

*The Dalkon Shield* This was introduced in 1970 in an attempt to overcome the expulsion problem. It was smaller and had plastic "teeth" to grip the uterine wall more effectively. However, it was gradually noted that the shield caused heavier menstrual bleeding, more pain, more infection and was often more difficult to remove than other IUDs; it also had a higher failure rate. In May 1974 the manufacturers, the A.H. Robins Company, sent a letter to some 120,000 American doctors informing them that thirty-six women who had become pregnant with the shield in place had suffered septic miscarriages and four of them had died.[19] That same month, the Food and Drug Administration heard the results of a six-month national survey into IUD complications that had been severe enough to require hospitalization; the Dalkon Shield accounted for nearly half the total number of complications.[20] The FDA did not bar the shield, which was redesigned, but Planned Parenthood clinics no longer prescribe it.

*Copper IUDs* The only copper IUD generally available in the United States at the time of writing is the Copper 7. The evidence suggests that it is probably as safe as the inert devices, although the complexity of the chemical reaction on which its contraceptive effect depends leaves several questions unanswered.

*Hormone-releasing IUDs* The Progestasert device, approved by the

FDA in February 1976, is the first to appear on the American market. This is a plastic T-shaped device with a hollow vertical stem containing progestogen which is gradually released into the uterus. The hormone-releasing IUDs have not solved the problem of expulsion, nor do they entirely prevent pregnancy, but they may eventually prove to be more effective than other IUDs. Their main drawback is that they have to be replaced after a year when the hormone runs out, whereas inert IUDs can be left in place forever providing all goes well, and copper devices have to be replaced only every two to four years.

*Potential effects on life and health* Unlike the pill, the most serious (or fatal) consequences from using an IUD happen when a woman becomes pregnant with the device in place. As IUDs are highly effective in preventing pregnancy, this risk is very small. The lesser risks are:

*Infection* Any bacteria present on an IUD is overcome by the body's natural defenses, and within a month of insertion the device is usually sterile. However, in the first six months of 1973 more than 3,500 women were hospitalized as a result of complications caused by IUDs, and of these, just under 2,000, or 34 percent, were attributed to pelvic inflammatory disease (PID). This infection can usually be cured by antibiotics, but it is potentially very dangerous. It is not entirely clear whether IUDs significantly increase the risk of developing PID, because there are no valid statistics on the disease in women who don't use IUDs. However there is growing evidence that this may be so. It is well known that an IUD insertion can trigger PID that is already present but dormant, as well as other infections such as venereal disease, vaginal and urinary infections.

*Ectopic pregnancies* IUDs are not thought to cause ectopic pregnancies, but they cannot prevent them in the same way that they prevent most uterine pregnancies. So women who become pregnant with an IUD in place run a higher risk of their pregnancies being ectopic: the chances are about one in twenty[21] or ten times the normal rate.

*Perforation* This happens when an IUD pierces the uterine wall. Though generally uncommon, perforation can occur during insertion. A great deal depends on the skill of the person who inserts the device, and some doctors believe there is an increased risk if IUDs are inserted immediately after abortion or childbirth. Perforation can also happen at a later stage. If the device has embedded itself only in the wall and is causing no discomfort, it is considered best to leave it alone. If a copper device is clearly working itself through the wall or is already outside, it should be removed since it can cause severe inflammation and adhesions (where tissue grows around the device) if left in the abdominal cavity. As far as inert devices are concerned, one authority recommends no immediate surgery unless pain is felt. But adhesions of tissue can grow around these too and, in extreme cases, may cause serious complications by damaging or obstructing the bowel. The main danger, however, comes from the risks of surgery if removal is necessary.

*Embolism* Blood clots (thromboembolism) are not directly caused by the IUD, as they sometimes are by the pill. However, the CDC survey[22] showed that two women died from blood clots which developed following an operation to remove IUDs: both devices had perforated the uterine wall and worked into the abdominal cavity. An early survey carried out by the American College of Obstetricians and Gynecologists revealed two deaths caused by amniotic fluid embolism. This extremely rare type of embolism occurs when a bubble of fluid from the amniotic sac surrounding a fetus escapes through the uterine wall into a blood vessel and works its way up into the lungs. Again, IUDs did not directly cause these embolisms, but IUDs had perforated the uteri of both women.

*Side effects* IUDs have far fewer known side effects than the pill. The two consistently reported are heavier menstrual periods and cramps or pain in the abdomen, both of which often lessen after the first two or three months of use.

*Pain during intercourse* Some women who use IUDs experience pain, or acute discomfort, when the penis thrusts deep into the vagina and pushes vigorously against the cervix. If this happens, you should consult a doctor promptly.

*Copper allergy* This is an extremely rare condition which makes one break out in a rash on contact with copper. Only one case has been reported of copper allergy in women wearing copper IUDs.

*Who should not use IUDs* You should not have an IUD inserted if any of the following conditions are present:

- *Venereal disease.* An IUD can make VD spread rapidly and may make it impossible to cure. Once a VD infection has been cured, an IUD may be used—although some doctors believe that women who change sex partners frequently and are exposed to VD should never use IUDs because of a danger that it can lead to sterility and other complications.

- *Pelvic inflammatory disease or vaginal or urinary infection.* IUDs can cause all these to flare up, spread and worsen.
- *Pregnancy.* It is dangerous to have an IUD inserted if you are pregnant because of the risk of infection.
- *Infection following abortion or childbirth.* This should be treated and cured at least three months before an IUD is inserted.
- *Cancer.* IUDs should not be used by women who suffer, or have suffered, from cancer of the cervix or uterus.
- *Endometriosis.* This happens when the tissue which lines the uterus grows abnormally elsewhere, most often in the genital or intestinal organs. Its symptoms include excessive menstrual pain and pain during intercourse—both of which are worsened by an IUD.
- *Retroverted or unusually small uterus.* The uterus commonly changes its position and sometimes becomes tipped (retroverted). If a uterus is permanently retroverted (quite rare) it would be impossible to insert an IUD. If a device is already inside when the uterus becomes retroverted it causes intolerable pain. The same is true of women with tiny uteri.
- *Anemia.* Iron deficiency anemia is considerably worsened by increased blood loss, which rules out the IUD.
- *Excessively heavy menstrual periods or cramps.* Women whose periods are normally very heavy and painful would probably find an IUD intolerable.

*If you have never had a child* It is much easier to insert an inert IUD into the uterus of a woman who had already had a child because the uterus has been stretched by childbirth, and the device is less likely to be expelled from her body. Today, most doctors recommend a copper device, which is smaller, for women who have not given birth. But some doctors believe that women who have never borne a child should not use IUDs at all on the grounds that it has not yet been disproved that IUDs can increase the risk of infertility in childless women.

*How to get fitted for an IUD* An IUD must be inserted by a well-trained person. This is usually a doctor, although it might be a specially trained nurse or midwife. Whomever you go to, try to make sure that he or she is experienced in fitting IUDs.

*Examination and tests* You should receive a full pelvic examination, and a Pap smear should be taken to check for cervical cancer. It is also wise to ask for a test for venereal disease.

*Choosing an IUD* The doctor will check the size and shape of your uterus to help decide which IUD will suit you best. Although they do not come in a sufficient variety of sizes to allow perfect customer fit, ideally you want one that fits snugly into the triangle of your uterus so that it is less likely to be expelled or cause cramps or pain after it has settled down. Whichever device is suggested, the doctor should thoroughly explain the reasons for the choice. If you are offered a device not mentioned here, or one that is still experimental, ask exactly what advantages this is supposed to have over existing well-tried IUDs. Remember that you have a right to know whether the IUD has been approved by the FDA, and the right to refuse an experimental device.

*Food and Drug Administration requirements* In 1975 the FDA drew up mandatory labeling requirements for IUDs. These give detailed information to doctors on the effectiveness and risks, and instructions for insertion. There is also a patient brochure containing similar information, including how to check regularly that the device is in place. The FDA requires that a doctor give the brochure to a patient to read *before* an IUD is inserted. She must also give her informed consent to the doctor, either orally or in writing, before insertion.

*When to have an IUD inserted* The best time is either during or immediately after your menstrual period. There are two reasons for this: (a) to ensure that you are not pregnant, which could make an IUD dangerous; (b) because the cervix is softer then, which makes insertion easier.

*Insertion procedure* In the technique recommended by the Population Council and major training centers, the doctor performs a pelvic examination to check the size and position of the uterus. A speculum, a duck-billed instrument which holds the vaginal walls apart so that the cervix is exposed, is placed in the vagina. The doctor grasps the cervix with a tenaculum or forceps and swabs the vagina and cervix with an antiseptic solution. At this point it is necessary to straighten the cervical canal and uterus by tugging slightly on the cervix, and to take a sounding to check the depth and direction of the uterus. If both these things are done, there is far less chance of perforation when the IUD is inserted. The IUD is straightened out in an inserter, which is a thin plastic tube. Both must be sterile. The doctor then gently pushes the tube through the small hole (os) in the cervix into the uterus. The inserter should be pushed far enough into the uterus so that when the IUD is released it stays in the upper part where it is less likely to be expelled or cause pain. Most modern inserters are "notched" to show uterine depth and to lessen the danger of forcing the IUD too high or causing perforation. When the IUD is released it springs back into its original shape, and the inserter is removed. The doctor should then check that the thread attached to the device is hanging down into the vagina correctly. Finally, the doctor removes the forceps and speculum. The whole procedure takes only a few minutes.

*Pain during and after insertion* The insertion can hurt quite a lot, particularly if the cervix is tight and the uterus small, as is often the case with women who have not given birth. Individual women's experiences vary enormously, and the skill of the doctor probably makes a difference. Several studies report that most women feel nothing worse than menstrual-like cramping. An ordinary pain-killing pill or a tranquilizer may help. Later on in the day there may be cramping and backache, as in a menstrual period. Any pain that persists should be reported to the doctor.

*Having an IUD inserted after pregnancy* IUDs are often inserted immediately after an abortion or the delivery of a child. But there is some disagreement among doctors as to whether this is the safest time.

*After an abortion* An IUD is easier to insert after an abortion when the cervix is already slightly stretched, and it is no less safe—providing there are no signs of infection. However, any infection which sets in as a result of abortion usually does not become noticeable until a few days or a week or two afterwards. So it may be safer (though less convenient) to wait for a couple of weeks—during which time sex is not recommended anyway in case of infection.

*After childbirth* IUDs are sometimes inserted while a woman is still in the delivery room, or a few days later before she leaves the hospital. This is considered safe, although infection can set in after childbirth too. But if more than a week goes by after delivery, it is thought wise to postpone an IUD insertion for about eight weeks. This is because some studies (mainly in Egypt and Singapore) have shown an exceptionally high rate of perforation in insertions performed between four and eight weeks after childbirth. The uterus is very soft at this time and probably more easily perforated. The chance of expulsion is very high, too, at this stage.

*Breast-feeding* There is no evidence that IUDs can, like the pill, affect the quantity and quality of breast milk. A study in Egypt (where, as in most developing countries, lactation is more vitally important than it is in the West) showed no differences in the milk of mothers wearing Lippes Loops.

*Checking that the IUD stays in place* This is easy to do. Squat down and insert a (clean) finger into the vagina. Your cervix is inside, feels like a knob and is harder than the surrounding area. The string of the IUD should be protruding a little way from the hole in the center. Sometimes the uterus tips and it is more difficult to find the cervix and locate the thread. Try again a couple of days later. This check should ideally be done every week, and particularly after a period: IUDs are more easily expelled during menstruation. If several days go by without your being able to find the thread—or if you feel a hard piece of plastic as well as the thread, which means that the device has slipped down into the cervix and may be coming out—call your doctor immediately. A doctor can diagnose whether an IUD is still in the uterus or whether any perforation has occurred.

*Medical check-ups and replacements* Although most IUDs can stay in place for years if all goes well, it is best to be checked by a doctor every year. If you have an annual gynecological examination, it can be done then. When you get your IUD inserted, check the patient brochure to find out how long that type remains effective before it needs to be replaced.

### The diaphragm
The rubber diaphragm, invented in the 1880s, was the first modern contraceptive to give women a reasonable degree of control over their own fertility. By the end of the 1950s, it was used by one-third of American couples who practiced birth control.[23] With the advent of the pill and IUD in the 1960s, the diaphragm was dismissed as "old-fashioned" because it did not give 100 percent protection, and "inconvenient" because the necessity of having to insert the device before having sex seemed not to fit the new mood of sexual freedom. By 1973, only about one in fifty (2.4 percent) married women was using it.[24]

Today, the diaphragm appears to be making a come-back among young women who, fed up with side-effects and worried about long-term safety, have abandoned the pill and IUD. In January 1976 an informal check around several state affiliates of Planned Parenthood revealed a small but distinct shift to the diaphragm, and diaphragm manufacturers report increased sales.

*How the diaphragm works* The diaphragm is a soft rubber cup with a sprung rim which you push into your vagina before sexual intercourse and leave there for several hours afterwards. When correctly in position, it fits snugly over the cervix and is held there by the spring tension of the rim, the pelvic bone and vaginal muscles. The main purpose of the diaphragm is to hold in place a cream that kills sperm before it can get into the uterus. It also acts as a barrier to prevent sperm passing through into the cervix (sperm trapped in the vagina cannot survive more than a few hours), but without a spermicidal cream some will get through anyway.

*Failure rate* A recent study[25] of 2,000 women aged thirteen to fifty-four, and mostly unmarried, showed a yearly pregnancy rate of only 2 percent—almost as good as the IUD.

*Causes of failure*

1. If you don't use it *every* time you have sex.
2. If it is the wrong size.
3. If it is not spread correctly with spermicidal cream.
4. If it is not positioned properly over the cervix.
5. If it is defective: any small holes will allow sperm to pass through.
6. If it becomes displaced during intercourse.
7. Even if you use the diaphragm perfectly and none of the possibilities listed above occurs, there is still a small chance you may become pregnant if sperm somehow manage to avoid the cream and slip around the diaphragm into the cervical canal.

*Getting fitted for a diaphragm* You can get a diaphragm from a doctor or at a birth-control clinic. A proper fit is essential, so never be tempted to borrow someone else's or buy one from a druggist without a doctor's prescription. The doctor will give you a general pelvic examination to make sure that your reproductive organs are in healthy shape (women with vaginal or uterine problems cannot wear a diaphragm), and to decide what size you need. If you have just given birth, you must postpone the fitting until about six weeks after the delivery, when your muscles and cervix are back to normal; the same is true after a second-trimester abortion. If you are still a virgin and wish to be fitted with a diaphragm before you have sexual intercourse, you will be advised to stretch your vaginal canal, gently using first one then two fingers, for several weeks beforehand. *Warning:* Try not to tense your vaginal muscles while the doctor is examining you for size, or he might diagnose a smaller diaphragm than you really need.

*Using the diaphragm correctly* It is absolutely essential that the doctor or nurse explains to you exactly how the diaphragm is inserted. Inserting a diaphragm always seems awkward at first. Once you have been told how to do it, keep on practicing right there in the doctor's office until you've got the hang of it. The doctor or nurse can help you check whether you've got it properly in place. If you know what it feels like when it is in right, you'll be more confident of using it at home. Within a very short time you'll find it as easy as inserting a tampon.

*The diaphragm and sexual intercourse* It is perfectly safe to insert your diaphragm up to two hours before you have sexual intercourse. This gives considerable leeway in anticipating sex, so that you don't always have to interrupt a passionate moment. Do not remove it until at least six hours after intercourse; by this time the sperm in the vagina will be destroyed. Do not douche or bathe before removing the diaphragm or you will dilute the cream and reduce its effectiveness. For maximum protection, you should probably insert more cream if your diaphragm has already been inside longer than two hours before you make love—or if you have sex again during the six-hour period. In this case, leave the diaphragm in place for another six hours.

There is some disagreement among doctors as to whether more cream is actually necessary. Dr. Hans Lehfeldt, director of family planning at Bellevue Hospital, New York City, is one of those who believe that spermicides remain potent for twenty-four hours regardless of how often the couple have sex in that time. He says that this was clearly demonstrated in a study[26] he made of spermicides in relation to the cervical cap (see p. 167). Although no other studies have been done to confirm his, as far as he knows, "my findings were very clear and what is true for the cervical cap must also be true for the diaphragm. I have advised my patients for years that extra cream is unnecessary, and they have not become pregnant any more frequently."[27]

*The diaphragm and menstruation* No harm is done if you start menstruating with the diaphragm in place. Some women find it conveniently holds back the blood if they have sexual intercourse during their periods.

Others who suffer from heavy periods find it provides additional protection against a sudden embarrassing flood on social occasions.

*Possible side effects* The diaphragm has none of the risks to health associated with the pill or IUD. It cannot get lost inside you, as some women fear. Very rarely, a few women experience the following minor effects:

*allergic reaction* Any itching or irritation may be due to an allergy to rubber or the spermicidal cream. An allergy to cream may be cured by switching brands. (This sometimes affects a man as well.) If the allergy is to rubber, then a plastic cervical cap may be used instead (see p. 167).

*infection* If the diaphragm is left in place for too long (more than twenty-four hours), there is a chance of infection developing around the cervix because bacteria trapped by the diaphragm will multiply more easily.

*painful intercourse* If this occurs, it is usually because the diaphragm is too big and is buckling against the vaginal wall. If this explanation is ruled out, you should consult a doctor: pain during intercourse can be a sign of several gynecological problems.

*Unanswered questions* The diaphragm seems a perfectly straightforward device. Nevertheless, women sometimes raise questions that cannot be answered with absolute conviction, even though doctors often reply in categorical terms.

*Cancer* It is not known what effect, if any, the diaphragm has on cervical cancer. It is extremely unlikely that it could cause cancer, and there is a possibility that it offers some protection against it, but so far research has not determined whether this is so.

*Vaginal and cervical infections* Cervicitis (inflammation of the cervix) and cervical erosion (sores on the cervix) could possibly be caused or worsened by a diaphragm if it is left in place too long. Whether cervicitis or any of the common vaginal infections could be caused or aggrevated by *normal* diaphragm use is not entirely clear. Studies show a low incidence of vaginitis and cervicitis among women using spermicidal creams so they may offer some protection.

*Looking after your diaphragm* Some women with very active sex lives find they are wearing their diaphragms virtually all the time. However, you should not leave it inside longer than twenty-four hours before taking it out and washing it. Wash it thoroughly with mild soap and warm water and dry it carefully. Dusting with cornstarch or baby powder may help prevent the rubber from perishing, but scented talcum powder should be avoided as it may cause irritation. Latex rubber may be damaged if exposed to any of the following: heat, bright light, oils (e.g. Vaseline), detergents, metals. Make sure that your nails don't pierce the rubber, especially when removing the diaphragm. Check it regularly for holes by holding it up to the light, or by filling it with water and watching for leaks. One should also do this before using it for the first time. In the United States, there is no government supervision on diaphragms (as there is for condoms) and quality control is left to the manufacturers; even with the most rigorous checks, a defective device occasionally gets through.

*Checkups and replacement* The doctor who fits the diaphragm may ask you to return a few weeks later to make sure that you are using it correctly and that there are no problems. This is a good idea, even if it seems like a hassle. If you were a virgin, or had had sex only a few times when the diaphragm was fitted, you will need a new size after a few weeks because your vaginal muscles will expand with sexual experience. You will also need a new size if you have a baby, a second-trimester abortion, pelvic surgery, or gain or lose more than fifteen pounds in weight. With proper care, a diaphragm should last up to two years. If you notice any sign of wear—such as a puckering of the rubber—get a new one.

## The cervical cap
The cap has fallen out of favor since the 1950s, mainly because physicians think that it is too complicated to handle. But this is not necessarily true, and the cap has advantages over the diaphragm that make it worth considering.

*How it works* The cap is similar in principle to the diaphragm but smaller and thimble-like in shape. It fits more securely around the cervix and is held in place by suction. Although some caps are rubber or even metal, most are rigid plastic; recently they have also been made of flexible polythene. Spermicidal cream is placed inside the cap before insertion. However, many women leave the cap in place for days or weeks at a time; plastic cannot corrode inside the body. In this case, more spermicidal cream or foam should be placed deep inside the vagina before every act of intercourse to give maximum protection.

*Failure rate* No recent investigation has been made. The most quoted study,[28] carried out in 1953, established a failure rate of 7.6 pregnancies per 100 women after a year of use. This was based on 28 failures among 143 women (a very small sample) during a period of two and one-half years, and most of the failures were attributed to faulty technique (e.g. not using spermicide cream) or irregular use (not using the cap every time).

*Causes of failure* One report[29] states: "So little is known about the cap's effectiveness that the reasons for its failures can only be surmised. The cap may be dislodged during intercourse if the wrong size has been prescribed, or it may not remain firmly in place if the user has an unusually long or short cervix. Because a properly fitted cap clings by suction deep inside the vaginal canal, however, it is less likely than the diaphragm to be displaced by the excitement phase of intercourse."

*Using the cervical cap* Like the diaphragm, the cap must be fitted initially by a doctor, and you must be taught how to insert and remove it. This process is somewhat more complicated than for the diaphragm, and it will help greatly if you use a speculum (the duck-billed instrument a doctor uses to hold the vaginal walls apart during an examination), and with a mirror and flashlight look inside your vagina.

*Advantages and disadvantages compared to the diaphragm* The main advantage is that it can be used by women with poor muscle tone, uterine prolapse or vaginal damage, or who are allergic to rubber. It can also be left in place for longer periods. It cannot be used by women who suffer from sores on the cervix (cervical erosion), inflammation of the cervix (cervicitis), lacerations of the cervix (when the cervix has been damaged in childbirth) or cervical malformations, such as an unusually long or short cervix. If left in place for long periods, a malodorous secretion may collect inside the cap. This may increase the risk of infection, although that has not been established. The cap may cause some women discomfort and, if made out of rigid plastic, the man may feel it during intercourse. It must always be removed before menstruation.

### The condom

The condom (also known as a rubber or prophylactic) is at present the only contraceptive that can be used by a man. It was first invented in the sixteenth century as a protection against venereal disease. Early versions were made of linen, silk and leather—which explains why Madame de Sévigné, writing to her daughter in the seventeenth century, bitingly put down condoms as "armor against love, gossamer against infection." Neither is true of today's condoms, which are made to high standards of quality from thin latex rubber. The condom was the most popular contraceptive before the pill and IUD were introduced in the 1960s, and in some countries (such as Britain) it still is. The decline of the condom in recent years has certainly contributed to the spread of VD. It has also meant that responsibility for contraception has been transferred from men to women.

*How it works* The condom is a fine but tough rubber sheath which the man rolls onto his erect penis immediately before sexual intercourse. Its purpose is to catch the ejaculated semen so that no sperm escapes into the woman's vagina.

*Failure rate* About 3 pregnancies per 100 couples in a year, if used properly. Two small British studies reported failure rates as low as 0.8 and 1.6. In the first of these, significantly, condoms were delivered to the couples every month to ensure that they did not run out.[30-31] If condoms are used together with spermicide creams (most often they are not) they should provide almost 100 percent protection.

*Causes of failure* The condom can fail if it has holes in it, if it bursts or splits during intercourse, if the man is not careful enough in withdrawing and lets some semen spill into the vagina. Another common cause of failure is when the penis is inserted into the vagina for a short while, before the condom is placed on it; some semen can leak from the penis well before the man has his orgasm.

*Types of condoms* The ordinary condom is a plain sheath of rubber with a rounded tip at one end and a rubber ring at the open end which helps keep the condom on the penis. But there are several variations: One type has a nipple at the end to catch the semen and help prevent the condom from bursting. Another is specially lubricated for couples who need extra lubrication. Condoms made from "skin"—actually membranes from the intestines of young lambs—are twice as expensive as rubber condoms and considered a luxury; they allow greater sensitivity during intercourse. Colored condoms have recently become popular.

*Using the condom* The condom can be put on only when the man's penis has become hard and erect. The man should put it on before his penis has touched any of your sexual parts. Unless he is using a condom with a nipple at the end, he should pinch the end of the condom as he rolls it on so that a space is left in the end to catch the semen. Otherwise some may be forced down the side of the penis, and the condom may burst. A lubricant will also help prevent tearing. This can be saliva or any jelly that is not oil-based (e.g., *not* Vaseline, which will damage the rubber); the best kind, however, is spermicidal cream or jelly which also gives more protection against pregnancy. The lubricant should be applied after the condom is on the penis. After the man has had his orgasm, he should hold the condom on with his fingers as he withdraws his penis so that no semen leaks inside your vagina. For absolute safety, he should withdraw before his penis goes soft and keep it well away from your vagina. *For your own protection,* keep some spermicidal cream or foam handy, even if you do not normally use it with the condom, for instant action if there is an accident.

*Possible side effects* The condom itself is absolutely safe. The only possible side effect is that it could cause irritation for a man or woman who is allergic to rubber, which is very rare.

*How to get condoms* Condoms do not require a doctor's prescription or prior fitting. They are made in a standard size which all men (except those with unusually large penises) can wear comfortably. High quality condoms are best obtained from drugstores or at birth-control clinics. Good, reasonably priced condoms can be ordered by mail from Population Planning Association, 403 Jones Ferry Rd., P.O. 400, Chapel Hill, North Carolina 27514. Commercial mail-order services advertise in some newspapers and magazines. Condoms obtained from slot machines in mens' rooms are not always of the highest quality. Some men are embarrassed the first time they buy condoms across the counter. It helps to know that if the drugstore assistant asks "What size?," he or she is not referring to the size of the man's penis but to the packet: condoms come in packets of three or twelve. There is no reason why women should not buy condoms—particularly as those bought by mail order come in unmarked packets.

*How long do they last?* If kept too long in a wallet or a pocket, body heat will cause the rubber to deteriorate. A high-quality condom may be used four or five times if properly looked after, although most men probably use a condom only once. It should be thoroughly washed and dusted with baby powder or cornstarch (to dry it) and rerolled.

## Spermicidal chemicals (foam, cream, jelly, suppositories)

The insertion of pastes, liquids and jellies into the vagina is one of the oldest forms of birth control. As early as the nineteenth century B.C. Egyptian women were using a mixture of honey and crocodile dung. In later centuries a variety of mixtures was tried, such as frankincense, rock salt dipped in oil, quinine, peppermint and fruit juices. Most were wishful thinking. Some were effective up to a point because their acid content helped to kill sperm, as does another cheap product used for this purpose in many developing countries today—Coca-Cola! However, do-it-yourself spermicides can be harmful and are not very good at preventing pregnancy.

Modern spermicide chemicals are the only female contraceptives that do not need a doctor's prescription, but advertisements for these products (particularly foam) often suggest that they are highly effective when used on their own. This is usually not so. They are effective as adjuncts to other methods and useful as back-ups. They also give some protection against venereal disease and may help counteract vaginal infections.

*How they work* The purpose of spermicides is to destroy sperms before they pass through the cervix and into the uterus. How they do this depends on their chemical ingredients which work in three different ways.[32] Some brands contain two or all three agents:

*Surface active agents* are thought to attach themselves to the sperm, breaking down the cell walls, denying them oxygen and upsetting their metabolism. These agents all have impressively long names, such as p-methanylphenyl polyoxyethylene. Brands available in the United States which contain these agents are: Koromex-A, Orthogynol, Preceptin, Ramses, Conceptrol, Delfen Cream, Delfen Foam, Immolin, Lorophyn, Emko Foam.

*Bactericidal agents* disrupt the metabolism of the sperm by combining with their sulfur and hydrogen bonds. Some of these agents contain phenyl mercuric acetate (PMA), a mercury compound suspected of causing toxic effects (see p. 173). Because the bactericides can also have a destructive effect on the surface of the sperm, they are highly potent when combined with surface active ingredients. American brands containing bactericides are: Koromex-A, Lorophyn, Emko Foam.

*Highly acid agents* are destructive to sperm, which cannot survive long in an environment that is either too acid or too alkaline. Ingredients used in spermicides include lactic acid, boric acid, tartaric and citric acids and gum acacia. American brands containing these are: Koromex-A, and Ramses.

*Failure rate* Theoretically, about 15 pregnancies per 100 women after a year if used on their own. In fact, the variation is enormous and failure rates as low as 2 per 100 and as high as 38 per 100 have been reported. Foam is more effective than cream or jelly, and these in turn are more effective than suppositories. But all of them work best when used with the diaphragm or condom.

To be effective when used alone, the spermicide must spread evenly and thickly high up in the vagina to form a barrier between the cervix and sperm. Whichever spermicide is used, it should be inserted into the vagina before sexual intercourse. More must be put in if you have sex again shortly afterwards.

## How to use spermicides

*Foam* This comes in aerosol cans with an applicator and looks something like shaving cream. The idea is to put two applicatorsful on and around your cervix no more than fifteen minutes before intercourse. Shake the can very hard to aerate the foam thoroughly: the thicker and bubblier it is, the more effective it will be. Put the applicator on the top of the can and force the foam into it according to the instructions. Insert the applicator gently about three or four inches into your vagina (remembering that the vagina tilts back and up) and release the foam onto your cervix. (Brands: Delfen and Emko.)

*Cream and jelly* These come in a tube with an applicator. Insert two lots of cream or jelly into your vagina, depositing it far inside around your cervix, not more than fifteen minutes before intercourse. (Cream brands: Conceptrol, Delfen, Immolin. Jelly brands: Koromex-A, Lorophyn, Orthogynol, Ramses. Koromex is reputed to be effective within an hour after insertion.)

*Suppositories* These are the same chemicals in tablet form. When pushed into your vagina with a finger, they are supposed to dissolve in the heat of your body and spread in the vaginal juices. They do not spread nearly so well as foams or creams and may not melt at all. For best results use about 15 minutes before and immediately after intercourse. (Brand: Lorophyn.)

*Note on all types* Don't confuse spermicides with vaginal sprays or preparations to treat vaginal infections, neither of which has any contraceptive effect. When using spermicides, do not wash or douche for at least six hours after intercourse. If you begin to "leak," a tampon will help.

*Possible side effects* Some women find that the delicate membranes of the vagina are irritated by spermicides. They affect some men in the same way. (As different products have different ingredients, this may be cured by changing to another brand.) That, as far as anyone knows, is the only side effect. However, spermicides contain powerful chemicals, and very few tests have been done to evaluate their safety.

*Unanswered questions* One important question is whether, on occasion, spermicides might have a detrimental effect on the fetus. Thousands of normal, healthy children have, of course, been born over the years to women who were using spermicides at the time of conception. No human abnormalities have ever been connected with spermicides. But there are two reasons why speculation still exists. One is that, biologically, a spermicide could damage the genetic material in the sperm head without destroying the sperm—which might go on to fertilize an egg and lead to abnormalities. The other possibility is that the mercury contained in phenyl mercuric acetate (PMA)—a compound used in some brands of spermicide—might have a toxic effect on a developing embryo in early pregnancy. Animal studies have shown fetal abnormalities as a result of PMA introduced into the vaginas of mice in early pregnancy. The presence of PMA in a spermicide is clearly stated in the labeling and easily avoided.

### Withdrawal
Withdrawal (known medically as "coitus interruptus") is the oldest form of birth control and still widely practiced throughout the world. In the United States it is used mainly by couples who have no information on, or no ready access to, birth-control care or who cannot afford the costs of contraception. It is often relied on by teen-agers.

*How it works* The man withdraws his penis just before he has his orgasm. The sperm is ejaculated outside the woman's vagina.

*Failure rate* Thought to be very high.

*Causes of failure* Sperm can leak from a man's penis long before he has his orgasm. It is very easy for a man to misjudge and fail to withdraw in time. If he ejaculates near the vagina, some sperms may still get inside and swim up into the uterus.

## The rhythm method

The rhythm method was first developed in the 1930s, based on what seemed to be, at that time, sound scientific principles. It was thought that ovulation occurred two weeks before a woman's next menstrual period; that the egg could be fertilized only within twenty-four hours; and that sperm could not remain functional longer than seventy-two hours. This led to the ingenious idea that if a woman could forecast the period during which ovulation was most likely, she could avoid pregnancy by not having sex during that time. It is now known that ovulation can occur *at any time*. And the actual survival time of egg and sperm is still a matter of speculation, so that even if ovulation could be pinpointed exactly, it would still be impossible to tell when it is "safe" to have sex.

Rhythm is still the only method of birth control approved by the Roman Catholic Church. Recently, new rhythm techniques have also been promoted among non-Catholics as "natural family planning"— phraseology that may appear attractive to women who are disenchanted by drugs and devices. It is therefore important to know what these techniques involve and how the claims made for them have been evaluated.

Rhythm does *not* mean simply avoiding sex for a few days in the middle of the menstrual cycle. Each technique depends on making complicated calculations.

*Calendar method* This, the oldest method, is based on the assumption that ovulation occurs between sixteen and twelve days before your next menstrual period starts. That gives five unsafe days; to this is added another three to allow for the time sperm might survive; an extra day for the survival of the egg; and yet another for luck. This already adds up to ten days when you must avoid sex, but applies only to women whose periods fall in absolutely regular twenty-eight-day cycles. Most don't. So you have to use a calendar record of your periods over the previous twelve months to calculate your own variation, which requires expert guidance. The Human Life Foundation, which sponsors research into rhythm, no longer recommends using this method alone.

*Temperature method.* This depends on the idea that when ovulation occurs your basal body temperature (BBT) rises by half a degree or more and stays at the higher level until a day or two before your next period. It is necessary to use a special thermometer, which registers much smaller changes than ordinary ones, and use it at the same time every day—ideally first thing in the morning before getting out of bed, since any activity at all can raise your BBT. If you detect a slight rise on the thermometer you assume you have ovulated; two days later you assume you are safe. For the best results you should use the calendar method as well, and have sex only *after* the rise in BBT and until your next period arrives—which leaves only ten to twelve days each month for intercourse. However it is not reliable: some women have conceived nine days *before* the thermometer recorded a shift in BBT.

*Cervical mucus method* This is the newest rhythm technique, recently promoted as the "ovulation method." Normal discharge, or secretion, from the cervix is linked to changing levels in the estrogen hormone during the menstrual cycle: there is a peak in cervical secretion around the time of ovulation. This has led to the idea that ovulation can be detected by a woman if she examines her cervical mucus every day and learns how to recognize changes in volume, color and consistency. These changes are gradual, but are said to go through five phases:

1. the "dry days" immediately after menstruation when there may be no secretion because of low estrogen levels;
2. the secretion is cloudy yellow or white and has a sticky consistency as estrogen levels begin to rise in the early preovulatory days;
3. the "wet days" immediately before and after ovulation when estrogen levels reach their peak: the discharge increases in volume and becomes clear and highly lubricative with the consistency of egg white;
4. the amount of mucus lessens rapidly, becoming cloudy and sticky, in the days immediately after ovulation when progesterone levels rise;
5. the mucus may again become clear and watery in the few days before menstruation, although this does not always happen.

It has been claimed that this method can be used on its own, without charts or thermometers, and allows sexual intercourse both before and after ovulation. However, the changes are not always easy to detect, particularly for the many women with vaginal infections which cause abnormal discharges. According to one report,[33] ". . . for the present, physicians, statisticians, and program administrators remain doubtful about the technique itself as well as statistics and tactics used to promote it."

*Self-examination method* The cervical os (the hole in the middle of the cervix) is closed in the early preovulatory period and after ovulation, but gradually opens as ovulation approaches, and the cervix itself becomes softer during ovulation. A woman may be able to observe these changes in herself if she uses a speculum and mirror (see p. 168). Some women in self-examination groups have attempted this. But again the changes are not always easily recognized, particularly in women with cervical damage.

*Sympto-thermal method* This is a combination of several techniques, recently promoted as "natural family planning." It combines taking one's basal body temperature with observing cervical mucus changes plus any other symptoms (such as the abdominal twinges some women feel at ovulation or observed changes in the cervical os). High motivation and considerable time are required.

*More information* To use any rhythm method properly, you need expert guidance. Any federally funded birth-control clinic should provide information, or your state or city department of health may be able to refer you to a physician or counselor trained to teach different methods. The Margaret Sanger Center (see p. 58) offers free information leaflets on rhythm. Basal thermometers are available from most pharmacies.

### Female sterilization

This is a surgical operation that makes it virtually impossible for a woman to have children. Until quite recently, prejudice against a woman being sterilized simply because she wanted no more children was strong in the medical profession. Today, voluntary sterilization has become one of the most popular forms of birth control in the United States. About 90 percent of female sterilizations are done for contraceptive reasons. In 1974, an estimated 1.3 million operations were performed.[34]

Far more controversial is the question of compulsory sterilization. Many states still have laws which permit people, particularly the mentally sick, to be forcibly sterilized. This had led to several cases of abuse in which normal women have been sterilized without their informed consent. At present, the issue is legally confused. It is therefore important to seek help immediately from your local American Civil Liberties Union if you find anyone trying to pressure you into being sterilized.

*How it works* The Fallopian tubes are cut and tied (tubal ligation) or blocked (tubal occlusion) or burned through (cautery) so that sperm cannot reach the egg and fertilization can no longer occur. Female sterilization always requires an operation. This may be performed in one of several ways:

*Laparotomy* This is the most traditional procedure for tubal ligation. A cut about 2 inches long is made in the abdomen and each tube is exposed in turn. Each is tied (ligated) with catgut in two places and the tube is then cut through between the ligations. This method is regarded as major surgery; it is usually performed under a general anesthetic and the woman must stay in the hospital for several days.

*Mini-laparotomy* This procedure (sometimes known as "mini-lap") is the most recent development in tubal ligation. Only a small incision, about an inch long, is made in the lower abdomen, below the pubic hairline. Because the cut is so small, mini-lap can be performed with a local anesthetic on an outpatient basis.

*Colpotomy* This is similar to laparotomy except that the surgeon, instead of cutting though the abdomen, makes an incision in the cul-de-sac of the vagina which is behind the cervix.

*Laparoscopy* This was the first technique to allow sterilizations to be done on an outpatient basis with local anesthetic. The surgeon inserts a needle into the abdominal cavity and fills it with gas (carbon dioxide) to make the abdomen taut. Two tiny holes are made: the surgeon inserts a laparoscope (an instrument with lights and mirrors) through one hole so that he can look directly at the Fallopian tubes; through the other he inserts electrocautery forceps, the tips of which heat up instantly to about 800 degrees F. The forceps grasp each Fallopian tube in turn and cauterizes them (burns them through so that the divided edges are sealed). A newer laparoscopic technique is to place rings or clips round the tubes to block them (occlusion), which avoids some of the risks involved in cautery. Another variation uses only one incision instead of two.

*Culdoscopy* As with colpotomy, the incision is made in the cul-de-sac of the vagina. As with laparoscopy, it can be done as an outpatient procedure and uses an instrument for viewing the Fallopian tubes directly (the culdoscope). The tubes are either cut and tied (ligated) or sealed off with clips (occluded).

*Hysteroscopy* This method is still regarded as experimental and has a high failure rate (often more than 10 percent). The approach to the Fallopian tubes is made through the vagina and uterus. An instrument similar to a laparoscope is inserted into the uterus, which is distended with gas (usually carbon dioxide), so that the opening of the tubes into the uterus can be seen. A small electrocautery probe is inserted into these openings, the tip is instantly heated and cauterizes the tube ends. Scar tissue then forms, blocking the tubes.

*A warning on hysterectomy* Hysterectomy is the removal of the entire uterus, performed mainly for medical reasons when the uterus has become badly damaged or diseased. However, hysterectomies have been increasingly performed simply to sterilize women or, in many cases, to abort and sterilize them at the same time. Gynecologists who defend this practice maintain that it prevents uterine disease (including cancer) later on. They also argue that the uterus is no more than a "baby carriage"—a useless organ for any woman who wants no further pregnancies. Those opposed point out that no one can yet say whether the uterus has a function other than for pregnancy and claim that hysterectomies are often performed solely for financial motives: a hysterectomy may cost up to $1,500 compared to $500 or less for tubal ligation or laparoscopy. What is certain is that the death risk from hysterectomy (estimated at 300 to 500 deaths per 100,000 operations) is far, far higher than for ordinary sterilizations (10 to 30 per 100,000), and the complication rate is correspondingly higher.[35]

*Failure rate* Sterilization is not always 100 percent successful. A few women do become pregnant after the operation. Studies show a range of between zero and two percent, but a great deal depends on the skill of the surgeon. When correctly performed, laparoscopy has the lowest pregnancy rate of four per 1,000 sterilizations or less.[36]

*Causes of failure* The commonest reason is not that the operation fails but that the woman, unknown to herself and the surgeon, is already pregnant at the time of the operation. To avoid this happening, it is best to be sterilized immediately after menstruation. Some doctors prefer to scrape out the uterus with a curette before sterilizing, to make sure there is no newly fertilized egg left in the uterine lining.

Occasionally the Fallopian tubes join up again naturally—a process known as re-anastomosis. This is more likely to happen when the tubes have been occluded by clips, which may work loose and fall off, than when the tubes are ligated or cauterized. Rarely, the surgeon may not succeed in completely cauterizing a tube during laparoscopy, so that sperm can still reach the egg. There have also been incidents of surgeons mistaking the tube and cauterizing or cutting the round ligament (a support ligament in the abdominal cavity) instead of the Fallopian tube. This is more easily done in those methods that use the vaginal approach and make it more difficult for the surgeon to see what he is doing.

*Reversibility* Sterilization is usually thought of as an irreversible procedure. In most cases, that is true. However, a few surgeons have succeeded in rejoining the tubes of women previously sterilized so that they have been able to have children, though most doctors take the view that a woman who has been sterilized should stick with her decision. But a growing minority acknowledge that women today are being sterilized very young, and if a woman's circumstances change (for example, if her children die or she remarries) she may bitterly regret that earlier decision. So there is a feeling among a few doctors that young women should be sterilized only by a method that gives some chance of reversal later on. The currently most popular method, cauterization by laparoscopy, makes it virtually impossible to rejoin the tubes. Traditional laparotomy has a higher chance of successful reversal, depending on the skill of the surgeon. The latest hope is the use of laparoscopy to block off the tubes with rings or clips that can later be removed, but it is not known yet how successful this might be.

*Making up your mind about sterilization* Sterilization will in no way interfere with your natural hormonal rhythms: you continue to ovulate and menstruate in the normal way, and your pleasure in sex should not be affected. Nevertheless, some women emotionally equate fertility with femininity, and a few have said that they cannot enjoy sex as much when they know they cannot conceive. You should confront the prospect honestly before having a sterilization operation. Some clinics, such as Planned Parenthood, offer counseling to women who are considering sterilization.

## How to get contraception when you are not married

Unmarried people can now obtain contraceptives much more easily than ever before. Two types of contraception—condoms and spermicides—are universally available without restriction from drugstores. However, three factors may inhibit women from seeking good contraceptive care: having to see a doctor to obtain the pill, IUD or diaphragm, the law in some areas which makes it difficult for a teen-ager to get those contraceptives without her parents' consent, and the matter of cost.

*Going to a doctor* To provide contraception for anyone who wants it counts as good medical care, and most doctors no longer discriminate against unmarried women. Very often a doctor will not even ask if you are married. Birth-control clinics such as Planned Parenthood have specific policies of treating all women alike, regardless of marital status. But of course there are always exceptions. Some doctors may not be able to resist delivering a lecture on morality to a single woman who requests contraceptive care. Such a situation can usually be avoided by going to a birth-control clinic or by choosing your doctor with care. However, if it should happen don't be intimidated; consult another doctor.

A more frequent cause for complaint these days is that a doctor may promote his or her own bias about which contraceptive is best. Some doctors are so pro-pill that they hardly consider another method, while some are so against it that they refuse to prescribe it to any patient. Or they go through phases: "I had to fight my doctor to get on the pill," said one woman, "and I had to fight him to come off it." Some are forthright about their own biases. For example, a gynecologist who runs a large student health center freely admitted that his own views probably accounted for the high proportion of his patients who use the diaphragm. "They often ask me what my own daughters use and I tell them —the diaphragm."

### If you are a minor

Can you obtain contraceptives without your parents' (or guardians') consent? The answer depends on the kind of contraceptives you require, the federal and state laws and the attitude of individual doctors.

*Nonprescription contraceptives* You can freely obtain condoms or spermicides at any age from pharmacies or clinics in every state.

*Contraceptives that require a doctor's prescription* Under federal law, you do not need parental consent to obtain the pill, IUD or diaphragm if:

(a) you ask for them under a family planning program that is subsidized by the government; or

(b) you are receiving welfare.

Aside from these two categories, however, it depends on the laws of your state. According to the latest survey,[37] you can get prescription contraceptives without parental consent at the following ages:

*At any age:* Alaska, Arkansas, California, Colorado, Florida, Georgia, Idaho, Illinois, Kansas, Kentucky, Maine, Maryland, Michigan, Minnesota (unless, in this state, a parent has already notified the doctor or clinic of an objection), Mississippi, New Hampshire, New York, Ohio, Pennsylvania, Tennessee, Utah, Virginia, District of Columbia

*At age 12:* Delaware (providing, the statute says, that you are *already* sexually active!)

*At age 14:* Alabama
*At age 15:* Oregon
*At age 16:* South Carolina
*At age 18:* Arizona, Connecticut, Hawaii, Indiana, Iowa, Louisiana, Massachusetts, Montana, Nevada, New Jersey, New Mexico, North Carolina, North Dakota, Oklahoma, Rhode Island, South Dakota, Texas, Vermont, Washington, West Virginia, Wisconsin
*At age 19:* Nebraska, Wyoming
*At age 21:* Missouri

*Doctors' attitudes* Some doctors give contraceptives to minors without asking for parental consent even when their state laws require it. This is also the policy of Planned Parenthood clinics.

*Financial responsibility* If your state law allows you to consent to your own contraceptive care, you must also take responsibility for paying for it. All states that have passed such laws have exempted parents from any financial liability.

*Special services for teen-agers* Some clinics and hospitals provide special birth-control services for young people, with a staff selected to be especially sympathetic to their needs. Check with your state, county or city department of health.

# Source References

## 1. Diagnosing Pregnancy

1. Christopher Tietze, "Probability of Pregnancy Resulting from a Single Unprotected Coitus," *Fertility and Sterility*, 11: 485 (1960).
2. "Diethylstilbestrol as a Post-Coital Oral Contraceptive; Patient Labelling," U.S. Food and Drug Administration, *Federal Register*, 40: 5351 (1975).
3. T. Crist, "Post-Coital Estrogen," *Journal of Reproductive Medicine*, 13: 198 (1974). Summarized in *Family Planning Perspectives*, Vol. 7, No. 2 (March/April 1975).
4. L. K. Kuchera, "Post-Coital Contraception with Diethylstilbestrol, Updated," *Contraception*, 10: 47 (1974).
5. J. Lippes, T. Malik and H. J. Tatum, "The Post-Coital Copper T," paper presented at the annual meeting of the Association of Planned Parenthood Physicians, Los Angeles, April 1975. Summarized in *Family Planning Perspectives*, Vol. 7, No. 4 (July/August 1975).
6. In interview with author.
7. "Menstrual Regulation in the United States: A Preliminary Report" (University of North Carolina), *Fertility and Sterility* (March 1975).
8. "Menstrual Regulation Update," Population Report, Series F No. 4, George Washington University Medical Center (May 1974).
9. International Fertility Research Program (University of North Carolina), analysis of data on menstrual extraction from 22 countries: quoted in *Population Report (ibid.)*.
10. Judy Stringer, "Menstrual Regulation," a report on clinical research at three London teaching hospitals, presented at a symposium on "Out-Patient Abortion," London, England (November 1974).
11. R. Landesman and B. B. Saxena, "Results of the First 1,000 Radioreceptorassays for the Determination of HCG: A New, Rapid and Sensitive Test for Pregnancy," paper presented at the annual meeting of the American Fertility Society, Los Angeles (April 1975) and summarized in *Family Planning Perspectives*, Vol. 7, No 3 (May/June 1975). "The Use of a Radioreceptorassay of HCG for the Diagnosis and Management of Ectopic Pregnancy," *Fertility and Sterility*, Vol. 26, No. 5 (May 1975).

12. Eve W. Paul, Harriet F. Pilpel, Nancy F. Wechsler, "Pregnancy, Teenagers and the Law, 1976," *Family Planning Perspectives,* Vol. 8, No. 1 (January/February 1976).
13. *New York Times* (July 11, 1974).
14. For example: "Abortion referrals—a web of complaints," by Mark Reutter, *Baltimore Evening Sun,* Md. (October 27, 1974); "Profit, Error in Abortions," by Elizabeth Duff, *Philadelphia Inquirer,* Pa. (August 19, 1973); "Doctors O.K. Needless Abortions," by Jeannie Borba and Nancy Smith, *Evening Outlook,* Los Angeles (October 14, 1972).

## 3. Marriage

1. Data provided by the National Center for Health Statistics (1976).
2. Kristin Luker, *Taking Chances: Abortion and the Decision Not To Contracept* (Berkeley: University of California Press, 1975).
3. "Nearly half of all teenage marriages break up within 5 years and the rates are even higher for young people who marry primarily in response to a pregnancy." *Congressional Record* S 16030 (September 17, 1975).

## 4. Abortion

1. *Williams' Obstetrics,* 14th edition (New York: Appleton-Century-Crofts Educational Division, Meredith Corp., 1971).
2. Report to the National Commission for the Protection of Human Subjects (1975).
3. C. Tietze, "Two Years' Experience with a Liberal Abortion Law," *Family Planning Perspectives*, Vol. 5, No. 1 (Winter 1973).
4. *Legalized Abortion and the Public Health,* Institute of Medicine, National Academy of Sciences, Washington D.C. (May 1975).
5. Charles G. Child III, "Mortality ratios of selected surgical procedures, U.S.A. 1969," from *Life and Death in Medicine* (San Francisco: W.H. Freeman, 1973).
6. C. Tietze and S. Lewit, "Joint Program for the Study of Abortion: Early Medical Complications of Legal Abortion," *Studies in Family Planning,* The Population Council (1972).
7. Report of the Committee on the Working of the Abortion Act (Chairman: The Hon. Mrs. Justice Lane DBE), Her Majesty's Stationary Office, London (1974).
8. J.K. Russell, "Sexual Activity and Its Consequences in the Teenager," *Clinics in Obstetrics and Gynecology,* I: 683–698 (December 1974).
9. J.F. Jekel et al., "A Comparison of the Health of Index and Subsequent Babies Born to School-Age Mothers," *American Journal of Public Health* 65: 370–374 (April 1975).
10. S. Fleck, "Some Psychiatric Aspects of Abortion," *Journal of Nervous and Mental Diseases,* 151: 44 (1970).

11. E. Weinstock, C. Tietze, F. Jaffe and J. Dryfoos, "Abortion Need and Services in the United States, 1974–5," *Family Planning Perspectives*, Vol. 8, No. 2 (March/April 1976).

12. "Fertility Related Insurance Coverage Found Limited," *Family Planning Perspectives*, Vol. 7, No. 5 (September/October 1975).

## 5. Pregnancy

1. "Effects of Childbearing on Maternal Health," Population Reports, Series J No. 8, George Washington University Medical Center (November 1975).

2. N. Shaw, *"So You're Going To Have A Baby"* (Elmsford, N.Y.: Pergamon Press, 1973).

3. Guidelines on Sex Discrimination, issued by the Equal Employment Opportunity Commission (March 31, 1972).

4. Elizabeth Ann Reinhardt v. Board of Education of Alton Community Unit School, Illinois State Circuit Court, Third Judicial Circuit, Madison County (1973). Quoted in *Employment Practice Decisions*, Vol. 7, p. 6431.

5. Guidelines on Sex Discrimination, issued by the Equal Employment Opportunity Commission (March 31, 1972).

6. *A Working Woman's Guide to her Job Rights*, U.S. Department of Labor Women's Bureau, U.S. Government Printing Office, Washington D.C. (revised 1975).

7. La Fleur et al. v. Cleveland Board of Education et al., and Cohen v. Chesterfield County School Board, U.S. Supreme Court (January 21, 1974). Quoted in *Family Planning/Population Reporter*, Vol. 3, No. 1 (February 1974).

8. HEW's Office of Civil Rights regulations for the enforcement of Title IX of the Educational Amendments, part B, section 86.37 (1975).

9. Dr. Luella Klein, Director of the Maternal and Infant Care Project, Emory University School of Medicine, Atlanta, Georgia, "Models of Comprehensive Service—Regular School-Based," *The Journal of School Health*, special issue on school-age parents, Vol. 45 No. 5 (May 1975).

10. Phillip J. Goldstein et al., Department of Obstetrics and Gynecology, San Francisco General Hospital, "Vocational Education: An Unusual Approach to Adolescent Pregnancy," *Journal of Reproductive Medicine* (February 1973).

11. Guidelines on Sex Discrimination, issued by the Equal Employment Opportunity Commission (March 31, 1972).

12. *Facts about Women's Absenteeism and Labor Turnover*, U.S. Department of Labor, Wage and Labor Standards Administration (August 1969).

13. Barbara Shacks, Assistant Director, New York Civil Liberties Union; statement before congressional hearings on the Economic Problems of Women (July 12, 1973).

14. *Ibid.*

15. *Women and Insurance,* California Commission on the Status of Women (February 1975).
16. "Supreme Court Upholds Jobless Pay During Pregnancy," *Family Planning/Population Reporter,* Vol. 4, No. 6 (December 1975).
17. "U.S. Supreme Court Rules the Unborn Not 'Dependent' for Purposes of AFDC," *Family Planning/Population Reporter,* Vol. 4, No. 2 (April 1975).

## 7. Bringing Up a Child on Your Own

1. U.S. Census Bureau statistics (1960 and 1970).
2. U.S. Census Bureau annual survey (March 1975).
3. *U.S. Working Women, A Chart-book,* U.S. Department of Labor, Bureau of Labor Statistics (1975).
4. Bruno Stein, *Work and Welfare in Britain and the USA* (New York and London: Macmillan, 1976).
5. Congressional hearings on the Child and Family Services Act 1975, Vol. I, p 135.
6. Elsa Ferri, *Growing Up in a One-Parent Family,* a National Children's Bureau Report, London (1976).
7. L. Kriesberg, *Mothers in Poverty* (Chicago: Aldine, 1970).
8. Testimony of Dr. Urie Bronfenbrenner before the Subcommittee on Children and Youth. *American Families: Trends and Pressures 1973,* p. 136.
9. Margaret O'Brien Steinfels, *Who's Minding the Children? The History and Politics of Day-Care in America* (New York: Simon and Schuster, 1973).
10. *U.S. Working Women, a Chart-Book, op. cit.*
11. Katie Mae Andrews et al. v. Drew Municipal Separate School District U.S. District Court, Greenville Division, Mississippi, No. GC 73–20-K (July 3, 1973). See *Employment Practices Decisions,* Vol 6, p. 5217.
12. Drew Municipal Separate School District v. Andrews. U.S. Supreme Court, No. 74–1318; CA 5, No. 73–3177 (May 3, 1976).

## 8. Contraception

1. Luigi Mastroianni, Jr., "Rhythm: Systematized Chance-Taking," *Family Planning Perspectives,* Vol. 6, No. 4 (Fall 1974).
2. Christopher Tietze, "Probability of Pregnancy Resulting from a Single Unprotected Coitus," *Fertility and Sterility,* 11: 485 (1960).
3. N.B. Ryder, "Contraceptive Failures in the United States," *Family Planning Perspectives,* Vol. 5, No 3 (Summer 1973).
4. "Oral Contraceptives and Health: an interim report," Royal College of General Practitioners, London 1974, published in the U.S. by Pitman Publishing Corporation, New York. This is the first report of an ongoing investigation into 23,611 British pill-takers compared with 22,766 nonusers.
5. Elizabeth B. Connell, "The Pill Revisited," *Family Planning Perspectives,* Vol. 7, No. 2 (March/April 1975).

6. D.H. Carr, "Chromosome studies in selected spontaneous abortions: conception after oral contraceptives," *Canadian Medical Association Journal*, 103: 343–348 (1970).

7. S. Rancharan, ed., "The Walnut Creek Contraceptive Drug Study, a prospective study of the side effects of oral contraceptives: Vol. I—Findings in Oral Contraceptive Users and Non-Users on Entry into Study," 1975. HEW, U.S. Government Printing Office, Washington D.C. This is the first report of a major American ongoing investigation into 21,000 women who currently use, formerly used or have never used the pill.

8. Collaborative Group for the Study of Stroke in Young Women: "Oral Contraceptives and Stroke in Young Women—Associated Risk Factors," *Journal of the American Medical Association*, 231: 718 (1975).

9. W.H.W. Inman and M.P. Vessey, "Investigation of deaths from pulmonary, coronary and cerebral thrombosis and embolism in women of childbearing age," *British Medical Journal*, 2: 193–9 (April 27, 1968).

10. J.I. Mann, M.P. Vessey, M. Thorogood and R. Doll, "Myocardial Infarction in Young Women with special reference to Oral Contraceptive Practice," *British Medical Journal*, 2: 241 (May 3, 1975).

11. J.I. Mann and W.H.W. Inman, "Oral Contraception and Death from Myocardial Infarction," *British Medical Journal, op. cit.*

12. J.I. Mann and W.H.W. Inman: unpublished data.

13. R. Hertz, "The problem of possible effects of oral contraceptives on cancer of the breast," *Cancer*, 24: 1140–1145 (December 1969). Also R. Hertz, "Report of the task force on carcinogenesis; appendix 3, Second report on oral contraceptives, U.S. Food and Drug Administration (August 1969).

14. S.G. Silverberg and E.L. Makowski, "Endometrial Carcinoma in Young Women Taking Oral Contraceptive Agents," *Journal of Obstetrics and Gynecology*, 46: 5 (November 1975).

15. "Oral contraceptives and venous thromboembolic disease, surgically confirmed gall bladder disease and breast tumors," Boston Collaborative Drug Surveillance Program, *Lancet* (June 23, 1973).

16. D.F. Hawkings, J. Bonnar, M. Smith et al., research papers published in the *British Medical Journal* (1974) and summarized in *Family Planning Perspectives*, Vol. 7, No. 4 (July/August 1975).

17. "IUDs Reassessed—A Decade of Experience," *Population Report*, Series B No. 2 (January 1975), Department of Medical and Public Affairs, George Washington University Medical Center, Washington D.C. 20009.

18. "Analysis of Intra-Uterine Contraception," edited by F. Hefnawi and S.J. Segal (North-Holland Publishing Company, distributed in U.S. by Elsevier Publishing Company Inc., New York, 1975). Proceedings of the Third International Conference on IUDs, held in Cairo, Egypt (December 1974).

19. Marshall E. Schwartz, "The Dalkon Shield: Tale of a Tail," *Family Planning Perspectives*, Vol. 6, No 4 (Fall 1974).

20. "Current Trends—IUD Safety: report of a nationwide physician survey," HEW Center for Disease Control, *Morbidity and Mortality*, 23: 226 (1974).

21. M.P. Vessey et al., "Outcome of Pregnancy in Women Using an Intra-Uterine Device," *Lancet*, 1: 495 (1974).

22. HEW Center for Disease Control Report, *op. cit.*

23. "The Diaphragm and Other Intravaginal Barriers," *Population Report*, Series H No. 4 (January 1976).

24. 1973 National Study of Family Growth, National Center for Health Statistics (1976).

25. Mary Lane et al., "Successful use of the diaphragm and jelly by a young population: report of a clinical study," *Family Planning Perspectives*, Vol. 8, No. 2 (March/April 1976).

26. H. Lehfeldt et al., "Spermicidal effectiveness of chemical contraceptives used with the firm cervical cap," *American Journal of Obstetrics and Gynecology*, Vol. 82 (2), 446–8 (August 1961).

27. Interview with Dr. Lehfeldt.

28. C. Tietze et al., "The effectiveness of the cervical cap as a contraceptive method," *American Journal of Obstetrics and Gynecology*, 66: 904–8 (October 1953).

29. Vessey et al, "Outcome of Pregnancy in Women Using an Intra-Uterine Device," 495.

30. J. Peel, "A male-oriented fertility control experiment," *General Practitioner*, 202: 677–81 (May 1969).

31. J. Peel, "The Hull Family Survey II: family planning in the first five years of marriage," *Journal of Biosocial Science*, 4 (3) 333–346 (July 1972).

32. "Vaginal Contraceptives—A Time for Reappraisal?", *Population Report*, Series H, No 3 (January 1975).

33. "Birth Control Without Contraceptives," *Population Report*, Series I, No. 1 (June 1974).

34. B. Gonzales, "Estimate of numbers of voluntary sterilizations performed," Association for Voluntary Sterilization, New York (1975).

35. "Elective hysterectomies," *Medical World News* (November 24, 1972).

36. B.H. Thompson and C.R. Wheeless, "Failures of Laparoscopy Sterilization," *Obstetrics-Gynecology*, 45 (6): 659–664 (June 1975).

37. E.W. Paul, H. Pilpel, N.F. Wechsler, "Pregnancy, Teenagers and the Law," *Family Planning Perspectives*, Vol. 8, No 1 (January/February 1976).

# Index

abortion, x, 7, 22, 32, 34, 41–65
  after-care, 61, 62–64
  Catholic counseling for, 26
  checking quality of, 59–62
    after-care, 61
    birth-control information, 61–62
    confirmation of pregnancy, 60
    counseling, 60
    emergency measures, 61
    medical history, 60
    medical screening, 60
    medical tests, 61
  cost of, 62
  criminal type of, 45–46
  D and C, 44, 46, 47, 49, 51
  decision for or against, 30
  within fourteen days (of overdue period), 46
  hysterectomy, 47, 48–49
  intra-amniotic injection, 47–48
  IUD insertion after, 162
  legal, 46–49
  medical thinking on, 42
  obtaining, 57–59
    hospital care, 59
    referrals, 58–59
    through clinics, 57–58
  prostaglandin, 47, 48
  publications on, 64–65
  rights organizations, 64
  safety and, 49–57
    long-term complications, 51–53

    minimizing the risks, 55
    psychological consequences, 53–55
    religious and moral feelings, 55–57·
    risk of complications, 50–51
    risk of death, 49–50
  saline (salt) solution, 48
  self-induced, 45
  after sixteen weeks, 47
  spontaneous, 44–45
  stages of pregnancy and, 41–44
  suction method, 47, 49
  Supreme Court on, 41, 45, 51
  between thirteen and sixteen weeks, 46
  under thirteen weeks gestation, 46
  *See also* menstrual extraction
*Abortion: A Woman's Guide* (Planned Parenthood of New York City), 64
abortion clinics, 17–18, 57–58
  availability of, 58
*Abortion Controversy, The* (Sarvis and Rodman), 64
abortion counselors, 25, 60
*Abortion Eve* (Lyvely and Sutton), 65
*Abortion Factbook* (Population Council), 65
*Abortion: Law, Choice and Morality* (Callahan), 55–56, 64

*Abortion Surveillance* (Department of Health, Education and Welfare), 65
*Abortion Two: Making the Revolution* (Lader), 64
activity, feelings of, 20
adoption, 87–98
  arrangements, 91–95
  agency, 91–92
  blackmarket, 83, 93
  consent, 94
  legal process, 93–95
  nonagency, 92–93
  relinquishment, 94–95
  decision for or against, 30
  pros and cons of, 87–91
  child's feelings, 88–89
  mother's feelings, 89–91
  single-parent, 95–96
  *See also* fostering
adoption agencies, 26, 91–92
  finding, 92
Adoption Resource Exchange of North America (ARENA), 96
Aid to Families with Dependent Children (AFDC), 82, 83, 100, 113–14, 115, 117, 121, 124, 126–30
  application form, 127
  basis of claim, 128
  decision for, 128
  emergency payments, 128
  help with welfare problems, 129
  how to apply, 127
  interview, 127
  people who can help, 130
  published information on, 129–30
  registering for work or training, 128–29
  verification, 128
Alan Guttmacher Institute, 65
alimony, 125
American Civil Liberties Union, 81, 123, 139, 176

American Civil Liberties Union Reproductive Freedom Project, 64
American College of Nurse-Midwives, 71
American College of Obstetricians and Gynecologists, 159
*American Families, Trends and Pressures,* 138
American Institute of Medicine, 49, 52, 54
American Medical Association, 16
American Society for Psychoprophylaxis in Obstetrics, 75
anxiety, feelings of, 66
apathy, feelings of, 20
Arms, Suzanne, 73
Atkin, Edith, 105

Barrett, Elizabeth, 120
basal body temperature (BBT), 174, 175
benign breast tumors, 151
Big Brothers, 137–38
Binder, Mary-Jo, 130
Bing, Elisabeth, 76
*Birth* (Milinaire), 73
Birth Center, The, 71–72
birth-control, *see* contraception
birthright or lifeline groups, 25
black market adoption, 83, 93
blood-clotting disorders, 149
blood tests, 12
Boston Women's Health Collective, 69, 72–73, 76
Bowlby, John, 114, 115
breast cancer, 151
breast changes, 4
breast-feeding, IUDs and, 163
Breibart, Vicki, 120
bringing up a child alone, *see* single-parent family

Caesarean birth, 48
Caine, Lynn, 136

Callahan, Daniel, 55–56, 64
cancer of the cervix (or vagina), 6
cancer and tumors, 151, 166
*candida albicans*, 153
Catholic Alternatives, 26
Catholic Charities, 25
Center on Social Welfare Policy, 130
cerebrovascular disease, 149–50
cervical cancer, 151
cervical cap, 167–68
  causes of failure, 168
  compared to diaphragm, 168
  failure rate, 168
  how it works, 167
  using, 168
cervicitis, 166
Chesler, Phyllis, 140
chicken pox, 153
child support, 124–25
Child Welfare League of America Inc., The, 84, 92, 95, 96, 137
childbirth, IUD insertion after, 162
childbirth preparation classes, 74–76
*Childbirth Without Fear* (Dick-Read), 76
Children's Defense Fund, The, 120, 137
Children's Foundation, The, 137
chloasma, 153
church welfare organizations, 25–26
Civil Rights Act of 1964, 77, 78, 122
Clergy Consultation Service on Abortion, 25, 59
Cleveland Women's Counseling Service, 25, 140
Coca-Cola, 171
cohabitation, 37–38
colpotomy, 177
*Common Sense in Child Rearing* (Wright), 76
*Common Wealth* (newsletter), 130
*Commonsense Childbirth* (Hazell), 76

Community Chest, 120
community counseling organizations, 26
community law centers, 138
Conceptrol, 171, 172
condoms, 168–70
  causes of failure, 169
  failure rate, 169
  how to get, 170
  how long they last, 170
  how it works, 169
  possible side effects, 170
  types of, 169
  using, 169–70
Connolly, Lisa, 135
*Constitutional Aspects of the Right to Limit Childbearing* (Commission on Civil Rights), 65
contraception, 141–81
  cervical cap, 167–68
  condom, 168–70
  diaphragm, 163–67, 179
  female sterilization, 176–79
  how to get, 179–81
    going to doctor, 179–80
    for minors, 180–81
  IUDs, 42, 61, 155–63, 179
  pill (oral contraceptive), 42, 142–55, 179
  rhythm method, 174–76
  spermicidal chemicals, 42, 171–73
  withdrawal (coitus interruptus), 173
copper allergy, 159
copper IUDs, 156, 157
cream and jelly, how to use, 172
credit, 131
criminal abortion, 45–46
crisis centers, 26
culdoscopy, 177
cystitis, 155

Dalkon Shield, 157
*Day Care Book, The* (Breibart), 120

day care centers, 116–21
  for children under six, 116–19
  for school-age children, 119–21
Day-Jermany, Catherine, 130
decisions (what to do when preg-
    nant), 19–31
  immediate reactions and, 19–21
    activity, 20
    apathy, 20
    doubts and fears, 20
    embarrassment, 20
    instant decisions, 21
    pleasure, 19–20
    running away, 21
    suicide, 21
  law and, 27–29
    below age of consent, 27–28
    forcible rape, 28–29
  who to tell, 21–27
    friends, 24
    man who made you pregnant,
      22–23
    parents, 23–24
    professional advice for, 24–27
  working toward a solution, 29–31
    abortion, 30
    adoption, 30
    bringing up child alone, 31
    marriage, 20
deep-vein thrombosis, 149
Delfen Cream, 171
Delfen Foam, 171
Delta Women's Clinic, The, 58
Department of Consumer Affairs
    (New York City), 17
depression, mental, 66, 67, 148
diabetes, 152
diagnosis, pregnancy, 3–18
  abortion clinic and, 17–18
  blood tests, 12
  and "bringing on" periods, 5–10
  cost of tests, 16–17
  free (or low-cost) tests, 17

internal examination, 12–13
  methods, 10–18
  minors (with or without parental
    consent), 14–16
  symptoms, 4–5
  urine tests, 11
  where to go, 13–14
diaphragm, 163–67, 179
  causes of failure, 164
  checkups and replacement, 167
  compared to cervical cap, 168
  failure rate, 164
  getting fitted for, 164–65
  how it works, 164
  looking after, 166–67
  menstruation and, 165–66
  possible side effects, 166
  sexual intercourse and, 165
  unanswered questions, 166
  using correctly, 165
Dick-Read, Grantly, 76
Diethylstilbestrol (DES), 6
dilation and curettage (D and C),
    44, 46, 47, 49, 51
disability insurance, 81
doubts and fears, feelings of, 20, 66
Drabble, Margaret, 74

*Early Medical Complications of
  Legal Abortion* (Population
  Council), 65
ectopic pregnancies, 158–59
Educational Amendments of 1972,
    79
embarrassment, feelings of, 20
embryo, development of, 43
Emko Foam, 171
Emma Goldman Clinic, The, 58, 75
emotional problems, help for,
    139–40
employment:
  during pregnancy, 76–78
  single-parent, 121–24

endometrial cancer, 151–52
Equal Employment Opportunity Commission (EEOC), 76–77, 78, 81, 123
estimated date of delivery (EDD), 72
*Experience of Childbirth, The* (Kitzinger), 73

Fair Housing Act of 1968, 131
*Family Planning Perspectives* (Alan Guttmacher Institute), 65
*Family Planning/Population Reporter* (Alan Guttmacher Institute), 65
family welfare departments, 26
fear or guilt, feelings of, 66
Federation of Jewish Philanthropies, 26
Federation of Protestant Welfare Agencies, 26
female sterilization, 176–79
  causes of failure, 178
  failure rate, 178
  how it works, 176–78
  making up mind about, 179
  reversibility, 178–79
feminist counseling therapy referral services, 140
Feminist Federal Credit Union, 131
Feminist Women's Health Centers, The, 58, 62
fetus, development of, 43
Fitzpatrick, Elsie, 73
fluid retention (edema), 147
foam, how to use, 172
folic acid deficiency, 153–54
Food Research and Action Center, 130–31
food stamp program, 83, 130–31
Ford, Betty, x
Ford, Susan, x

fostering, 96–98
  difference between adoption and, 96
free (or low-cost) pregnancy diagnosis, 17

Gager, Nancy, 136
gallbladder disease, 152
general (money) assistance, 82–83
George Washington University, 142
gestation, 41
Graefenberg Ring, 155
Grimstad, Kirsten, 137
group disability insurance plans, 81
*Guide to the Food Stamp Program*, 130
*Guidelines for Women Seeking Psychotherapy*, 140

*Handbook of Public Assistance Administration*, 129
Hazell, Lester D., 76
Health Insurance Association of America, 62
heart attack, 150–51
high cholesterol levels, 154
Hope, Karol, 135
hormone-releasing IUDs, 156, 157–58
hospital, abortions, 59
hot lines, 26
housing:
  living in a family, 84–85
  maternity homes, 84
  residential jobs, 85, 122
  single-parent and, 131–33
*How to Organize a Multi-Service Women's Center*, 136
human chorionic gonadotropin (HCG), 11
Human Life Foundation, 174
Human Rights for Women Inc., 139

Hundred Woman Years (HWY), 142, 155
hypertension (high blood pressure), 152
hysterectomy, 47, 48–49, 177–78
hysteroscopy, 177
hysterotomy, 47, 48

*Immaculate Deception: A New Look at Women and Childbirth in America* (Arms), 73
Immolin, 171, 172
individual disability insurance, 81
inert IUDs, 155–56
instant decisions, making, 21
internal examination, 12–13
International Childbirth Education Association, 75
intra-amniotic injection, 47–48
intra-uterine device (IUD), 42, 61, 155–63, 179
 after an abortion, 162
 breast-feeding and, 163
 causes of failure, 156–57
 checking that it stays in place, 163
 after childbirth, 162
 failure rates, 156
 getting fitted, 160–62
  choosing an IUD, 161
  examination and tests, 160–61
  FDA requirements, 161
  insertion procedure, 161–62
  pain during and after insertion, 162
  when to have inserted, 161
 how it works, 155–56
 inserted postcoitally, 7–8
 inserted after pregnancy, 162–63
 medical checkup and replacement, 163
 potential effects, 158
  ectopic pregnancies, 158–59
  embolisms, 159
  infection, 158

 side effects, 159
 types of, 157–58
 when not to use, 159–60
 for women who have not given birth, 160

*Jane* (Wells), 74
Joint Program for the Study of Abortion (JPSA), 50, 51, 54

Kaiser Permanente Medical Center, 148
Karmel, Marjorie, 76
Kitzinger, Sheila, 73
Klein, Carole, 96, 136
Klein, Luella, 79
Koromex-A, 171, 172
Kuchera, Lucile K., 6–7

La Leche League International, 76
Lader, Lawrence, 64
Landesman, Dr. Robert, 12
Lane Committee (England), 52, 54–55
Lanham Act of 1941, 115
laparoscopy, 177
laparotomy, 176–77
last menstrual period (LMP), 41, 44
legal abortion, 46–49
Legal Aid, 138
legal problems, help with, 138–39
Legal Services Administration, 139
Legal Services Corporation, 130
Legal Services Program, 130
"Legalized Abortion and the Public Health" (American Institute of Medicine), 49, 52
*Legalized Abortion and the Public Health* (National Academy of Sciences), 65
Lehfeldt, Dr. Hans, 165
Lippes, Dr. Jack, 8, 157
Lippes Loop, 157
liver disorders, 152

living together ("without benefit of marriage"), 37–38
local health department, 14
Lorophyn, 171, 172
low blood sugar, 154
Luker, Kristin, 32
Lyvely, Chin, 65

Manpower Development and Training Act, 124
Margaret Sanger Center, The, 58, 64, 176
marriage, 32–40
  that both want, 33–35
  boyfriend not sure (and you are), 36–37
  decision for or against, 30
  living together without, 37–38
  not sure about, 35–36
  of single-parent, 112–13
  with someone else, 39
  if underage, 39–40
Mastroianni, Luigi, Jr., 141
maternity homes, 84
maternity leave, 80–81
*Maternity Nursing* (Fitzpatrick), 73
Maternity Service Association, 71, 75
Medicaid, 17, 62, 69
Medvin, Jeannine O'Brien, 76
menstrual extraction, 7, 8–10
  acceptability of, 10
  clinical practice, 9–10
  cost of, 10
  effectiveness, 9
  how it works, 9
  safety, 10
  timing, 9
menstruation, diaphragm and, 165–66
Milinaire, Caterine, 73
military hospitals, abortion in, 59
*Millstone, The* (Drabble), 74
mini-laparotomy, 177

missed period, 4, 5
  oral contraceptives and, 144–45
Mitchell, Juliet, x
Modicon, 143
MOMMA, 135, 138
money:
  AFDC, 82, 126–30
  alimony, 125
  child support, 124–25
  credit, 131
  disability insurance, 81
  establishing paternity and, 125–26
  food stamps, 130–31
  general assistance, 82–83
  help from other sources, 83
  paid maternity leave, 80–81
  pregnancy and, 80–83
  single-parent and, 124–31
  social security, 126
  unemployment insurance, 81–82
  welfare, 82
mood changes, 4
morning sickness, 4
"morning-after" pills, 5–7, 42
*Ms Magazine*, 137

National Academy of Sciences, 65
National Alliance Concerned with School-Age Parents, 80
National Center for Comprehensive Emergency Services to Children, 137
National Child Development Study, 101
National Children's Bureau, 100
National Legal Aid and Defender Association, 139
National Organization of Women, 14, 57, 59, 130, 131, 136
NOW Legal Defense and Education Fund, 139
*NOW Marriage and Divorce Task Force Legal Kit*, 139

National Paralegal Institute Inc., 130

National Welfare Rights Organization, 130

*New Woman's Survival Sourcebook, The* (ed. Rennie and Grimstad), 137

Office of Federal Contract Compliance (OFCC), 78

*One Parent Family* (journal), 135

Operation Peace of Mind, 86

Ortho Pharmaceutical Company, 143

Orthogynol, 171, 172

Ota Ring, 155

*Our Bodies, Ourselves* (Boston Women's Health Collective), 69, 72–73

paid maternity leave, 80–81

Parent Locater Service, 124

parents, telling, 23–24

Parents Anonymous, 140

Parents Without Partners, 134–35

*Part-Time Father* (Atkin and Rubin), 105

paternity, establishing, 125–26

periods:
"bringing on," 5–10
IUDs, inserted postcoitally, 7–8
menstrual extraction, 8–10
"morning-after" pills, 5–7
missed, 4, 5, 144–45

Peterson, Deena, 137

phenyl mercuric acetate (PMA), 171, 173

phlebitis, 149

pill (oral contraceptive), 42, 142–55, 179
causes of failure, 143
changing brands, 153
examination for 143
failure rate, 143
how it works, 142–43
periods and, 144–45
planned pregnancy and, 145
potential dangers, 149–53
"progestogen-only," 155
side effects, 145–49
break-through bleeding, 147
breasts, 146
changed sexual desire, 148
delayed or premature menopause, 149
eyes, 146
fatigue, 147–48
fluid retention, 147
hair, 146
headaches and dizziness, 147
increased blood pressure, 148–49
leg cramps or pains, 147
nausea and vomiting, 146
skin, 146
varicose veins, 149
weight gain, 146–47
starting, 143, 144
staying healthy and, 153–55
cholesterol level, 154
folic acid deficiency, 153–54
low blood sugar, 154
potassium and sodium, 154
vitamin $B_6$ deficiency, 154
vitamin C, 154–55
vitamin E deficiency, 154
temporarily coming off, 153

Planned Parenthood, 7, 14, 16, 17, 57, 59, 64, 151, 157, 179
national headquarters, 25

pleasure, feelings of, 19–20

Population Council, 45, 65

Population Planning Association, 170

potassium and sodium deficiency, 154

*Practical Guide to the Women's Movement, A* (ed. Peterson), 137
Preceptin, 171
pregnancy:
    abortion and the stages of, 41–44
    attitudes and feelings, 66–68
    calculating day of, 41
    chances of (after one act of intercourse during a month), 5
    and childbirth, finding out about, 72–76
        preparation classes, 74–76
        through books, 72–74
    decisions (what to do), 19–31
        immediate reactions, 19–21
        law and, 27–29
        who to tell, 21–27
        working toward a solution, 29–31
    diagnosis, 3–18
        abortion clinic and, 17–18
        and "bringing on" periods, 5–10
        methods, 10–18
        symptoms, 4–5
    employment during, 76–78
    housing and, 83–85
        living in a family, 84–85
        maternity homes, 84
        residential jobs, 85
    IUD inserted after, 162–63
    keeping secret, 85–86
    money and, 80–83
        AFDC, 82
        disability insurance, 81
        general assistance, 82–83
        help from other sources, 83
        paid maternity leave, 80–81
        unemployment insurance, 81–82
        welfare, 82
    school education through, 79–80
    "trimester" periods, 42
pregnancy counseling, 24–27
prenatal care, obtaining, 68–72
    assessing quality of, 70–72

*Prenatal Yoga and Natural Childbirth* (Medvin), 76
Preterm (clinic), 58
private health insurance plans, 62
private hospital abortions, 59
professional advice, 24–27, 40
    how to approach, 27
    types of, 25–27
professional counselors and therapists, 26
progestasert device, 157–58
progestogen-only pill (mini-pill), 155
prophylactic, *see* condoms
prostaglandin, 47, 48
public hospital abortions, 59

"quickening" stage, 43
radioassay, 12
radioreceptorassay (RRA), 12
Ramses, 171, 172
rape, 5, 27–29
    forcible, 28–29
    statutory, virginity and, 28
Rape Crisis Center, The, 29
rapists, penalty for, 28
referrals, abortion clinic, 58–59
Religious Coalition for Abortion Rights, 64
Rennie, Susan, 137
residential jobs, 85, 122
Revenue Act of 1971, 120
reversibility, sterilization, 178–79
Rhogam injection, 61, 62
rhythm method, 174–76
    calendar, 174
    cervical mucus, 175
    self-examination, 175–76
    sympto-thermal, 176
    temperature, 174–75
*Rights of Women, The* (Ross), 139
Robins Company (A.H.), 157
Rodman, Hyman, 64
Roman Catholic Church, 174

Ross, Susan Deller, 139
Royal College of General Practitioners (Great Britain), 144
rubbers, *see* condoms
Rubin, Estelle, 105
running away, feelings of, 21
Ryder, Norman B., 142

Saf-T-Coil, 157
saline abortion, 48
San Francisco General Hospital, 80
Sanger, Margaret, ix
Sarvis, Betty, 64
Saxena, Dr. Brij B., 12
self-induced abortion, 45
Sévigné, Mme. de, 168–69
sexual intercourse, diaphragm and, 165
Shacks, Barbara, 81
sickness and nausea, 4
*Single Parent Experience, The* (Klein), 96, 136
Single Parent Resource Center, The, 135
single-parent adoptions, 95–96
single-parent family, 99–140
  children and, 101–6
    aspirations, 102
    does not know his/her father, 105
    family health, 102
    knows his/her father, 103–5
    poverty, 101
    school adjustment, 102
    school performance, 102
  day care (for children under six), 116–19
    family, 117–18
    nonprofit centers, 116–17
    playgroups, 119
    privately hired, 118–19
    profit making centers, 117
    work-related, 118
  day care (for school-age children), 119–21
    finding, 120
    setting up your own, 120
    tax deductions, 120–21
  decision for or against, 31
  employment, 121–24
    discrimination, 122–23
    free-lance, 121–22
    full-time, 121
    part-time, 121
    residential jobs, 122
    vocation training opportunities, 123–24
    working at home, 122
  housing, 131–33
    group living, 133
    living alone, 132
    living with parents, 132
    sharing a home, 132–33
  life of your own, 109–12
    new relationships with men, 110–12
  marriage, contemplating, 112–13
  money and, 124–31
    AFDC, 126–30
    alimony, 125
    child support, 124–25
    credit, 131
    establishing paternity, 125–26
    food stamps, 130–31
    social security, 126
  number of (1975), 99
  problems, 106–9
    building confidence, 107–9
    child's problems, 107
    tension and strain, 106–7
  survival strategy, 134–40
    community self-help, 137
    for emotional problems, 139–40
    help for children, 137–38
    for legal problems, 138–39
    publications, 135–36

self-help for women, 136–37
work and education, 113–16
*Six Practical Lessons for an Easier Birth* (Bing), 76
*Smoking and Pregnancy* (Department of Health, Education and Welfare), 73
social security, 126
social service departments, 26
social welfare departments, 26
social workers, 26
Spalding, Elizabeth, 139
spermicidal chemicals, 42, 171–73
  bactericidal agents, 171
  failure rate, 172
  highly acid agents, 171–72
  how to use, 172
  how they work, 171
  note on types of, 172–73
  possible side effects, 173
  surface active agents, 171
  unanswered questions, 173
spontaneous abortion, 44–45
*Stanley v. Illinois*, 94
statutory rape, virginity and, 28
sterilization, female, 176
suction method of abortion, 47, 49
suicide, feelings of, 21
suicide prevention services, 139–40
*Summary of the Aid to Families with Dependent Children* (Day-Jermany), 130
suppositories, how to use, 172
Sutton, Joyce, 65
symptoms, pregnancy, 4–5

teaching hospitals, 69–70
*Thank You, Doctor Lamaze* (Karmel), 76
thromboembolism, 6, 149, 159
Tietze, Christopher, 45–46
toxemia, 68

unemployment insurance, 81–82
U.S. Commission on Civil Rights, 65
U.S. Department of Defense, 59
U.S. Department of Health, Education and Welfare, 62, 65, 73, 82, 129–30
U.S. Department of Labor, 121, 124
U.S. Food and Drug Administration (FDA), 6, 153, 157, 161
U.S. Supreme Court, ix, 32, 41, 45, 51, 62, 81, 82, 94
University of Michigan, 124
urine, passing frequently, 4
urine tests, 11

vaginal infections, 152–53, 166
venereal disease, 153, 169
  contraception and, 159–60
Vermont Women's Health Centers, 58
vitamin $B_6$ deficiency, 154
vitamin C, 154–55
vitamin E deficiency, 154
vocational training opportunities, 123–24

welfare, 82, 113–14, 121; *see also* Aid to Families with Dependent Children (AFDC)
Wells, Dee, 74
*Widow* (Caine), 136
withdrawal (coitus interruptus), 173
Womancare of Feminist Women's Health Center, 75
*Women and Credit* (National Organization for Women), 131
*Women and Madness* (Chesler), 140
Women in Transition, 135
*Women in Transition, A Feminist Handbook on Separation and Divorce*, 125, 131, 135–36

Women's Action Alliance, The, 59, 69, 136, 137

Women's Bureau (Department of Labor), 121, 124

women's counseling services, 25

*Women's Rights Almanac* (ed. Gager), 136

*Women's Rights Law Reporter*, 139

*Work in America*, 129

Work Incentive Program (WIN), 124, 128–29

Wright, Emma, 76

zero population growth, 14, 16

Zigler, Dr. Edward, 119

zygote, 43

## About the Author

PATRICIA ASHDOWN-SHARP is a British journalist who specializes in social policy as it relates to women. She was born in England in 1941 and has been Woman's Editor of the *Birmingham Post* and feature writer on the *Daily Mail,* London; since becoming a free-lancer in 1971, she has written mainly for the *London Sunday Times.* She spent six months in the United States researching this book, an American version of her first book, *The Single Woman's Guide to Pregnancy and Parenthood* (London: Penguin, 1975). She lives in London.

## VINTAGE WOMEN'S STUDIES

V-72    BERNIKOW, LOUISE (ed.) / The World Split Open: Four Centuries of Women Poets in England and America, 1552-1950
V-227   DE BEAUVOIR, SIMONE / The Second Sex
V-359   DeCROW, KAREN / Sexist Justice
V-642   GLUCK, SHERNA (ed.) / From Parlor to Prison: Five American Suffragists Talk About Their Lives
V-407   HARDWICK, ELIZABETH / Seduction and Betrayal: Women and Literature
V-896   HATCH, JAMES AND VICTORIA SULLIVAN (eds.) / Plays By and About Women
V-880   LERNER, GERDA / Black Women in White America: A Documentary History
V-685   LESSING, DORIS / A Small Personal Voice: Essays, Reviews, Interviews
V-422   MITCHELL, JULIET / Psychoanalysis and Feminism
V-905   MITCHELL, JULIET / Woman's Estate
V-851   MORGAN, ROBIN / Monster
V-539   MORGAN, ROBIN (ed.) / Sisterhood is Powerful: An Anthology of Writings from the Women's Liberation Movement
V-151   MOFFAT, MARY JANE AND CHARLOTTE PAINTER (eds.) / Revelations: Diaries of Women
V-960   OAKLEY, ANN / Woman's Work: The Housewife, Past and Present
V-151   PAINTER, CHARLOTTE AND MARY JANE MOFFAT (eds.) / Revelations: Diaries of Women
V-621   ROWBOTHAM, SHEILA / Hidden From History: Rediscovering Women in History from the 17th Century to the Present
V-954   ROWBOTHAM, SHEILA / Women, Resistance and Revolution: A History of Women and Revolution in the Modern World
V-41    SARGENT, PAMELA (ed.) / Women of Wonder: Science Fiction Stories by Women about Women
V-738   SCHNEIR, MIRIAM (ed.) / Feminism
V-806   SHERFEY, MARY JANE / The Nature and Evolution of Female Sexuality
V-896   SULLIVAN, VICTORIA AND JAMES HATCH (eds.) / Plays By and About Women